ECONOMIC ESSAYS ON
VALUE, COMPETITION AND UTILITY

<u>В. К. Дмитріевъ.</u>

ЭКОНОМИЧЕСКІЕ ОЧЕРКИ.

(Серія I-ая: Опытъ органическаго синтеза трудовой теоріи цѣнности и теоріи предѣльной полезности).

Очеркъ I-й.
Теорія цѣнности Д. Рикардо.

Очеркъ II-й.
Теорія конкурренціи Ог. Курно

(великаго „забытаго" экономиста).

Очеркъ III-й.
ТЕОРІЯ ПРЕДѢЛЬНОЙ ПОЛЕЗНОСТИ.

Заключеніе.

МОСКВА.
Типо-литографія В. Рихтеръ, Тверская, Мамоновскій пер., с. д.
1904.

Title-page of first edition

V. K. DMITRIEV
ECONOMIC ESSAYS ON VALUE, COMPETITION AND UTILITY

TRANSLATED BY D. FRY
AND EDITED WITH AN INTRODUCTION BY
D. M. NUTI

Lecturer in Economics in the University of Cambridge

CAMBRIDGE UNIVERSITY PRESS

Published by the Syndics of the Cambridge University Press
Bentley House, 200 Euston Road, London NW1 2DB
American Branch: 32 East 57th Street, New York, N.Y.10022

This edition © Cambridge University Press 1974

Library of Congress Catalogue Card Number: 73–77176

ISBN: 0 521 20253 1

First published 1974

Printed in Great Britain
by William Clowes & Sons, Limited
London, Beccles and Colchester

CONTENTS

		page
Introduction		7
V. K. Dmitriev: A biographical note		29
Editorial note		33

V. K. DMITRIEV'S ECONOMIC ESSAYS
FIRST ESSAY. THE THEORY OF VALUE OF
DAVID RICARDO ... 37

1	Introduction: the theory of 'production costs' before Ricardo	39
2	Ricardo's theory of value	50
3	The theory of monopoly prices	80
4	Ricardo's theory of rent	83
5	Ricardo's theory of the value of infinitely reproducible goods	91

SECOND ESSAY. THE THEORY OF COMPETITION OF
AUGUSTINE COURNOT ... 97

1	Cournot's theory of competition	99
2	A critique of Cournot's theory of competition	116
3	The case of production costs greater than zero	123
	Appendix to Section 3	145
4	The significance of unlimited free competition from the point of view of the national economy	147
	Appendix to Section 4	149
5	Some consequences of the unequally favourable situation of individual entrepreneurs	150
6	Complications raised by the assumption that potential and actual production of enterprises are independent variables	161
	Appendix to Section 6	167
7	The economic consequences of technical progress	168

THIRD ESSAY. THE THEORY OF MARGINAL UTILITY ... 179

| 1 | The evolution of 'marginal utility theory' (1750–1854) | 181 |

Contents

2 An analysis of the relationship between price of a product and
demand   197

3 The psychological foundations of marginal utility theory   208

CONCLUSION. SUMMARY AND RESULTS
OF THE ANALYSIS IN THE FIRST, SECOND
AND THIRD ESSAYS   213

Bibliography   221

Index   225

INTRODUCTION

Vladimir Karpovich Dmitriev (1868–1913) was the first Russian mathematical economist, and his *Economic Essays*, published between 1898 and 1902, are a classic text in economic literature.

The interest of this text for the modern reader is threefold. First, Dmitriev anticipated and formulated in rigorous and unambiguous terms a number of propositions and techniques which are an essential part of modern economics; these range from the foundations of input–output analysis to the correct determination of labour values and prices of production, including what is now known as Samuelson's 'non-substitution theorem' and some of Sraffa's propositions on prices and distribution. Second, Dmitriev developed a highly original version of the theory of competition which we could characterise as perfect competition in present markets in the absence of forward markets; this is a fresh and highly relevant contribution to a field where research has come to a standstill. Third, now that there are raging controversies between schools laying different emphasis on the relative role of individual choice and of macroeconomic relations, Dmitriev's attempt at 'an organic synthesis of the labour theory of value[1] and of the theory of marginal utility' is a most topical reminder of the necessity of considering aspects of the theory of prices and distribution neglected either by one school or the other. In addition, the rediscovery of Dmitriev's work in the 1960s has had a salutary influence on current Soviet economic thought and planning practice; although Dmitriev is not a Marxist, his system of thought is compatible with Marxian economics; he provides opportunities for appealing to a Russian tradition in mathematical economics and his book has greatly contributed to the legitimacy of the use of mathematical methods in both economic investigations and planning practice.

Labour values

Dmitriev uses 'value' in the sense of 'exchange value', interchangeably with 'price', not in the Marxian sense of *labour value* or labour embodied in commodities. However, Dmitriev is the first economist to go beyond the mere definition of 'labour embodied' and to provide a theoretical and

[1] Here 'labour theory of value' should really be understood as 'theory of prices of production', see p. 13.

7

computational framework for the actual calculation of the 'labour embodied' in commodities. This he does by means of a system of equations expressing the labour value of each commodity in terms of its input coefficients and the labour values of its inputs.

At the beginning of the First Essay, Dmitriev considers the question 'how is it possible to calculate the amount of labour expended for the production of a given economic good from the very beginning of history, when man managed without capital, down to the present time' (p. 43). He answers that there is no need for 'historical digressions' of this kind; the quantity of labour N_A which goes, directly and indirectly, into the production of commodity A is expressed by the equation

$$N_A = n_A + \frac{1}{m_1} N_1 + \frac{1}{m_2} N_2 + \cdots + \frac{1}{m_M} N_M \tag{i}$$

where n_A is the *direct* labour input of a unit of commodity A; $1/m_i$ is the amount of the ith commodity *used up* in the production of commodity A, where $i = 1, 2, \ldots, M$; and N_i is the labour directly and indirectly embodied in the ith commodity (this is equation (6) in the First Essay, p. 44). The coefficient $1/m_i$ here is to be interpreted either as the intermediate inputs requirement for the production of the A commodity, or as the straight-line amortisation of the ith fixed capital good (assuming uniform productiveness over its lifetime); some of these coefficients may be equal to zero, as in Dmitriev's system of equations (7) in the First Essay. For each of the M other commodities there is an equation of the same form, relating labour (directly and indirectly) embodied to input coefficients and the labour embodied in the inputs (p. 44). We obtain a system of $(M+1)$ equations in $(M+1)$ unknowns, 'which is always adequate for the determination of N, giving the required sum of the labour expended on the production of product A. Therefore, without any digressions into the prehistoric times of the first inception of technical capital, we can always find the total sum of the labour directly and indirectly expended on the production of any product *under present day production conditions*, both of this product itself and of those capital goods involved in its production' (p. 44, emphasis in the text).

This is clearly a full-fledged input–output system, where N_i are the full coefficients of labour, the n_i are the direct labour inputs, and the $1/m$ are identical with Leontief's input–output coefficients.[1] The analytical apparatus provided by Leontief four decades later adds two things: (i) a method for the actual computation of the solution, namely the inversion of the matrix $(\mathbf{I} - \mathbf{A}')$, where $\mathbf{I}$ is the identity matrix and $\mathbf{A}'$ is the transpose

[1] W. W. Leontief, *The Structure of the American economy 1919–1939*, New York, 1941; W. W. Leontief *et al.*, *Studies in the structure of the American economy*, New York, 1953.

of the matrix of technical coefficients; and (ii) the generalisation of the notion of full input (i.e. direct and indirect input requirements) from labour to other production inputs. In Leontief's type of notation, if we call a_{ij} the amount of ith product required per unit of the jth product, $\mathbf{A}$ the $[a_{ij}]$ matrix; a_{oj} the direct labour input of product j, and $\mathbf{a}$ the column vector $[a_{oj}]$; and f_{ij} the full-input coefficient, i.e. the element of the $(\mathbf{I} - \mathbf{A}')^{-1}$ matrix, we obtain

$$f_{ik} = \sum_{j=1}^{n} a_{ij} f_{jk} + \delta_{ik} \qquad \text{(ii)}$$

where $i, k, j = 1, 2, \ldots, n$; and δ_{ik} is Kronecker's delta, i.e. is equal to zero except for $i = k$ when it is equal to unity. If we indicate full labour inputs (i.e. Dmitriev's N's) by f_{ok}, Leontief's approach gives

$$f_{ok} = \sum_{j=1}^{n} a_{oj} f_{jk} \qquad \text{(iii)}$$

or

$$\mathbf{f}_o = (\mathbf{I} - \mathbf{A}')^{-1} \mathbf{a} \qquad \text{(iv)}$$

where $\mathbf{f}_o = [f_{ok}]$. Dmitriev's formulation of full labour inputs is

$$f_{ok} = a_{ok} + \sum_{j=1}^{n} f_{oj} a_{jk} \qquad \text{(iii')}$$

or

$$\mathbf{f}_o = \mathbf{a} + \mathbf{A}' \mathbf{f}_o \qquad \text{(iv')}$$

which is just another way of rewriting Leontief's equation (iv).

Soviet and Western writers have not failed to notice the similarity between Dmitriev's and Leontief's equations. V. S. Nemchinov writes that Leontief 'gave a mathematical interpretation of the balance sheet of an economy by constructing equations relating input and output as Walras and Dmitriev had in their day suggested';[1] he refers repeatedly to the 'iteration equations of Dmitriev–Leontief'[2] and speaks of 'the identity of the results obtained from Dmitriev's equation and Leontief'.[3] The Soviet economists V. D. Belkin, D. M. Grobman and A. L. Lunts maintain the identity of Leontief's full-input coefficients with Dmitriev's results and offer a proof of 'correlation of two ways of determining full

[1] V. S. Nemchinov, 'The use of mathematical methods in economics', in V. S. Nemchinov (Ed.), *The use of mathematics in economics*, Moscow, 1959, English translation edited by A. Nove, London, 1964, p. 12 of the English edition.
[2] V. S. Nemchinov, 'A model of an economic region', Moscow, 1961, translated in *Mathematical studies in economics and statistics in the USSR and Eastern Europe*, Vol. I, 1964, p. 14; 'Basic elements of a model of planned price formation', *Voprosy Ekonomiki*, n. 12, 1963, translated in A. Nove and D. M. Nuti (Eds.), *Socialist Economics*, Penguin, 1972, p. 414.
[3] Nemchinov, 'Basic elements . . .', p. 414, footnote.

Introduction

inputs'.[1] The similarity of the two approaches has also been emphasised by A. Zauberman and A. Nove in the West.[2] Zauberman gives a conveniently shortened version of the proof offered by Belkin–Grobman–Lunts. Arguing from analogy, the authors of the theorem write down for Dmitriev an equation of full inputs c_{ik} of any ith commodity per unit of a kth product:

$$c_{ik} = a_{ik} + \sum_{j=1}^{n} c_{ij} a_{jk} \qquad (v)$$

for $i, k, j = 1, 2, \ldots, n$. If we compare this extension of Dmitriev's approach with Leontief's equations (ii) above for full inputs, it can be proved that $f_{ik} = c_{ik}$ if $i \neq k$, and $f_{ik} = c_{ik} + 1$ if $i = k$. Following Zauberman's version of the proof, with $\mathbf{A} = [a_{ij}]$, $\mathbf{F} = [f_{ij}]$ and $\mathbf{C} = [c_{ij}]$, and by definition unit matrix $\mathbf{I} = [\delta_{ij}]$, we have $\mathbf{F} = \mathbf{A}' + \mathbf{IF}$, $\mathbf{C} = \mathbf{A}' + \mathbf{CA}'$. Solving the two sets of equations, we have $\mathbf{F} = \mathbf{I}(\mathbf{I} - \mathbf{A}')^{-1}$, $\mathbf{C} = \mathbf{A}'(\mathbf{I} - \mathbf{A}')^{-1}$; hence the difference of the two matrices $\mathbf{F} - \mathbf{C} = (\mathbf{I} - \mathbf{A}')(\mathbf{I} - \mathbf{A}')^{-1} = \mathbf{I}$, i.e. $\mathbf{F} = \mathbf{C} + \mathbf{I}$, so that Leontief's matrix of full coefficients is different from an analogous Dmitriev matrix only along the leading diagonal.[3] Zauberman explains the difference by saying that 'on the Leontief route full coefficients are computed per unit of output passing into final uses; on the "analogous" Dmitriev route they would be computed per unit of produced outputs'; but 'only by resorting to "*analogy*" have Belkin–Grobman–Lunts formulated the equation for a generalised case of c_{ik}, which is indeed theirs, not Dmitriev's'.[4]

If one wishes to extend Dmitriev's notion of full labour coefficients to the full coefficients of other inputs as well, it is perfectly clear that the full-input coefficient of a commodity into one *net* unit of the same commodity (i.e. along Leontief's leading diagonal) is given by one unit of itself as well as by the sum of all direct and indirect requirements of that commodity to produce itself. Dmitriev's and Leontief's approaches then turn out to be identical, and the Belkin–Grobman–Lunts proof is unnecessary. The question whether the extension is legitimate is a matter of opinion; as to labour, the identity of equations (iv) and (iv') is incontrovertible, and the problem does not arise. Here priority in discovery is immaterial; whether or not Leontief as a Russian student in the 1920s was acquainted with the

[1] V. D. Belkin, 'Natsionalnyi dokhod i mezhotraslevoy balans' [National income and intersectoral balance], in *Primenenie matematiki i elektronnoy tekhniki v planirovanii* [The use of mathematics and electronic techniques in planning], ed. by A. G. Aganbegyan and V. D. Belkin, Moscow, 1961, p. 28.

[2] A. Nove and A. Zauberman, 'A resurrected Russian economist of 1900', *Soviet Studies*, July 1961; A Zauberman, 'Few remarks on a discovery in Soviet economics', *Bulletin of the Oxford Institute of Economics and Statistics*, 1962.

[3] See Zauberman, 'Few remarks on a discovery . . .', p. 422.

[4] *Ibid.*, pp. 422–3.

10

work of an economist whose death in 1913 was recognised as 'a great loss for Russian economic science', and was already hailed as the 'first Russian economist-mathematician',[1] Dmitriev's achievement is remarkable all the same.

The importance of Dmitriev's approach for socialist planning was already understood in the 1920s, and A. V. Chayanov developed Dmitriev's scheme of the economy into an input–output table for agriculture.[2] From the beginnings of Soviet planning, the consistency between gross and net output in different sectors was attempted mainly by means of the method of material balances; these are budget-type accounts, showing the resources and uses for each product or group of products; intermediate uses are assessed on the basis of planned input coefficients ('norms') so that each material balance contains the information corresponding to one row of an input–output table. Even in the absence of input–output techniques, the procedure generally used to construct material balances corresponds to a large extent to the process of inverting a matrix of the technological coefficients of an input–output table, to obtain the $(\mathbf{I} - \mathbf{A}')^{-1}$ matrix.[3] But the Stalinist attitude to the use of mathematical methods as a bourgeois deviation inhibited their further development and retarded the use of input–output methods until the late 1950s.[4] Lange had tried to rehabilitate input–output techniques by maintaining the similarity between input–output tables and Marxian reproduction schemes[5] – a far-fetched interpretation in view of the use of value categories in those schemes, and the absence of the notion of input–output coefficients. The ability to claim Russian priority in the discovery of input–output equations in the work of Dmitriev was an important step in the struggle for the use of mathematical methods in socialist planning.

In 1962 the Central Statistical Administration produced an 83×83 intersectoral balance of labour outlays in the Soviet economy for 1959–60, using the first *ex-post* input–output tables for the Soviet economy, compiled for 1959. This balance shows, in terms of labour, the inter-

[1] N. N. Shaposhnikov, *Pervyi Russkii ekonomist-matematik Vladimir Karpovich Dmitriev, Doklad v posvyashchennom pamyati Dmitrieva zasêdanii O-va im. A. I. Chuprova* [The first Russian mathematical economist V. K. Dmitriev, a lecture at a meeting of the A. I. Chuprov Society, held in memory of Dmitriev], Moscow, 1914.

[2] A. V. Chayanov, *The theory of peasant economy* (1926), English translation, 1966; quoted by M. Kaser, *Soviet Economics*, 1970, p. 65.

[3] See H. S. Levine, 'The centralised planning of supply in Soviet industry', in Joint Economic Committee, Congress of the United States, *Comparison of the United States and Soviet Economics*, Washington, 1959; J. M. Montias, 'Planning with material balances in Soviet-type economies', *American Economic Review*, December 1959 (reprinted in Nove and Nuti, *Socialist Economics*).

[4] See V. G. Treml, 'Input–output analysis and Soviet planning', in J. P. Hardt *et al.*, *Mathematics and computers in Soviet economic planning*, London, 1967.

[5] O. Lange, *Introduction to Econometrics*, Warsaw, 1958, pp. 218–29 of the English translation from Polish, London, 1959.

industrial flows, the formation of the final bill of goods, the formation of national product and cost incurred in the non-productive sphere.[1] This calculation corresponds exactly to the Dmitriev–Leontief full labour coefficients. It shows that, for instance, out of 97 million man-years, about 50 million are ultimately devoted to the production of consumer goods; 34 million to that of clothes and footwear alone. The non-productive sphere, including administration, absorbs 17 million man-years and about 30 million go to capital formation, exports and other items. Soviet writers have regarded these computations as methods of measuring the Marxian 'socially necessary labour' contained in different commodities. Eidel'man suggested that this kind of labour balance should be used in an analysis of the price system and as an aid to an empirical price formation.[2] This however is a misapplication of Dmitriev's approach. In Marxian theory labour values are but a step in the understanding of the origin of profit in a capitalist economy, not prices to be charged in a socialist economy;[3] Marx had a theory of prices as *transformed* values,[4] which are higher or lower than respective values because of the basic requirement of a uniform profit rate throughout the economy. No wonder that actual Soviet prices do not correspond to the 'labour content' computed in Soviet tables; making average full labour content per rouble equal to 100, it has been found that the actual full labour input coefficients per rouble ranged from 33 in the gas industry to 198 for animal husbandry,[5] but this cannot *per se* be regarded as evidence of irrationality in Soviet pricing. However, in addition to his solution of the determination of labour embodied in commodities, Dmitriev also had a theory of *prices of production* which is a reformulation and development of Ricardian price theory and corresponds to Marxian production prices.

Prices of production

Imagine an economy where production takes place under constant

[1] See M. R. Eidel'man, 'Pervyi mezhotraslevoi balans zatrat truda v narodnom khoziaistve SSSR' [The first intersectoral balance of labour expenditures in the national economy of the USSR], *Vestnik Statistiki*, n. 10, 1962; A. Zauberman, 'A note on the Soviet inter-industry labour input balance', *Soviet Studies*, 1963.

[2] See Eidel'man, 'Pervyi mezhotraslevoi . . .'; 'Mezhotraslevoi balans obshchestvennogo produkta i ego ekonomicheskie soderzhanie' [Intersectoral balance of social product and its economic content], *Voprosy Ekonomiki*, 1961.

[3] For Marx, the proposition that prices *in terms of labour embodied* are equal to labour values is not an assertion about what happens in economic reality, but an *assumption* under which the origin of profit is investigated, on the ground that if profit cannot be explained under that assumption, it cannot be explained at all (see K. Marx, *Wages, price and profit*, 1898). In Marx's view, the equality of prices and labour values is not a feature of the socialist economy; see K. Marx, *Critique of the Gotha Programme*, 1891.

[4] See K. Marx, *Capital*, Vol. III, 1894, Chs. 9 and 10.

[5] Treml, 'Input–output analysis and Soviet planning', p. 117.

returns to scale, with the assistance of one primary (i.e. non-produced) input, i.e. labour, which is paid a given real wage, and of produced capital goods. Suppose also that there is only one method of producing each commodity. If the composition of output has been correctly anticipated, and if competition equalises the profit rate on the value of capital goods (including advances to labourers), it can be proved that prices (in Dmitriev's terminology, *values* or *exchange values*) are equal to prices of production. Prices of production are made up of the wage and material costs of production plus profit on capital at a rate determined by the production coefficients and the real wage rate. In modern literature, this proposition can be found in P. Sraffa's *Production of commodities by means of commodities*, 1960, if we add the assumption of constant returns to scale (although Sraffa insists that he is not assuming constant returns to scale, and therefore his analysis holds only for a scale and composition of output which are taken as given). If we assume that labour and produced inputs can be combined in an infinite number of different alternative proportions, profit maximisation by competitive producers leads to the choice of the combination of productive methods that maximises the profit rate; it turns out that, although in principle there exists 'substitutability' between inputs, under the given assumptions only one combination of methods will be in use and the composition of output does not lead to substitution between inputs. Demand conditions will affect the relative quantities demanded at those production prices, but relative prices are the same whatever the composition of demand turns out to be at those prices (as long as this composition is correctly anticipated by producers). This proposition, which for a timeless economy has been put forward in 1951 independently by P. A. Samuelson, who labelled it 'non-substitution theorem' and by N. Georgescu-Roegen,[1] can be found in its 'dynamic' version (i.e. for the economy we have described, where production takes time, and intermediate inputs are circulating capital) in Sraffa's book, and is now referred to as the 'dynamic non-substitution theorem'.[2] These propositions can be found in Dmitriev, although the additional necessary assumption of no joint production is not explicit.

Dmitriev starts from the refutation of the criticism levied in his time against the 'classical' theory of price determination based on production costs, 'that it defines price from prices, that it defines one unknown from other unknowns' (p. 41). Among others, Walras had criticised 'the

---

[1] P. A. Samuelson, 'Abstract of a theorem concerning substitutability in open Leontief models', in T. C. Koopmans (Ed.), *Activity analysis of production and allocation*, 1951; N. Georgescu–Roegen, 'Some properties of a generalised Leontief model', *ibid*.

[2] J. Mirrlees, 'The dynamic nonsubstitution theorem', *Review of Economic Studies*, January 1969.

English economists' for expressing price as the sum of profit and wage, and at the same time profit as the difference between price and wage: 'In the language of mathematics' – Walras wrote – 'one equation cannot be used to determine two unknowns'.[1]

This allegation, Dmitriev argues, can be levied against Adam Smith, who did not deal with the problem of the determination of the profit rate, except for a vague reference to the demand for and supply of capital, i.e. going outside the sphere of production.[2] But Ricardo is not subject to this criticism; indeed 'The most important point in Ricardo's theory is undoubtedly his theory of the conditions defining the "average" profit rate . . .' and 'Ricardo's immortal contribution was his brilliant solution of this seemingly insoluble problem' (pp. 50 and 58, First Essay).

For the study of *prices* (or *values*, in his terminology) Dmitriev uses a framework slightly different from that employed for the study of *labour values* (or labour embodied in commodities). Instead of extending his *point input–point output* framework, whereby commodities are produced by means of labour and other commodities (equation (i)), he uses an Austrian-type model where commodities are produced by dated labour, i.e. a *flow input–point output* framework, whereby commodities are produced by dated labour. For each commodity Dmitriev formulates a price equation of the type:

$$X_A = n_A a X_a (1+r)^{t_A} + n_1 a X_a (1+r)^{t_{A1}} + \cdots + n_m a X_a (1+r)^{t_{Am}} \qquad \text{(v)}$$

where X_A is the price of commodity A, a is the amount of wage good (say, corn) consumed by workers, X_a is the unit price of the wage good; $n_A, n_1, \ldots, n_m$ are the labour inputs required respectively $t_A, t_{A1}, \ldots, t_{Am}$ time units before the output of commodity A becomes available (this is equation (25), p. 54). If there are M commodities in addition to the wage good, we have $(M+1)$ equations; there are M relative prices to be determined, in terms of an arbitrary commodity whose price is taken as unit of account, plus the profit rate; the system is complete and can simultaneously determine relative prices and the profit rate. 'It is to Ricardo's credit that he was the first to note that there is one production equation by means of which we may determine the magnitude of r *directly* (i.e. without having recourse for assistance to the other equations). This equation gives us the production conditions of the product a to which in the final analysis the expenditure on all the products, $A, B, C, \ldots$

[1] L. Walras, *Elements of pure economics* (1874), Lesson 40, § 368, p. 425 of the Jaffé edition, 1954.

[2] A. Smith, *Wealth of nations*, Book I, Ch. 9, p. 143 of the 1814 edition; see also Dmitriev's First Essay, p. 49.

is reduced' (p. 59). For the wage good, with labour inputs N_i,

$$X_a = aX_a[N_a(1+r)^{t_a} + N_1(1+r)^{t_{a1}} + \cdots + N_q(1+r)^{t_{aq}}]. \qquad \text{(vi)}$$

From this (equation (44), First Essay) we can obtain

$$a = \frac{1}{\sum_i N_i(1+r)^i} \qquad \text{(vii)}$$

which today is familiar as the 'wage–profit frontier'; Dmitriev writes it instead in the perfectly equivalent form

$$r = F(N_a, N_1, \ldots, N_q; t_a, t_{a1}, \ldots, t_{aq}; a). \qquad \text{(viii)}$$

The proposition that 'a reciprocal relationship will exist between the profit rate and the level of wages' could already be inferred from Smith's analysis, but the actual quantification of this relation – Dmitriev argues (p. 58) – should be credited to Ricardo.

Dmitriev then extends his analysis to the case where workers consume not a single commodity but a number of commodities α, β, γ, $\ldots$, in fixed proportions. He indicates by a, b, c, $\ldots$ the quantities of consumption goods consumed by a unit of labour, and by X_a, X_b, X_c, $\ldots$ their respective prices. His price equations become:

$$\left.\begin{aligned}
X_a &= N_a(aX_a + bX_b + cX_c + \cdots)(1+r)^{t_a} + \\
&\qquad N_{a1}(aX_a + bX_b + cX_c + \cdots)(1+r)^{t_{a1}} + \cdots \\
X_b &= N_b(aX_a + bX_b + cX_c + \cdots)(1+r)^{t_b} + \\
&\qquad N_{b1}(aX_a + bX_b + cX_c + \cdots)(1+r)^{t_{b1}} + \cdots
\end{aligned}\right\} \text{(ix)}$$

$\ldots$

(this is his system of equations (48), p. 60). As in the case of a single wage good, 'the level of the profit rate r is determined by the production costs of products consumed by the workers'[1] (p. 61); hence 'To level at Ricardo's theory the hackneyed reproach that it "defines price in terms of price" is to manifest a complete lack of understanding of the writings of this very great theoretical economist' (p. 61). The condition for a positive profit rate to arise is that 'we can obtain a *larger* quantity of the same product within some finite period of time as a result of the production process' (p. 62).

These statements can easily be put in a modern formulation. If we consider the simpler case where production takes place in a single uni-

---

[1] The idea that for a given real wage the production conditions of wage goods determine the profit rate has now been noted by Soviet economists; see A. A. Konius, 'Trudovaya teoriya stoimosti i ekonometrika' [The labour theory of value and econometrics], in P. A. Baran and others, *On political economy and econometrics, Essays in honour of Oskar Lange*, Warsaw, 1964, pp. 240–1.

form period, which is taken as the time unit, the system of equations (ix) becomes

$$X_a = (1+r)N_a(aX_a+bX_b+cX_c+\cdots) \Big\}$$
$$X_b = (1+r)N_b(aX_a+bX_b+cX_c+\cdots) \Big\}$$

$$\cdots$$

(x)

For simplicity, we introduce the following matrix notation (where vectors are *column* vectors): $\mathbf{w} = (a, b, c, \ldots, z)$; $\mathbf{a}_o = (N_a, N_b, N_c, \ldots, N_z)$; $\mathbf{B} = \mathbf{a}_o\mathbf{w}'$; $\mathbf{p} = (X_a, X_b, X_c, \ldots, X_z)$. We can now write equation (x) as

$$\mathbf{p} = (1+r)\mathbf{B}'\mathbf{p} \qquad \text{(xi)}$$

i.e.

$$\mathbf{B}'\mathbf{p} = \frac{1}{1+r}\mathbf{p}. \qquad \text{(xii)}$$

In the language of modern algebra, the profit rate turns out to be equal to $(1-\sigma)/\sigma$, where σ is the eigenvalue of the unique positive eigenvector of the positive matrix $\mathbf{B}$; a positive profit rate requires $\sigma < 1$. This is equivalent to Dmitriev's statement above; in fact, to say that 'we can obtain a *larger* quantity *of the same* product within some finite period of time as a result of the production process' means that for some vector $\hat{\mathbf{x}}$ of gross output $\mathbf{x}$, such that

$$\mathbf{B}\hat{\mathbf{x}} = \lambda\hat{\mathbf{x}} \qquad \text{(xiii)}$$

the condition is satisfied

$$\lambda < 1. \qquad \text{(xiv)}$$

The dominant eigenvalue of $\mathbf{B}$ is in fact the same as the dominant eigenvalue of $\mathbf{B}'$, hence if condition (xiv) is satisfied there is a positive profit rate.

It is interesting to compare this with the Sraffian price equations. Sraffa assumes that wages are post-paid, and that commodities – as well as labour – are needed for the production of commodities. Hence following Sraffa we could write:

$$\mathbf{p} = (1+r)\mathbf{A}'\mathbf{p}+\mathbf{a}\mathbf{w}'\cdot\mathbf{p}. \qquad \text{(xv)}$$

If we modify the Sraffa model to allow for wages being anticipated, we obtain

$$\mathbf{p} = (1+r)\,(\mathbf{A}'+\mathbf{a}\cdot\mathbf{w}')\mathbf{p}. \qquad \text{(xvi)}$$

Comparing this with equation (xi), we can see that the Dmitriev equation corresponds to the Sraffa equation under the assumption that wages are anticipated and that there are no intermediate inputs. But beside this difference the formal structure of the model is the same, and we find in Dmitriev an anticipation of the notion of 'basic commodities', i.e. the commodities entering directly or indirectly in the production of all commodities. The production conditions of these commodities (in Dmitriev's case, wage goods) determine the profit rate in the economy and the relative prices of *all* commodities, including those which do not enter into the wage basket. However, the Sraffian notion of 'standard commodity', i.e. the composite commodity obtained by combining the basic commodities in proportions such that the surplus has the same composition as the inputs, is not explicit in Dmitriev, other than in the generic statement of the condition 'we can obtain a *larger* quantity *of the same* product within some finite period of time as a result of the production process'. Sraffa's discovery of the 'standard commodity' and its properties could not possibly be ascribed to Dmitriev.

Dmitriev, in sum, considers 'production of commodities by means of dated labour', not 'production of commodities by means of commodities' (at least when discussing the determination of the profit rate), with wages being advanced, not 'posticipated' as in Sraffa. Their similarity descends from the common Ricardian root. They also bear a similar relation to Marx: both Dmitriev and Sraffa provide the correct solution to the determination of prices of production, of the kind sought by Marx, but their prices are not, as in Marx, a *transformed* form of *labour values*; they are determined directly from technology and the real wage rate, without the intermediate route of labour values, and therefore without necessarily drawing the Marxian inference of labour exploitation. There is, however, a difference between Dmitriev's and Sraffa's relations to Marx. Dmitriev, like Marx, finds the origin of profit in the production conditions of the real wage. Sraffa, on the contrary, because of his assumption of post-paid wages and his measurement of wages in terms of the 'standard product' (i.e. the net product of a hypothetical economy having the same labour force and producing only the 'standard commodity') loses the Marxian connection between the productive conditions of workers' consumption and the profit rate. In Sraffa the profit rate appears to depend on the distribution in the standard system, while the production conditions of wage goods determine the level of workers' real consumption, not the profit rate.[1]

Although Dmitriev's approach is closer to Marx than Sraffa's, Dmitriev goes out of his way to *deny* the Marxian theory of exploitation and to

---

[1] In a sense Sraffa loses, in this way, also something of the Ricardian approach to production and distribution. Sraffa's 'standard commodity' has in common with Ricardo's corn the fact that input and output have the same physical specifications; but unlike Ricardo's corn, the 'standard commodity' is not consumed directly by workers. In general, unless workers happen to consume the 'standard commodity', no commodity will have both these properties of Ricardo's corn.

show, 'proceeding from Ricardo's analysis, that the origin of industrial profit does not stand in any "special" relationship to the human labour used in production' (p. 64). In order to do this, Dmitriev investigates the properties of an imaginary system where work is performed exclusively by animals and machines.

Workers, animals and machines

In an imaginative piece of analysis, Dmitriev argues that although 'The *starting point* for Ricardo's analysis was provided by the present-day *capitalist system* based on the use of *hired human labour* it would, however, be extremely erroneous to imagine that the *conclusions* at which [Ricardo] arrived have a bearing only on the present time' (p. 61). The conditions for a positive profit rate are quite general: '... whenever a known quantity of some product *a* has been used up in the production of *a* and we can obtain a *larger* quantity *of the same* product within some definite period of time as a result of the production process, the profit rate in the given branch of industry will be a fully-determined quantity greater than zero, irrespective of the price of the product *a*. If the production costs of the other goods *A*, *B*, *C*, ... are reduced *in the final analysis* to the same product *a*, the same profit rate should also be established in these branches under conditions of free mobility from one branch of production to another. ... Whether the potential energy incorporated in the production good *a* is released and used in production in the form of *human labour*, as happens at present, or by means of some other process (*not involving the participation of human labour*) is a matter of indifference' (pp. 62–63). 'It is theoretically possible to imagine a case in which all products are produced exclusively by the work of machines, so that no unit of *living labour* (whether human or of any other kind) participates in production, and nevertheless an industrial profit may occur, in this case, under certain conditions, a profit which will not differ essentially in any way from the profit obtained by present-day capitalists using hired workers in production' (p. 63). Dmitriev realises that for a process not requiring human labour to be actually employed in production, it is necessary not only that such a process should yield a positive profit rate (equal to the rate of self-reproduction of animals or machines, to whose input any output can be reduced) but also that this profit rate should be greater or equal to that obtainable by using labour: 'for any given process *actually* to determine the profit rate, it is still insufficient that it *could in general* serve as a source of profit, and it is further necessary that it should yield *a higher profit rate* than all other possible processes' (pp. 64–65); 'in reality one out of all these equation systems [describing alternative technologies] will be in force, namely the one which will

18

yield the greatest value for *r*...' (p. 66); 'when different constant profit rates exist in different branches of production, a balance will be established either when products yielding a high profit rate pass into the realm of *free goods* or when the production of products with a low rate of profit is discontinued' (p. 68).

So far so good; this is a neat and modern-tasting piece of analysis. But Dmitriev rather overreaches himself with the claim that '*therefore* ... the origin of industrial profit does not stand in any "special" relationship to the human labour used in production' (p. 64, emphasis added). This is a splendid *non sequitur*. What Dmitriev has actually shown is that if no *human* labour is used in production there can be no exploitation of human labour; but then profit will arise from a 'special relation' of capital to animal labour, or robots' labour, and the fact that we do not usually talk of 'exploitation' of animals and machines does not in any conceivable sense rule out the proposition of *human* exploitation when *human* labour *is* actually used in production.[1]

In view of Dmitriev's claim that profit has nothing to do with the relation between capital and hired labour, it seems apt that he should be classified, in Soviet handbooks on the history of economic thought, as belonging to 'the Russian bourgeois literature'.[2] This classification also seems correct in view of Dmitriev's approach to income distribution; although in his First Essay he says that 'the level of [the real wage] at which equilibrium is established is a question of fact and will be dependent on the strength of the contending parties' (p. 74) and seems to suggest some scope for class struggle in the determination of income distribution, he later seems to have subscribed to J. B. Clark's marginal productivity theory,[3] i.e. to bourgeois economics at its worst, in a formulation now entirely discredited in the modern discussions on capital theory.[4]

Dmitriev as an anti-Ricardian

In the scanty references to Dmitriev's work, especially in modern economic literature, Dmitriev is generally regarded as a Ricardian.[5]

[1] See H. Denis, Postface to V. K. Dmitriev, *Essais Économiques*, with an Introduction by A. Zauberman, Centre National de la Recherche Scientifique, Paris, 1968, p. 265.

[2] A. I. Pashkov (Ed.), *Istoriya Russkoi ekonomicheskoi mysli* [History of Russian economic thought], Moscow, 1966, Part I, Tome 3, p. 182.

[3] V. K. Dmitriev, 'A review of Tugan–Baranovsky's *Principles of Political Economy*', *Russkaya Mysl*, n. 11, 1909, p. 113.

[4] For a survey of these discussions, see G. C. Harcourt, *Some Cambridge controversies in the theory of capital*, Cambridge, 1972.

[5] See for instance, P. Struve, *Russkaya Mysl*, 1913, n. 10, as quoted in Zauberman, 'Few remarks...', p. 440; M. H. Dobb, 'The Sraffa system and critique of the neoclassical theory of distribution', *De Economist*, Vol. 118, 1970.

This is due to the importance of Dmitriev's contribution to the clarification and extension of Ricardo's economics, to Dmitriev's great admiration for Ricardo, and to the wider popularity of his First Essay whose broad contents were cited at length by Bortkiewicz.[1] But any reading of Dmitriev's three Essays should quickly dispel the impression that he is a Ricardian.

The purpose of Dmitriev's work is clearly stated in the subtitle of the Essays: 'An attempt at an organic synthesis of the labour theory of value and the theory of marginal utility.' The preoccupation with providing some *synthesis* (*reductio ad unum*) of conflicting theories is a typical feature of continental (i.e. European versus Anglo-Saxon) intellectuals; in Russian economic thought, a 'reconciliation' of the labour theory of value (understood here as a theory of prices of production) and Austrian utility theory was attempted by M. Tugan-Baranovsky and P. Struve,[2] and Dmitriev falls neatly into this tradition, although his contributions were more original and substantial. Having formulated and developed Ricardian propositions on prices of production Dmitriev proceeds to show that these propositions hold only under the most restricting assumptions. Among these are constant returns to scale, i.e. zero rents, *and* perfect competition of a kind that brings prices down to the (constant) necessary costs of commodities (including profit at a rate determined by technology and the real wage). He decidedly parts company from Ricardo and shows that whenever at least one of these conditions is not satisfied prices depend on *demand conditions* as well, and not even 'long-run' equilibrium prices can be obtained purely from the knowledge of technology and the real wage.

Already at the end of the First Essay, Dmitriev shows that a price theory based exclusively on production conditions, i.e. independently of demand conditions (even for a given real wage) cannot handle the cases of monopoly prices and of positive rent. He follows Cournot in his analysis of monopoly and Auspitz and Lieben in his analysis of rent. In both cases, predictably, prices depend not only on production conditions, but also on *demand*, or the 'conditions of consumption'.[3] But the greatest

---

[1] L. von Bortkiewicz, 'Wertrechnung und Preisrechnung im Marxschen Sistem' (in three parts), *Archiv für Sozialwissenschaft und Sozialpolitik*, 1906, Band 23, Heft 1; 1907, Band 25, Heft 1; 1907, Band 25, Heft 2. The second and the third parts are translated into English, as 'Value and Price in the Marxian system', *International Economic Papers*, 1952, n. 2.

[2] M. I. Tugan-Baranovsky, *Osnovy politicheskoy ekonomii* [*Principles of political economy*], 1909; P. V. Struve, *Khozyaistvo i tsena, Kriticheskie issledovaniya po teorii i istorii khozyaistvennoi zhizni* [Economy and price, critical researches on the theory and history of economic life], Moscow, 1916; Pashkov, *Istoriya . . .*, p. 178. See also Zauberman, 'A few remarks . . .'.

[3] There is a warning against the use of *average* costs in price determination (First Essay, Section 4) which should be carefully thought upon by Soviet planners; and there is an interesting analysis of the effects of discontinuities in production costs.

blow to the Ricardian theory of price determination is given in the Second Essay, where Dmitriev most emphatically argues that demand conditions contribute to price determination also for 'goods which are infinitely reproducible by labour under conditions excluding the possibility of the occurrence of rent' (p. 92) even under competitive conditions. In order to do this, Dmitriev challenges the proposition that 'competition lowers prices' (p. 93) and starting from Cournot's analysis of competition he constructs a theory of unrestricted but not-so-perfect competition.

Dmitriev's theory of competition

The key to Dmitriev's approach to market competition is contained in his quotation from Thornton at the beginning of the Second Essay: 'Dealers do not undersell each other merely for fun. Each is quite content that all the rest should sell dearly, provided he himself can sell as dearly . . .' (p. 97). Why then does the price–output combination prevailing when sellers are many differ as a rule from that maximising *joint* profits for sellers as a whole? Because, if a price prevails equal to the monopoly price, each seller expects a 'temporary profit' (Cournot's *bénéfice momentané*, p. 103) from expanding his individual output, and all sellers acting *independently* on the same expectation bring about a greater joint output and lower price and joint profit from the monopoly level. 'It would be a correct economic calculus for each separate entrepreneur to abstain [from expanding output] only if he could be certain that other entrepreneurs would similarly abstain. It is, however, impossible to derive such certainty from the fact that all other entrepreneurs are guided in their action by correct economic calculus' (p. 109). The greater the number of competing sellers, the greater the output and the lower the price, and for the number *n* of sellers tending to infinity, the competitive price tends to the necessary production cost of the last unit of the product (including profit). When costs are constant, this leads to Ricardo's proposition. This is the picture of competition drawn by Cournot.

Dmitriev points out that there is a crucial implicit assumption in Cournot's analysis, namely that each producer–seller must assume that his competitors' supply is equal to their production (p. 116), i.e. that they do not carry stocks and do not have spare productive capacity. Otherwise, an individual producer's attempt to expand supply would not lead to a *bénéfice momentané* for him, as his competitors' reaction would be *immediate*, and whoever disturbs monopoly-type equilibrium is worse off along with everybody else. Dmitriev argues that the assumption that supply = production contradicts not only economic reality, but also the other basic hypothesis of competitive analysis, 'that every individual tends to pursue the greatest advantage' (p. 118). He relaxes the assumption that production = supply, and produces a most refreshing piece of economic analysis, which stands the test of time beautifully and remains an original and unrivalled contribution to the theory of competition.

If production costs were zero, there would be no limit to the extent production could exceed supply (= sales), and '. . . when an instantaneous expansion of supply is possible for any number of isolated entrepreneurs competing in the market, the most advantageous general volume of supply will be the same for a monopolist entrepreneur (or when the competitors have reached an agreement)' (p. 118). More generally, i.e. also for positive production costs, *whatever the quantity produced, for a given quantity of production, the market price will be fixed at the same level, whether the total quantity produced is in the hands of one owner or of any number of entrepreneurs.* Competition has an effect on the volume of production, but no effect at all on the volume of supply *for a given volume of production* (p. 121). In other words, Dmitriev postulates that *for a given volume of production* rational behaviour of producers leads them to a tacit collusion on price, but (i) such collusion is enforceable only because of the existence of a potential threat in the form of a potential supply greater than the collusion sales level, and (ii) competition between producers takes the form of expanding the level of potential supply, with sales lagging behind. Some readers may take the view, at this stage, that this is not simply a way of bringing consistency to Cournot's assumptions, but an entirely different model; whether or not this is the case, the point is that by relaxing Cournot's assumption that production = supply Dmitriev is able to obtain new and interesting results. For a given number n of producers there is an equilibrium potential supply such that the price corresponds to what would be charged by a monopolist, who happened to have that level of potential supply, but none of the n producers can expect to obtain a 'temporary profit' by violating the tacit collusion. For n tending to infinity, the cost of the potential supply tends to equal the revenue from actual sales; profit (over and above the interest component of production costs) is zero, as in the customary competitive equilibrium, not because price is equal to the necessary production cost of the output sold, but because the additional cost of holding stocks or installing unused capacity brings the total cost of potential output up to the level of actual sales revenue and wipes out profits completely (p. 134). This general result is worked out in detail by Dmitriev.

First he considers the case of a perishable product producible at a constant cost u. Suppose Q_m is the level of overall supply that maximises the industry's revenue. Dmitriev shows that if the industry's output happens to be lower than or equal to Q_m, supply equals production as in Cournot's case; if the industry's output is greater than Q_m, supply is equal to Q_m and price is equal to what the monopoly price would be if production costs were zero (p. 127). If, at that price, there is a positive profit calculated over the *whole* output produced, individual producers may have an incentive to expand their individual output. The crucial factor determining whether or not they do in fact expand output is the number of competitors (assumed here to have equally favourable production and sale conditions, so as to *expect* that their share of sales increases if their output increases). It remains true that 'several competing entrepreneurs will establish the total volume of output at a higher level than a monopolist' (p. 129), but this output will not be entirely sold; when the number of competing entrepreneurs tends to infinity, the level of output tends to a quantity equal to $Q_m p_m / u$, for which overall profit (over and above the interest component of costs) is zero (pp. 132–3). Competition involves a waste equal to

$$u \left(\frac{Q_m p_m}{u} - Q_m \right) = (p_m - u) Q_m \qquad \text{(xvii)}$$

which Dmitriev names sales cost or 'realisation cost' (*izderzhki po realizatsii*, p. 134), which the economy has to bear in addition to the necessary production costs of the quantity actually sold. Under unlimited competition price is lower and output is greater, as a rule, than under monopoly, but total (production and realisation) unit costs are greater under competition than under monopoly (p. 136). The exception is the case of a product whose production cost is greater than the revenue-maximising price p_m, in which case output is equal to supply, and price is equal to Cournot's competitive price, equal in turn to necessary cost u (Ricardo's price of production; p. 144). Dmitriev's proposition is therefore *testable* to this extent, as it leads to the prediction that the price of a perishable commodity produced under constant costs is fixed at a level where demand elasticity is equal to unity (this is in fact the definition of p_m), unless $u > p_m$, in which case the price is equal to production cost u and demand elasticity is greater than unity at that price. It also follows that, if the demand curve changes, as long as the point where elasticity is unity remains the same, price will also remain unchanged, whatever the shape or the position of the demand curve (because p_m remains unchanged).

If the commodity is storeable (i.e. if storage costs are lower than production costs), the analysis changes slightly. Now the difference between output and sales is not entirely lost, because it can be carried over into the next period at a cost; for competition to eliminate profits it is now necessary for the industry to reach an output level *higher* (other things being equal) than in the case of the perishable product. Actual price as a rule is not now equal to p_m (which is the price a monopolist would charge if he obtained the commodity at zero cost). Dmitriev's result can be stated by saying that in this case price is equal to $p'_m < p_m$, where p'_m is the price that a monopolist would charge, if he could produce at a unit production cost equal to the difference between actual production and storage cost, i.e. equal to $(u-v)$, where v is storage cost.[1] Therefore when output is storeable, other things being equal the price is higher and the quantity sold is lower than when it is perishable; output produced is greater because otherwise the conservation of part of excess output would yield a positive profit. In equilibrium, if demand production and storage conditions do not change, production equals sales (footnote 1, p. 137) but the industry carries a certain amount of 'dead' inventories, serving only the purpose of eliminating any potential *bénéfice momentané* that individual producers otherwise would get from expanding individual supply; 'potential' supply is greater than actual sales. Unlike the previous case of perishable commodities, these results hold even if necessary productions costs u are greater than p_m; even then, in fact, '*the equilibrium price would nevertheless be established at a level higher than the necessary production costs of the product*' (p. 144). It also follows from Dmitriev's theory that unrestricted competition leads to a price/output combination in the industry, such that the elasticity of demand at that price is greater than unity. Ricardian price theory based on necessary costs therefore does not apply, even under the assumption of constant production costs. In any case, Dmitriev holds that production costs higher than the revenue-maximising price are 'a *transient* phenomenon corresponding to a low state of technology and would disappear with further improvement in production methods' (p. 145).

The existence of production capacity in excess of actual production is regarded by Dmitriev simply as a substitute for holding 'dead' unproductive stocks (Section 6). This is therefore a case perfectly symmetrical with that of a storeable commodity. If the cost of carrying unproductive stocks is greater than the cost incurred in installing an equivalent amount of additional capacity, competing producers will use excess capacity as a cheaper method of producing a potential threat in order to dissuade each other from failing to conform to their tacit price-collusion. A further instance of unproductive expenditure is mentioned by Dmitriev in his Conclusion, namely 'advertising, in the broad sense', 'not . . .

[1] In fact, for any given production level $Q^* > D$ the total cost of the quantity sold D is equal to necessary costs uD plus the cost of storing excess output, or $v(Q^*-D)$, where v includes all the costs involved in postponing the sale of output to the next period (not only storage in a strict sense, but also interest, insurance, physical wastage, etc.); while the cost of producing excess output is not included in the total cost, because this excess output is carried over and all the costs involved in postponing the sale are already included in v. For a total cost equal to $uD + (Q^*-D)v$, marginal cost of sales is $(u-v)$ and the joint-profit-maximising price in the industry is that for which marginal revenue equals $(u-v)$.

advertising to expand the market for a given commodity, but only a special category of advertisements to expand sales of an individual entrepreneur *when the total sales level remains the same.* . . . A distinguishing feature of such advertisements is that they are effective in expanding sales only if used by one or a few of the sellers of a commodity; they are ineffective once used simultaneously and equally by *all* entrepreneurs' (p. 219). Like the other forms of waste, this kind of expenditure raises costs above necessary costs and wipes out profit at a higher price level and a lower sales level than would prevail under traditional competition.

Dmitriev shows that these basic results remain unchanged when production costs are not constant, and entrepreneurs produce under unequally favourable conditions of production, storage and sale (Section 5): '*for non-productive costs to arise in sale when rent in the Ricardian sense exists, it is sufficient that the necessary costs of the last unit out of a total output equal to the supply yielding the greatest gross revenue should be less than the price at which this quantity yielding the greatest gross revenue may be sold*' (p. 159).

It follows from this analysis that unrestricted competition has a cost for the economy, i.e. a *social* cost of wasted output, excess inventories, unused capacity or redundant advertising. This is only partly compensated by consumers' gain from prices lower than monopoly prices. '*When monopoly prevails, the national economy as a whole loses nothing; what is taken from the consumers over and above the necessary production costs is at the disposal of the monopolist as a particularly high monopoly profit; conversely, when free competition prevails, the entire sum paid by consumers over and above the necessary production costs is lost without trace to the national economy, by its expenditure on non-productive costs (i.e. costs the expenditure of which does not increase the sum total of benefit or satisfaction).*' This undermines, in Dmitriev's view, 'the thesis that free competition ensures the greatest productivity of existing means of production, which has become practically axiomatic in classical political economy . . .' (p. 148). In a notable passage Dmitriev compares the role of commodity stocks with the strategy of 'intensified armament of the Powers in peace time' (pp. 148–9).

A most important implication of Dmitriev's analysis is his account of 'the economic consequences of technical progress' (Section 7). The lowering of necessary production costs over time, in conditions of unrestricted competition, results only partly in lower prices; technical progress raises the level of potential supply (which includes stocks, production and excess capacity) at which the *bénéfice momentané*, obtained by individual producers breaking their tacit price-collusion, disappears. '*Therefore an expansion of output following a reduction of production costs will, in general, extend not only to an expansion of supply but also to an increase in excess commodity inventories*' (p. 171). The building up of excess commodity inventories following technical progress gives rise to fluctuations in the levels of output capacity, capacity utilisation, and inventory levels (pp. 173–8). When technical progress takes place, 'overproduction' periodically occurs, and this '*is in no sense a result of errors of economic judgement,* i.e. it is not a consequence of the inability of production to adapt to excessively variable demand . . . but is a direct result of the struggle of competing entrepreneurs, *each of whom is motivated in his own actions by quite correct economic judgement*' (p. 177). Here again Dmitriev's modernity is apparent; and his dramatic description of the phases of the cycle is a striking piece of economic literature.

The rise of non-productive costs in conditions of unrestricted competition has nothing to do with the presence of middle men between producers and direct consumers of commodities (Appendix to Section 6), although their presence amplifies the fluctuations generated by technical progress (pp. 172–3). The only way of eliminating wasted output, excess inventories and unused capacity, and the non-productive costs which these involve, is the establishment of forward markets (*Terminhandel*): 'forward contracts make non-productive "reserve stocks" unnecessary since they make it possible to sell goods which have still not been produced but merely can be produced . . .' (p. 178, footnote 1). Dmitriev relegates this qualification to a footnote, but this is really a central point in his argument, because if there was a full-fledged system of forward markets his whole analysis would collapse. The observable fact that forward markets for manufactured commodities are conspicuously absent in all the economies of the world as we know it makes his analysis infinitely more relevant to the understanding of economic life than the wishful picture of conventional competitive analysis.

Utility, production, competition

Having established that under no circumstance, not even under constant production costs, is the Ricardian theory of prices based on necessary production costs valid, Dmitriev in his Third Essay naturally turns to the investigation of the 'conditions of consumption' which concur necessarily to price determination.

In a fascinating excursus into the history of economic thought Dmitriev marshals German, French, Italian, English and Russian literature on the subject of utility. He takes the view that 'we find *all the information* needed for the construction of a *finished* theory of marginal utility in the work of such an "old" economist as Galiani, the first "positivist" in political economy . . .'; while 'An impartial analysis must lead to the conclusion that the Austrian school as such (Menger, Böhm-Bawerk, von Wieser and others) *added very little* (unless much significance is given to the introduction of new terms) to what had been done before them *for the solution of the problem* ' (p. 181). A fuller formulation of Galiani's approach, however, is credited to a group of economists who used the mathematical method, which is 'the method of precise knowledge'; 'These included Walras (who may justifiably be regarded as the creator of marginal utility theory), Launhardt, Auspitz and Lieben and Jevons . . .' (p. 182).

Dmitriev gives the Walrasian equations for the case of pure exchange, and accepts them as a rigorous model for the exchange relations of an arbitrarily large number of individuals and products. For Dmitriev, the short-run equilibrium of an economic system is determined by the given levels of supply and the demand functions. (Dmitriev does not enquire into the conditions for the existence, economic meaningfulness, uniqueness and stability of the solution; since he ends up by rejecting this approach, an implicit assumption that all these conditions are satisfied does not harm the following reasoning.)[1] If prices of commodities happen to coincide with their necessary reproduction costs, actual prices will correspond to the solution of the Walrasian system. But if the supply level of a commodity is such that its price exceeds its necessary reproduction costs, the question of the distribution of the extra-normal profit lies, for Dmitriev, 'outside the sphere of economic research', because it is the result of a 'struggle' and is taken as a question of fact by economic theory. There may be 'a general *sociological* solution' (p. 207); 'Otherwise we should have to admit that the question cannot have any *general* solution at all' (*ibid.*). The behaviour of supply in subsequent periods – in the absence of generalised forward markets – is expected by Dmitriev to be regulated in this case by his competition theory: output capacity, output, inventory levels and actual sales are expected to take the values determined by the analysis in the Second Essay (p. 206). This competition analysis, in turn, can only obtain from utility theories certain minimum basic features of utility functions (pp. 210–11), but should not rely on 'hasty and false generalisations' such as the use of logarithmic functions.

We can see now the basic outcome of Dmitriev's 'attempt at an organic synthesis between the labour theory of value and the theory of marginal utility'. There is a special case where Ricardo's theory of prices and the profit rate holds, regardless of what we can broadly label 'demand conditions'; this is the case of constant costs for a given real wage rate, provided 'competition lowers prices' to the level of necessary costs, including profit (First Essay). But unrestricted competition in the absence of forward markets leads to tacit price collusion among entrepreneurs, and generates non-productive costs (excess inventories, unused capacity, advertising) and therefore raises price above necessary cost, up

---

[1] 'Stability' here means simply the ability of the system to reach the equilibrium solution, when production and consumption plans are made by individuals on the basis of prices different from equilibrium prices, as in Walras's case of prices *criés par hazard*.

to a level which depends on the shape of the demand curve and the number of competitors; in no case, therefore, can price determination be independent of demand conditions, either in the short or in the long run (Second Essay). Because of the absence of forward markets, general equilibrium theory can handle only the special case where equilibrium prices correspond to the necessary reproduction cost (of the last unit produced of each commodity). Outside this case, which is just as special as the 'pure' Ricardian case, price theory becomes the theory of the self-defeating attempts, by economic agents, to gain from a social struggle which is rational by the standards of individuals though not of society, and the theory of the ensuing waste and fluctuations (Third Essay).

This may be regarded as a work of destruction, rather than the promised 'synthesis', but it is also a blueprint for economic investigations. The criticisms put forward by Dmitriev in 1902 are still valid, today, equally against those neo-Ricardians who, unduly extrapolating Sraffa's results, believe they can neglect the role of demand in the theory of prices and distribution, and against those neo-Walrasians who believe that general equilibrium theory contains the answers to every economic question. Marxists and Keynesians should receive support and inspiration from Dmitriev's work. But there is enough in these Essays to shake anybody's complacency.

King's College   Domenico Mario Nuti
Cambridge

V. K. DMITRIEV: A BIOGRAPHICAL NOTE

Vladimir Karpovich Dmitriev was born on 24 November 1868 on the Rai estate in Smolensk Gubernia, Smolensk Uezd. He was educated first in the Tula Classical Gymnasium, where he completed his studies in 1888. He then went to Moscow University to study Medicine, but subsequently transferred to the Law Faculty, where he began his studies on Political Economy. After graduating in 1896 he married T. A. Vatatsi and left to take the post of excise controller in the small town of Von'kovitsy in Podol'sk Gubernia. He served there for three years, but contracted pulmonary tuberculosis and had to leave the service. This serious disease never abandoned him, and finally caused his death on 30 November 1913. N. N. Shaposhnikov, who recorded these basic data in his memorial lecture at a meeting of the A. I. Chuprov Society held in 1914 in honour of Dmitriev, adds that 'Dmitriev was in great need all his life. The harsh material conditions and lack of resources for adequate treatment un-doubtedly hastened his end'.[1]

Dmitriev's First Essay appeared in 1898, under the title:

Ekonomicheskie Ocherki, Vyp. I, 'Teoriya tsênnosti D. Ricardo (opyt' tochnago analyza)' [*Economic Essays*, Issue I, The theory of value of D. Ricardo, an attempt at a rigorous analysis], Moscow, pp. 65.

The Second and Third Essays appeared in 1902, under the title:

Ekonomicheskie Ocherki, 'Chast' l-aya (opyt' organicheskago sinteza trudovoi teorii tsênnosti i teorii predêl'noi poleznosti)', Vypuski 2–i i 3–i. Ocherk 2–i: 'Teoriya konkurrentsii Og. Kurno (Velikago "zabytago" ekonomista)'. Ocherk 3–i: 'Teoriya predêl'noi poleznosti' [*Economic Essays*, Part i, Attempt at an organic synthesis of the labour theory of value and the theory of marginal utility, Issues 2 and 3. Second Essay: The theory of competition of A. Cournot (the great 'forgotten' econo-mist). Third Essay: The theory of marginal utility], Moscow, p. 152. The volume includes a Zakliuchenie (Conclusion).

The three essays were reissued together in 1904, under the title:

Ekonomicheskie Ocherki (Seriya I-aya: 'opyt' organicheskago sinteza trudovoi teorii tsênnosti i teorii predêl'noi poleznosti') [*Economic Essays*, First Series: Attempt at an organic synthesis of the labour theory of

[1] Shaposhnikov, 'Pervyi . . .', p. 13.

value and the theory of marginal utility], Moscow, pp. 65 + 152. The text of this issue is completely unchanged, including the page numbers of the original Essays.

According to Shaposhnikov, the Essays were completed long before their publication, but 'Dmitriev had to seek a publisher for years' for this as well as for his next book. 'These first three essays' – wrote Dmitriev in his Conclusion – 'which are united by a common plan, constitute a complete theory of the general elements of value'. In his intention the three Essays represented 'the *first part* of our attempt at analysing the basic propositions of theoretical economics' (p. 213). He was planning to write a second series of at least three further Essays, on the theory of rent (p. 156, pp. 160–1), on the theory of industrial crises (p. 173) and on the theory of monetary circulation (p. 178, p. 213). These Essays were apparently never written, or at any rate there is no record of their publication. Copies of the 1898, 1902 and 1904 issues are available at the Lenin Library, Moscow, and at the Saltykov Shchedrin National Library, Leningrad. The only original copy of the 1904 edition traced in the West belongs to the Sraffa collection; a microfilm of the same edition is available at the Library of the London School of Economics.

Dmitriev's next book was:

Kriticheskie izslêdovaniya o potreblenii alkogolya v Rossii, s predisl. P. B. Struve, Issledovaniya i raboty po polit. ekonomii i obshchestv. znaniyam, izd. pod red. P. B. Struve, Vyp. I [*Critical studies on the consumption of alcohol in Russia*, with an introduction by P. V. Struve; Studies and works in political economy and social sciences, edited by P. V. Struve, Issue I], Moscow, 1911, pp. xii + 283 (with an English translation of the table of contents).

Dmitriev also published the following articles and reviews:

1. A Review of A. Manuilov, *Ponyatie tsênnosti* [*The concept of value*], *Russkoe Ekonomicheskoe Obozrênie*, 1901, n. 7.
2. 'Teoriya tsênnosti (obzor literatury na russkom yazyk)' [The theory of value, a survey of Russian literature], *Kriticheskoe Obozrênie*, 1908, n. 2.
3. 'Alkogolizm, kak massovoe yavlienie v Rossii (obzor literaturno-statisticheskikh materialov)' [Alcoholism as a mass phenomenon in Russia, a review of literary and statistical materials], *Kriticheskoe Obozrênie*, 1908, n. 8.
4. 'Teoreticheskaya statistika (obzor nauchnoi i nauchno-popularnoi literatury na russkom yazyk)' [Theoretical statistics, a survey of scientific and popularising publications in Russian], *Kriticheskoe Obozrênie*, 1909, n. 6.

5. 'Novyi Russki traktat po teorii politicheskoi ekonomii (razbor *Osnov' politicheskoi ekonomii* Tugan-Baranovskago)' [A new Russian treatise on the theory of political economy, an analysis of Tugan-Baranovsky's *Principles of Political Economy*, 1909], *Russkaya Mysl*, 1909, n. 11.

6. 'Novyi Opyt' "rêsheniya" problemy raspredêleniya (razbor knigi Solntseva *Zarabotnaya Plata*)' [A new attempt to 'solve' the problem of distribution, a review of S. I. Solntsev's book *The wage as a problem of distribution*, 1911], *Russkaya Mysl*, 1912, n. 3.

In addition, Dmitriev published a number of other minor reviews, in *Kriticheskoe Obozrênie* and *Russkaya Mysl*.

The importance of Dmitriev's contribution to economic theory was recognised soon after the publication of his *Essays*. L. von Bortkiewicz refers to a 'very favourable' review by A. I. Chuprov, in *Mitteilungen des St. Petersburger Polytechnischen Instituts*, 1905, which drew his attention to the *Essays*.[1] Dmitriev's price equations were extensively used and acknowledged by Bortkiewicz in his work on Marx; he wrote of this 'remarkable work': 'Since the author employs algebraic and geometrical means of exposition and of demonstration, it is hardly surprising that his publication (apparently a first work!) has received very little notice (I mean of course from Russians), although it bears evidence of an exceptional theoretical talent and presents something really new.'[2] P. Struve in 1913 hailed Dmitriev as a 'logically and mathematically thought-out and tested Ricardo'.[3] N. N. Shaposhnikov, in his memorial lecture a year after Dmitriev's death, said that 'Russian economics has suffered a heavy loss and has been deprived of one of its most talented and devoted servants'; 'Dmitriev was the first Russian member of the mathematical school of political economy, and Russian economics may take pride in such a member'; 'Dmitriev's study will always be of great significance for a person who acknowledges the value of and the need for abstract analysis of economic problems'.[4] Until shortly after the October Revolution Dmitriev was widely mentioned in Russian economic literature; M. Kaser remarks that 'there are . . . more references to him than to Marx in Yurovsky's *Essays on Price Theory*, published in Saratov in 1919'.[5] But from then on Dmitriev was entirely forgotten in Soviet economic literature, until Academician Nemchinov brought him out of official oblivion in 1959 (see p. 9). Since then Dmitriev has been repeatedly quoted and referred to in Soviet literature. His books have

---

[1] von Bortkiewicz, 'Wertrechnung . . .', p. 22 of the English translation.
[2] *Ibid.*
[3] P. Struve, *Russkaya Mysl*, 1913, n. 10.
[4] Shaposhnikov, 'Pervyi . . .', pp. 3, 6, 11.
[5] Kaser, *Soviet Economics*, p. 31.

not been reprinted to date (1972) and he is still being described in Soviet handbooks on the history of economic thought as a 'bourgeois economist',[1] but he is now unanimously considered as the father and founder of Russian mathematical economics.[2]

DMN

---

[1] See Pashkov (Ed.), '*Istoriya* . . .', p. 182.

[2] A. L. Vainshtein, for instance, calls Dmitriev 'our first and eminent mathematical economist'; see his 'Vozniknovenie i razvitie primeneniya linenogo programmirovaniya v SSSR' [The birth and development of linear programming in the USSR] in L. E. Mints (Ed.), *Ekonomiko-matematicheskie metody* [Economic-mathematical methods], Moscow, 1966.

EDITORIAL NOTE

This translation has been made from a microfilm of the 1904 edition, kindly lent by the London School of Economics. Transliteration of Russian words follows the British Standard (2979C:1959) throughout, with the exception of names ending in -ii, oi and -yi, which have been transliterated as -y because most authors are already known in English with such an ending (e.g. Tugan-Baranovsky, Zalessky, etc.). When it is clear that the word *produkt* means 'product *for the market*', it has often been rendered as 'commodity', as if it were *tovar*. Dmitriev follows the convention, introduced by Auspitz and Lieben, of calling 'demand curve' what is today generally known as 'gross revenue curve'; this has been rendered according to modern usage, unless specific reference to Auspitz and Lieben was made in the text. The Russian text contains many printers' errors in addition to those noted on the Russian errata slip at the end of the First Essay; self-evident errors have been corrected without comment. A number of mathematical slips or misprints in the equations have also been corrected, whenever they did not affect the argument; some apparent actual mistakes have been left in, with an editorial note. Lettering of diagrams did not always correspond to the description in the text; this has been corrected, and the lettering system has been standardised (e.g. Greek letters are used for angles only) and does not correspond to the original letters. One particularly overcrowded diagram (Figure 5 in the original, Second Essay) has been split into two separate diagrams (Figures 2.6 and 2.7, same Essay) for the sake of clarity. Diagrams and equations, which were variously identified in the original (by Roman and Arabic numbers, Latin and Greek, capital and lower case letters, with or without subscripts) are numbered in one sequence, with Arabic numbers in each Essay; unlike the original, *all* equations are now identified by a number. Dmitriev used only a handful of symbols to indicate a large number of different concepts and functional relationships: mostly f and F for functions, and x and y (or X and Y) for variables; even then he was not consistent in his notation (for instance, price is indicated as x, or X, or Y in the First Essay, and in the same pages X is also used to indicate labour embodied; in the Second Essay the quantity produced is indicated alternatively as x, y, X, Y, Q, D); since there is no ambiguity in the text about the meanings of the equations, notation has been standardised to spare the reader unnecessary confusion. Mathematical notation is rather archaic (i.e. longhand expressions, with frequent use of subscripts) but any appreciable simplification would have required rather drastic alterations, and has therefore not been attempted (except that double subscripts of the kind A_{t_1} have been simplified to single subscripts of the kind A_{t1} for typographical convenience, without loss of clarity).

Original cross references (mostly of the kind 'as we have said *in the appropriate place* . . .') have been supplemented, and a number have been added. Bibliographical references in the original tended to be scanty, inadequate and often inaccurate, possibly quoted from memory; bibliographical details have been checked and supplemented; a very few references are untraceable. A bibliography has been compiled, giving accessible editions of the texts and, where possible, citing the original edition. Most of Dmitriev's quotations from non-Russian authors were in the original language; these have been translated into English, and whenever possible have been taken from already existing English editions of the works. Dr B. Schefold has translated German passages. Quotations in Russian from non-Russian authors have been traced and either translated from the original language or taken from an existing English translation; with the exception of those quotations on the title page of each essay, for which Dmitriev gives no information other than the author; these have been retranslated from their Russian translation. In the original Russian text, bibliographical data were sometimes given in the body of the text, sometimes in footnotes; on the other hand, minor digressions which one would normally expect to find in footnotes were often embodied in the text, sometimes preceded by the words *Note* or *N.B.*; conversely, brief sentences obviously belonging to the text are often found in footnotes. There were many exceedingly long sentences, with a most profuse use of brackets. To some extent, this was due to the stratified nature of the text, to which Dmitriev must have repeatedly returned in the long delay between writing and printing. An attempt has been made here at a more organic presentation of the material: sentences have been broken, many brackets have been removed, and some material and bibliographical information has been moved from the text to the footnotes and *vice versa*. All these apparently extensive changes do not go, however, beyond the changes that nowadays would normally be introduced by a sub-editor in any manuscript unfit for the printer; they have been introduced in the belief that because Dmitriev had a bad publisher this should not spoil the enjoyment of a classic text by the modern reader. The text is of course unabridged. Those readers who wish to sample the difficult and at times almost unintelligible reading of the original may turn to the French edition of this book (Paris 1968) where equations, diagrams, text and footnotes, references and bibliography are virtually untouched.

DMN

FIRST ESSAY

THE THEORY OF VALUE OF DAVID RICARDO

An attempt at a rigorous analysis

No study made by man can be said to be true knowledge unless it has been mathematically demonstrated. Leonardo da Vinci

I assert that the amount of true science to be found in any knowledge in the natural sciences is no greater than the amount of mathematics to be found in it. E. Kant

The mathematical method is invariably applicable as a tool whatever the subject under investigation. H. C. Carey

Mathematics is the prototype of deductive science; as its complication increases, every deduction becomes mathematical and it is precisely the complexity of deductive reasoning which makes essential the language of mathematical signs. E. Wundt

Anyone who accepts abstract analysis ought also to accept all its natural logical tools (including the mathematical method). L. Slonimsky

Mathematics should be used where it is impossible to arrive at the truth without its assistance. Were there to be such antipathy to mathematical analysis in other branches of knowledge as there is in political economy, we should have remained in total ignorance of the most important laws of nature.
J. H. von Thünen

Writers (economists) would appear to have formed a false idea concerning the way in which mathematical analysis is applied to the theory of wealth. They have imagined that the use of symbols and formulae can have no other purpose apart from numerical operations . . . However, those who have a knowledge of mathematics know that mathematical analysis is not concerned solely with figures, that it also serves to establish relationships between quantities which cannot be numerically defined, between functions whose law cannot be expressed by algebraic symbols . . . It is natural to use mathematical notations whenever the need is to establish relationships between quantities. Even were mathematical notations not to be strictly necessary, it would obviously be unscientific to reject them solely because they are not equally comprehensible to every reader, given that they can facilitate the exposition, make it more accurate, lead to more detailed explanations and avoid the digressions of vague argument . . .
A. Cournot

I. INTRODUCTION: THE THEORY OF 'PRODUCTION COSTS' BEFORE RICARDO

The simplest formula expressing the relationship between price and production cost is

$$\text{Price} \geqslant \text{production costs.} \qquad (1)$$

This formula is not a result of a scientific analysis of the phenomena of economic life, but a simple statement of the self-evident fact that production cannot continue (at least for any appreciable length of time) if the price of the product does not cover the costs incurred.

It is strange, therefore, to ascribe the discovery of this truth to any given economist.[1] What had to be done to pass from this *fact* to a complete *theory of production costs* in economics was, first, to state the laws defining the magnitude of that surplus which is incorporated in a price over and above the costs incurred; second, to analyse actual costs incurred in production by the entrepreneur. The first problem was not satisfactorily solved even by Smith: he, of course, defines profit in terms of the relationship between demand and supply of capital, i.e. by a feature dependent on market conditions. Very little had been done before Smith also for the analysis of real production costs in the narrow sense, *not including profit.*

Note that we completely disregard, as having nothing in common with science, all the *unsubstantiated* assertions concerning laws of value proclaimed by various 'thinkers' without any more foundation than the 'authority' of their propounders. They include, for example, the 'theory' which states that value is determined by the amount of labour expended on the production of the product (Franklin and Petty)[2] or by the amount of labour and land (Cantillon, Locke and others).[3]

[1] See for instance P. Bois-Guillebert, *Les détails de la France*, Paris, 1843; K. Marx, *Zur Kritik der politischen Oekonomie*, Berlin, 1859, p. 32, and N. Sieber, *D. Ricardo i K. Marx v' ikh ekonomicheskikh issledovaniakh* [D. Ricardo and K. Marx in their economic research], Moscow, 1885.

[2] See *The Works of Benjamin Franklin*, edited by J. Sparks, 1856 ['Trade in general being nothing else but the exchange of labor for labor, the value of all things is . . most justly measured by labor'], Vol. 2, p. 267. Petty, however, attempts to make his assertion less arbitrary by stipulating *caeteris paribus*: 'If a man can bring to *London* an ounce of Silver out of the Earth in *Peru* in the same time that he can produce a bushel of Corn, then one is the natural price of the other; now if by reason of new and more easie Mines a man can get two ounces of Silver as easily as formerly he did one, then Corn will be as cheap at ten shillings the bushel, as it was before at five shillings *caeteris paribus*'; W. Petty, *A treatise of taxes and contributions*, London, 1662, Ch. 5, pp. 50–1 of the 1899 edition. The approach is undoubtedly scientific, but even so it limits the very meaning and sphere of application of the law as stated.

[3] R. Cantillon, *Essai sur la nature du commerce en général*, London, 1755; edited with an English translation by H. Higgs, London, 1931; Locke, *Works*, London, 1823, Vol. 5, *Of civil government*, para. 40.

We find the most detailed analysis of production costs in the works of Smith's immediate forerunner, Steuart. According to Steuart's theory (*Principles of Political Economy*, 1767, Book 2) the actual value of a thing is made up of the following elements: 'The value of the workman's sub-sistence and necessary expense both for supplying his personal wants and providing the instruments belonging to his profession' and 'the value of the materials, that is the first matter employed by the workman'.

According to Steuart, these three elements combined define the lower limit, below which the market price of the product cannot fall. What we see here is essentially a simple, detailed list of the expenditure which the capitalist producer incurs (as before, profit is related to market conditions, i.e. to the supply and demand of the given commodity); no traces of *scientific* analysis are, as yet, to be noted in this 'theory' of production costs. The only exception is the subsistence wage theory. Even before Adam Smith's work appeared, the theory had become established in economic science that wages tended toward the means of subsistence. It is even possible to find a fairly detailed development of the concept of the 'means of subsistence' (Cantillon, Petty and Turgot).[1]

However, it was only in Adam Smith's work that an explanation was given of the mechanism of the process by which wages are constantly maintained at the level of the means of subsistence. To sum up what has been said, we may express the state of the theory concerning the relation-ship between value and production costs at a time immediately preceding the appearance of Adam Smith's work by the following formula:

Price = outlay on wages (= the number of working days × the
daily subsistence of the worker *in terms of the product* ×
the price of the produce consumed by the workers)
+ outlay in the replacement of tools and materials (= the
quantity of tools and materials consumed in production
× *the price of the tools and materials*)
+ *the total of profit*
+ *rent* (= the sum paid for 'the assistance of natural
forces'). (2)

The quantities set in italics are the unknowns.

Naturally, at this stage of development the theory of production costs

[1] See Cantillon, 1755, who is quoted by Smith himself.

W. Petty defines the value of the average daily pay by what the worker needs to live, work and reproduce himself (*The Political Anatomy of Ireland*, London, 1691, p. 64, p. 181 of 1899 edition). Turgot states 'Workers are continuously obliged to lower the price one against the other. For all kinds of labour it must happen and does in fact happen that the worker's wage is limited to what is necessary for his subsistence' (A. R. J. Turgot, *Réflexions sur la formation et la distribution des richesses*, 1770, § vi, p. 10 of the 1844 edition).

1. The theory of 'production costs' before Ricardo

fully merits the reproach so often levelled at the theory of production costs *in general* (consequently also in its fully developed form), that it defines price from prices, that it defines one unknown from other un-knowns.[1] The problem facing Adam Smith was not an easy one, and it is therefore not surprising that his solution of it was far from complete. It was only in the writings of his successor, Ricardo, that the theory of production costs was completed. Nevertheless, Smith did contribute a very great deal to the correct solution of the problem. Above all, we find in Adam Smith a correct formulation of the problem to be solved which is undoubtedly very important for its correct solution.

Smith states that 'the relative or exchangeable value of goods' is determined by 'rules which men naturally observe in exchanging them either for money or for one another'.[2] This first eliminated any question of the *intrinsic* value of commodities: the object of research should be merely the *relative* value of commodities, their ratio of exchange (the term is borrowed from Jevons[3]) to avoid confusion arising from the use of the word value in two senses: exchange value and use value; use of the term 'ratio of exchange' eliminates the need for any qualification concerning the different meanings of the word 'value', such as is made by Smith[4] and Ricardo.

Smith then proceeds to an analysis of the concept of production costs or, to be more precise, to an analysis of those elements from which they are made up for the capitalist entrepreneur. In his theory of wages Adam Smith merely develops and provides greater basis for the hypothesis

[1] E.g. Sieber, 1885, p. 109. Sieber quotes the words of Kamorzhinsky: 'It may be objected against theories of production costs that they explain the price of a good not from such elements as would be independent of price, but from other prices, because production costs are calculated from the price of all the goods needed for production'. Sieber adds to this: 'The formulation of the question of production costs given by us is a clear expression of the discontent which arises in the minds of some, unfortunately very few of the newest economists when discussing terms which *only seemingly* contain a known and definite meaning. . . .'

[2] A. Smith, *An enquiry into the nature and causes of the wealth of nations* (1776), Book I, Ch. 4, p. 42, of the 1814 edition.

[3] Jevons uses the term 'the ratio of exchange'; Zalessky translates this in our opinion, quite unsuccessfully in our opinion, by the words *otnoshenie obmena* [exchange relation]. See Zalessky *Uchenie o tsennosti* [Theory of value], Kazan, 1893, Book II, p. 122.

[4] 'The word *value*', states Smith, 'has two different meanings and sometimes expresses the utility of some particular object, and sometimes the power of purchasing other goods which the possession of that object conveys. The one may be called "value in use"; the other, "value in exchange"' (Book I, Ch. 4, p. 42 of the 1814 edition).

Although Adam Smith explained the concept of exchange value excellently he did not venture to give an equally precise definition of 'use value' or 'usefulness'. The first completely correct definition of the concept of 'usefulness' is found in F. Galiani, an Italian economist of the last century: 'I call utility the attitude of an object to procure us happiness', *Della moneta* (1750), Ch. 2, p. 59.

41

already stated by preceding economists that real wages have a tendency to coincide with the essential means of subsistence of the worker.[1]

The main changes made by Smith to the formula of production costs relate to the second and third terms of the second part of equation (2). Smith was the first to point out that the second term, the value of the tools and materials used in production, could invariably be broken down, in its turn, into *wages, profit* and *rent* (by 'profit' and 'rent' we shall invariably understand *the sum of profit* and the *sum of rent* in money) so that all production costs may be reduced to the three elements: wages, profit and rent. These three parts, states Smith,

> 'seem either immediately or ultimately to make up the whole price of corn. A fourth part, it may perhaps be thought, is necessary for replacing the stock of the farmer, or for compensating the wear and tear of his labouring cattle, and other instruments of husbandry. But it must be considered that the price of any instrument of husbandry, such as a labouring horse, is itself made up of the same three parts; the rent of the land upon which he is reared, the labour of tending and rearing him, and the profits of the farmer who advances both the rent of this land, and the wages of this labour. Though the price of the corn, therefore, may pay the price as well as the maintenance of the horse, the whole price still resolves itself either immediately or ultimately into the same three parts of rent, labour and profit.'

This hypothesis is subsequently extended by Smith to all other products (Smith, Book I, Ch. 6, p. 81 of 1814 Edition).

Smith himself notes instances when one (and sometimes even two) of these three basic elements of price are absent, so that the price of the product is reduced in the last analysis to only two elements, *wages and profits* (*Ibid.*).

In view of the inconsistency of Smith's views on rent, we shall subsequently consider only the latter case. Since, as is explained by Ricardo, the cause for the appearance of rent is that different portions of the same commodity sold in the same market (and consequently commanding the same price) are produced with different costs, in order to exclude rent from price, we have to make the *conventional* assumption that all units of a given commodity are produced with equal costs (and as a corollary of this, that all portions of the capital employed in the given production are *equally productive*). Formula (2) then becomes:

$$X_A = (n_A a X_a + n_1 a X_a + n_2 a X_a + \cdots + n_m a X_a) + (y_A + y_1 + y_2 + \cdots + y_m) \quad (3)$$

---

[1] Smith himself cites Cantillon on this question (Smith, Book I, Ch. 8, p. 110 of 1814 edition); the theory of the 'iron' law of wages reached its final development, of course, in the writings of David Ricardo, and we shall therefore defer closer examination of this question until we analyse Ricardo's theory of value.

where X_A is the price of product A; $n_A, n_1, n_2, \ldots, n_m$ are the number of working days expended in production; a is the amount of a product, e.g. corn, consumed by a worker in a day (in order to simplify the formula we assume that a worker consumes one product, e.g. corn, which is of course a simplification that Ricardo also makes in his analysis; we shall see subsequently that nothing is altered in our analysis if we accept that the workers consume several products); X_a is the price of product a; $y_A, y_1, y_2, \ldots, y_m$ are the profits incorporated in the price of product A; these include both the profit obtained by the producer of product A himself, and the profit of the producers of the tools and materials consumed in the production of product A. Or if

$$\begin{cases} n_A + n_1 + n_2 + \cdots + n_m = N_A \\ y_A + y_1 + y_2 + \cdots + y_m = Y_A \end{cases} \tag{4}$$

then we obtain

$$X_A = N_A a x_a + Y_A, \tag{5}$$

where N_A is the total sum of the labour directly or *indirectly* expended in the production of product A, and Y_A is the total sum of the profit received by all the producers involved directly or *indirectly* (i.e. by the production of materials and tools) in the production of commodity A.

Therefore, the total price of product A is, in the absence of rent, made up of only two elements: wages and profit. Smith repeatedly objected to this hypothesis;[1] these objections have once again been advanced comparatively recently, as an argument against the labour theory of value, by economists of the 'Austrian school', supporters of the theory of marginal utility.

What these objections amount to is that because capital is essential in all branches of production in the *modern* economy, it is impossible to eliminate the element of capital when calculating production costs. For the production of capital it is once again capital which is invariably needed. It is asked how it is possible to calculate the amount of labour expended for the production of a given economic good from the very beginning of history, when man managed without capital, down to the present time. There is no doubt that at present capital is invariably produced by capital; it is also correct that it is an impossible task to calculate the amount of labour expended in a given product from the time of the creation of the first capital by labour alone. However, there is no need for such a calculation: the sum of the labour expended on the production of a given product may be determined without such historical digressions.

[1] See K. Marx, *Capital*, Vol. I (1867), Part 3.

Let us denote by N the total amount of labour directly and indirectly expended on the production of a unit of commodity A; let the amount of labour directly consumed in production be n_A; let several kinds of 'technical capital' $K_1, K_2, \ldots, K_m$ be involved in production; let there be consumed in production $1/m_1$ of the capital K_1, $1/m_2$ of the capital $K_2, \ldots, 1/m_M$ of the capital K_M; further, let the amount of labour directly and indirectly expended on the production of the capital K_1 be N_1, that expended on production of the capital K_2 be $N_2, \ldots$, that expended on production of the capital K_M be N_M, in which case the total sum of the labour expended on the production of a unit of commodity A will be:

$$N_A = n_A + \frac{1}{m_1} N_1 + \frac{1}{m_2} N_2 + \cdots + \frac{1}{m_M} N_M. \qquad (6)$$

Since n_A and $m_1, m_2, \ldots, m_M$ are here quantities given by the technical conditions of production of the product A, N_A, N_1, $N_2, \ldots$, N_M are unknowns.

Other capital goods, some of which are included in this series and others not, are involved in their turn in the production of capital goods $K_1, K_2, \ldots, K_M$, to which the quantities of labour $N_1, N_2, \ldots, N_M$ of this equation correspond. Let the number of all the *different* capital goods involved both directly and indirectly in the production of the product A be M (the number is always finite).[1]

For the amount of labour needed for the production of any capital K_1 out of the M capital goods it is obviously possible to compile an equation completely similar to equation (6); quantities N corresponding to the capital goods involved in the production of the capital K_I will be incorporated in the second part of such an equation, and since M is a finite number, we shall obtain M equations with M unknowns (N_1, N_2, $N_3, \ldots, N_M$); adding in equation (6), we obtain a system of $(M+1)$ equations with $(M+1)$ unknowns (N_A, N_1, N_2, N_M) which is always adequate for the determination of N, giving the required sum of labour expended on the production of the product A. Therefore, without any digressions into the prehistoric times of the first inception of technical capital, we can always find the total sum of the labour directly and indirectly expended on the production of any product *under present-day production conditions*, both of this product itself and of those capital goods involved in its production. As we have seen, the fact that all capital under *present-day* conditions is itself produced with the assistance of other capital in no way hinders a precise solution of the problem.

It should not, however, be thought that the whole system of our $(M+1)$ equations is indispensable for the determination of the total

---

[1] This is because, despite the diversity and complexity of present-day technology, even the number of *all possible* qualitatively different capital goods is always a finite quantity.

labour expended on the production of any product I; all the unknowns incorporated in the expression of this sum may frequently be excluded from the smallest number of equations. For example, let the capital good K_1 be involved in production of the product; the capital goods K_2 and K_3 in production of capital good K_1; K_1 and K_3 in production of K_2; K_1 and K_2 in production of K_3 and so on; in that case, using the same notations as before, we shall have a system of four equations with four unknowns, from which N_I is determined by successive substitution:*

$$
\left.
\begin{aligned}
N_I &= n_I + \frac{1}{m_1} \cdot N_1 \\[2ex]
N_1 &= n_1 + \frac{1}{m_2} \cdot N_2 + \frac{1}{m_3} N_3. \\[2ex]
N_2 &= n_2 + \frac{1}{m_4} \cdot N_1 + \frac{1}{m_5} N_3 \\[2ex]
N_3 &= n_3 + \frac{1}{m_6} \cdot N_1 + \frac{1}{m_7} N_2
\end{aligned}
\right\}
\qquad (7)
$$

It is, of course, possible to imagine even simpler cases.[1]

Thus the production costs formula may always be reduced to the expression:

$$ X_A = N_A a X_a + Y_A. \qquad (8) $$

* *Ed. note.* The system of equations given by Dmitriev does not lend itself to solution by substitution: commodities 1 and 3 require commodity 2 and vice versa; commodity 1 requires commodity 3 and vice versa, i.e. there are feedbacks in the determination of the price system by substitution. However, Dmitriev is right in thinking that the solution of the system is simplified by the existence of a number of zero-technical coefficients (for instance, when the input–output matrix is triangular, or quasi-triangular) and that it can sometimes be solved by substitution, although in the following footnote he rejects the idea of progressive 'layers' of production.

[1] We are absolutely unable to agree with the opinion of Tugan-Baranovsky who, while quite correctly opposing von Wieser's objection to the labour theory of value, states that 'In passing from one branch of industry to another manufacturing goods of increasingly higher orders relative to our product . . . we ultimately arrive at branches of industry which manufacture their own constant capital (in the terminology of Marx)' (*Yuridicheskii Vestnik*, October 1890, p. 223). Such a completely arbitrary assumption deprives the solution of the problem of the generality which is required. Nor can we accept, either in form or in content, the 'mathematical' solution of the problem which he proposes at the end of the paper; the conclusion at which he arrives may be obtained only thanks to the completely arbitrary and unreal assumption that the denominator of an infinite descending progression remains continuously the same. Furthermore, it is impossible to equate incommensurate quantities.

If we take the appropriate formula for any product, $B, C, \ldots$

$$\left.\begin{array}{l} X_B = N_B a X_a + Y_B \\ X_C = N_C a X_a + Y_C \end{array}\right\} \tag{9}$$

$\ldots$

and if we bear in mind that the task of the theory of value is to determine the proportion in which products are exchanged, we shall have

$$\left.\begin{array}{l} X_{AB} = \dfrac{X_A}{X_B} = \dfrac{N_A a X_A + Y_A}{N_B a X_A + Y_B} \\[3mm] X_{AC} = \dfrac{X_A}{X_C} = \dfrac{N_A a X_A + Y_A}{N_C a X_A + Y_C} \end{array}\right\} \tag{10}$$

$\ldots$

and so on, where X_{AB} will denote the value of product A in terms of B, i.e. the number of units of the product B given in the market for a unit of the product A.[1] For X_{AB} to be known, the quantities Y_A and Y_B must be given; Adam Smith's second important contribution to development of the theory of value was the analysis of these quantities. Smith first notes that the quantity Y is always related to the sum of the capital expended in production and to the time during which it is in circulation (in the production concerned). If, therefore, we denote the capital by Z and the time by T and assume that all the other quantities on which the amount of profit may depend are constant, we shall have:

$$Y = F(Z, T). \tag{11}$$

If we denote the sum of the profit attained in the given production A by a unit of capital (expressed in the same unit of value as the sum of the profit) in a time unit[2] by r_A (which we shall refer to as 'the rate of profit in the production of A'), the sum of the profits attained in the same production by Z units of capital in unit time will be Zr_A, if we take into consideration our assumption made above (with the methodological aim of excluding the phenomenon of rent from our analysis) that *all capital goods* expended in production *are equally productive*. Adding this profit in unit time to the initial capital Z, we obtain $Z + Zr_A = Z(1 + r_A)$; if this

---

[1] We adopt the condition $X_{AB} = X_A/X_B$ without special proof as being sufficiently evident; for a detailed proof see L. Walras, *Eléments d'économie politique pure*, Lausanne, 1874, Lesson 11, pp. 153–63 of the English translation of the 1926 edition, by W. Jaffé, *Elements of pure economics*, London, 1954. Walras shows by mathematical analysis that '*We do not have* perfect, *or general* market equilibrium unless the price of any two commodities in terms of the other is equal to the ratio of the prices of these two commodities in terms of any third commodity' (p. 157 of the English edition). See also Smith, *Wealth of nations*, Book I, Chs. 6 and 10.

[2] The 'period of the production concerned' may be taken as the unit in the interests of simplicity.

sum is left in production, after a further unit of time (assuming that the conditions of production remain unaltered) we have: $Z(1+r_A)(1+r_A) = Z(1+r_A)^2$, and repeating T times, we shall have $Z(1+r_A)^T$, from which the sum of the profit from Z units of capital in T units of time will be:

$$Y_A = Z(1+r_A)^T - Z = Z[(1+r_A)^T - 1]. \qquad (12)$$

(See Smith, Book I, Ch. 9, p. 160–1 of the 1814 edition.)

In setting this expression of profit as a function of the sum of capital and of time in our formulas of production costs, we obtain for the simplest case in which N_A working days are expended on the production of a unit of the product without the participation of technical capital:

$$Y_A = N_A a X_a[(1+r_A)^{T_A} - 1] \qquad (13)$$

where T_A will denote the time having elapsed between expenditure of the capital $N_A a x_a$ (it is assumed in the interests of simplicity that the whole sum is expended simultaneously) and sale of the product.

In addition to the labour directly expended in the production of A, let there also be expended some capital K_1, and let this capital itself be produced by n_1 days of labour with the assistance of the capital K_2, and let us assume in the interest of simplicity that this capital K_2 is itself produced without the participation of new technical capital by n_2 days of labour (this methodological approach is, of course, regularly used by Ricardo in his researches on value with the object of simplifying formulas and thus making them more suitable for analysis). Let the capitals K_1 and K_2 involved in the productions A and K_1 be completely used up in production without residue (such an assumption will undoubtedly simplify the formulas more than the equally arbitrary assumption made by Ricardo that capital goods are perpetual).

Suppose the time expended in production of the capital K_2 be T_{K2}, in which case, assuming in the interests of simplicity that the whole sum expended on production of the capital K_2, which equals $n_2 a X_a$, is expended simultaneously, we shall have as an expression of the price of the capital K_2:

$$X_{K2} = n_2 a X_a (1+r_{K2})^{T_{K2}} \qquad (14)$$

where r_{K2} is the 'rate of profit' in the production of K_2. Further, let the time expended on production of the capital K_1 be T_{K1}, in which case, deliberating in the same way as before (and making the same arbitrary assumptions), we shall have for X_{K1}:

$$X_{K1} = n_1 a X_a (1+r_{K1})^{T_{K1}} + n_2 a X_a (1+r_{K2})^{T_{K2}} (1+r_{K1})^{T_{K1}}. \qquad (15)$$

47

If, finally, the time expended on manufacture of the product A is equal to T_A, we shall have for X_A

$$X_A = n_A a X_a (1+r_A)^{T_A} + n_1 a X_a (1+r_{K1})^{T_{K1}}(1+r_A)^{T_A} +$$
$$+ n_2 a X_a (1+r_{K2})^{T_{K2}}(1+r_{K1})^{T_{K1}}(1+r_A)^{T_A}. \quad (16)$$

If we compare this expression of price with the former expression

$$X_A = N_A a X_a + (y_A + y_1 + y_2 + \cdots + y_m) \quad (17)$$

we see that instead of the unknowns $y_{A1}, y_1, \ldots$, which denoted the *sums* of the profits of the different entrepreneurs directly or indirectly involved in production of product A, we now have another series of unknowns r_A, $r_{K1}, r_{K2}, \ldots$ denoting the *rate of profit* in the different branches of industry involved in the production of A. Therefore, the number of unknowns still remains the same (T_A, T_{K1}, T_{K2}, $\ldots$ incorporated in the new expression of price are known quantities dependent on the technical conditions of production of A, K_1, $K_2 \ldots$ and so on). The importance of the transformations made by us to the production costs formula is revealed only in connection with another hypothesis of prime importance established by Adam Smith, namely the hypothesis that the 'rate of profit' tends to be equalised in all branches of industry. By virtue of this hypothesis we shall have $r_A = r_{K1} = r_{K2} \ldots = r$, where r is taken to mean the *general* level towards which the rate of profit of individual branches of industry tends.[1]

Adam Smith arrives at this hypothesis deductively from the basic premise that every man aspires to the greatest advantage (Smith, Book I, Ch. 10, p. 162 of 1814 edition). Smith reasons as follows: if profit in some branch of industry A is higher than in others, this will compel industrialists from other branches to convert to production of the product A; *as a consequence of this production will expand, the supply of the product A will increase* and the price of the product which is, *caeteris paribus*, inversely proportional to the supply, will fall. But since *production costs will remain the same*, the profit on capital, which is the difference between the price and the production costs, will fall; if, nevertheless, it were still to be above the general level, this would cause a new conversion of producers from other branches and a new reduction of the price until, finally, profit reached the general level; there could be no further reduction of profit, since this would destroy the motive (exceptional profit) for the conversion of producers from other branches.

At this point we shall not make a critical analysis of this theory, which is completely accepted by Ricardo: we shall demonstrate its incorrectness and arbitrary nature in the Second Essay when analysing the 'theory

---

[1] We naturally assume that r, r_{K1}, r_{K2}, $\ldots$ are all adjusted to a common unit of time and unit of value expended.

of competition' (all that we have done here has been to indicate the arbitrary assumptions by setting them in italics). The whole of Smith's reasoning in this case is based on the arbitrary assumption that the amount of a given good may be increased without limit by the application of labour and capital and that its production is under the influence of free competition, and that therefore the law of the equality of the 'profit rate' in different branches of production applies only to goods which satisfy this *arbitrary* assumption.

If we make the corresponding transformations to the expressions X_A, X_B, ... we shall have

$$X_A = n_A a X_a (1+r)^{t_A} + n_1 a X_a (1+r)^{t_A+t_{A1}} + n_2 a X_a (1+r)^{t_A+t_{A1}+t_{A2}} + \cdots$$

(18)

for any product A, where the terms t_{A1}, t_{A2}, ... denote the periods of time expended on the production of capital goods of the first, second and higher orders involved in manufacture of product A, and

$$X_B = m_B a X_a (1+r)^{t_B} + m_1 a X_a (1+r)^{t_B+t_{B1}} + m_2 a X_a (1+r)^{t_B+t_{B1}+t_{B2}} + \cdots$$

(19)

for any product B [where m_B, m_1 and m_2 are labour outlays occurred respectively t_B, t_{B1}, t_{B2} time periods earlier].

We take the ratio of X_A to X_B and obtain:

$$X_{AB} = \frac{n_A a X_a (1+r)^{t_A} + n_1 a X_a (1+r)^{t_A+t_{A1}} + n_2 a X_a (1+r)^{t_A+t_{A1}+t_{A2}} + \cdots}{m_B a X_a (1+r)^{t_B} + m_1 a X_a (1+r)^{t_B+t_{B1}} + m_2 a X_a (1+r)^{t_B+t_{B1}+t_{B2}} + \cdots}.$$

(20)

If r is given, X_{AB} will also be a quite definite quantity and, consequently, the problem of the exchange proportion will be solved (since all the other exchange proportions may be similarly determined for a given product A: X_{AC}, X_{AD}, X_{AE} etc.).

However, Adam Smith did not proceed any further in his analysis of production costs. The honour for a complete solution of the problem belongs to his great successor Ricardo. Smith himself related the magnitude of r to the abundance of the supply of capital. He says: 'The increase of stock, which raises wages, tends to lower profit. When the stocks of many rich merchants are turned into the same trade, their mutual competition naturally tends to lower its profits; and when there is a like increase of stock in all the different trades carried on in the same society, the same competition must produce the same effect in them all' (Smith, Book I, Ch. 9, p. 143 of the 1814 edition).

If we denote the supply of capital by D, then $r = \phi(D)$ and $\mathrm{d}\phi(D)/\mathrm{d}D < 0$, i.e. as the supply of capital increases the profit rate declines. The actual form of the function ϕ is taken by Smith to be empirically given, despite the fact that the relationship between r and D undoubtedly already belongs to the sphere of *economic analysis* (as is shown by the writings of Ricardo); Smith does not give us any such analysis, although we find a completely accurate statement of the cause of the reduction in profit when capital goods increase *independent of competition* (see Smith, Book I, Ch. 9, p. 151 of the 1814 edition).

2. RICARDO'S THEORY OF VALUE

The most important point in Ricardo's theory is undoubtedly his theory of the conditions defining the 'average' profit rate to which, according to Smith's theory, profit tends in the individual branches of industry. As we have seen, this question was left unanswered in the writings of Smith, if we disregard his references to the relationship between the demand and supply of capital. We have to ask ourselves whether it was actually solved by Ricardo. Strange as it may seem, in view of the remarkable clarity of Ricardo's writings, negative answers to this question are still to be found in economic literature. It will suffice to mention the critical writings on the question of profit of E. Böhm-Bawerk (*Kapital und Kapitalzins*, Vol. 1, *Geschichte und Kritik der Kapitalzins Theorien*, pp. 101–11) and Zalessky (*Uchenie o proiskhozhdenii pribyli na kapital* [The theory of the origin of profit on capital], Kazan, 1898, Vol. II, p. 52); such views are particularly surprising when they are expressed by economists who have used the precise mathematical method for their analysis.[1]

Thus, in his most interesting analysis of Ricardo's theory of value[2] (which contains a model analysis of the theory of rent), Yu. Zhukovsky states, after having expounded Ricardo's theory of profit,

'But all this defines only the relative magnitude of the profit on capital or the order of its reduction. Ricardo however does not provide any answer to the question of how to determine the initial magnitude of the profit from which wages are subsequently deducted, the initial magnitude of the percentage on capital, and we would note that from this aspect the question still remains unanswered' (p. 345).

'... Ricardo gave no answer at all on how to determine this absolute initial magnitude of the percentage *and whether this initial magnitude of the percentage*, from which wages have to be subtracted, *remains constant* when the product becomes dearer; from this aspect this quantity remains completely undefined' (pp. 356–7).

[1] We should also include here in part the general criticisms which Thünen makes of the theory of production costs; see p. 58, footnote 2.

[2] Yu. Zhukovsky 'Istoriya politicheskikh uchenii XIX veka' [A history of nineteenth century political theories], Vol. I.

2. Ricardo's theory of value

'The only theory to which we may point as defining the initial level of the profit which may be taken by the capitalist *consists in the level or excess of capital goods*, and this level should be dependent *on the ratio between the supply and demand for capital* or r/s' (p. 357).

'Ricardo assumes that capital goods may flow freely like a fluid under the influence of gravity from one place and point to another and may tend toward equalisation of profits and to a general level of them, *the height of which is determined by nothing other than their greater or lesser excess*'. . .

'If we denote the volume of the capital goods by (a), the space over which they are poured by (b), and the height by (h), we shall have the condition: $hb = a$; from which $h = a/b$' (p. 342).

We would be in complete agreement with all these remarks by Zhukovsky had they been made in relation to Smith's theory, but to assert that we find no other definition for the general level of profit in Ricardo's work than the formula $x = r/s$ is to fail to understand the very basis of Ricardo's theory.

Walras states the same criticism even more clearly.

'Let P be the aggregate price received for the products of an enterprise; let S, I and F be respectively the wages, interest charges and rent laid out by the entrepreneurs, in the course of production, to pay for the services of personal faculties, capital and land. Let us recall now that, according to the English School, the selling price of products is determined by their costs of production, that is to say, it is equal to the cost of the productive services employed. Thus we have the equation

$$P = S + I + F$$

and P is determined for us. It remains only to determine S, I and F. Surely, if it is not the price of the products that determines the price of productive services, but the price of productive services that determines the price of the products, [we must be told what determines the price of the services]. This is precisely what the English economists try to do. To this end, they construct a theory of rent according to which rent is not included in the expenses of production,

$$P = S + I.$$

Having done this, they determine S directly by the theory of wages. Then, finally, they tell us that "the amount of interest or profit is the excess of the aggregate price received for the products over the wages expended on their production", in other words, that it is determined by the equation

$$I = P - S.$$

It is clear now that the English economists are completely baffled by the problem of price determination; for it is impossible for I to deter-

51

mine P at the same time that P determines I. In the language of mathematics one equation cannot be used to determine two unknowns. This objection is raised without any reference to our position on the manner in which the English School eliminates rent before setting out to determine wages' (Walras, *Elements*, 1874, Lesson 40, § 368, pp. 424–5 of the English edition).

The subsequent analysis will show us how justified these reproaches are.

The last formulas derived by us on p. 49, expressing the farthest point reached by Adam Smith in his analysis of the connection between the price of a product and its production costs relate, as we have noted, only to commodities: (1) whose quantity may be increased without limit by the application of labour and capital, (2) separate portions of which are produced with identical production costs (in order to exclude rent), (3) whose production and sale take place under the influence of 'unlimited competition'. These are precisely the forms that are also the starting point for Ricardo's analysis;

'In speaking, then, of commodities, of their exchangeable value, and of the laws which regulate their relative prices, we mean always such commodities only as can be increased in quantity by the exertion of human industry, and on the production of which competition operates without restraint.'[1]

Before turning to an examination of the conditions determining 'the general rate of profit' r, Ricardo pauses to analyse instances in which the sought-after quantities X_{AB}, X_{AC}, X_{AD} and so on (i.e. the value of any product A in terms of the value of the product B, C etc.) may be determined *independently* of the magnitude of r. Let the products A, B and so on be produced solely by 'current labour', without the use of capital goods (i.e. of tools and materials which are themselves a result of the expenditure of labour). Let N_A days of labour have been expended on the production of a unit of product A, N_B days of labour on the production of product B and so on; further, let the time needed for manufacture and delivery to the market be t_A for product A, t_B for the product B and so on (Ricardo invariably assumes that a product is sold immediately on delivery to the market). If in each period a worker consumes a units of corn (which Ricardo assumes is the only consumption of workers) and the price of corn is X_a, the price of N_A days of labour is $N_A a X_a$ and the price of N_B days of labour is $N_B a X_a$. If we now assume that the 'profit rate' in industries

[1] D. Ricardo: *On the principles of political economy and taxation*, London, 1817, Ch. 1, 'On Value'; throughout this chapter Ricardo assumes that individual units of the same product are obtained at the same cost, *but he does not specifically state* this assumption; the conditions under which rent may arise are not introduced until the second chapter.

A, B and so on is r, and assume for simplicity that the capital used to hire workers is all expended simultaneously at the beginning of production, we shall have the following expression for X_{AB}:

$$X_{AB} = \frac{N_A a X_a (1+r)^{t_A}}{N_B a X_a (1+r)^{t_B}} \qquad (21)$$

If $t_A = t_B$ in this expression, we shall have for X_{AB}, after the appropriate simplifications:

$$X_{AB} = \frac{X_A}{X_B} = \frac{N_A}{N_B} \qquad (22)$$

i.e. the relative value of products A and B equals the ratio of the amount of labour expended on the production of a unit of product A to the amount of labour expended on the production of a unit of product B; the cost of a unit of product A is related to the cost of a unit of product B as the amount of labour expended on the production of a unit of product A is related to the amount of labour expended on the production of a unit of product B.

Suppose the same number of workers are occupied from the beginning to the end in the production of A and in the production of B; this number will be N_A/t_A for A and N_B/t_B for B; let the payment to these workers be advanced not for the whole time until production of the product is completed, but only for a unit of time (e.g. for one day); in this case the expenditure at the beginning of each unit of time will be expressed by $N_A a X_a/t_A$ for product A and $N_B a X_a/t_B$ for product B; if the profit from a unit of capital over a unit of time remains equal to r, we shall have for X_{AB}:

$$X_{AB} = \frac{N_A a X_a (1+r)^{t_A}/t_A + N_A a X_a (1+r)^{t_A-1}/t_A + \cdots + N_A a X_a (1+r)/t_A}{N_B a X_a (1+r)^{t_B}/t_B + N_B a X_a (1+r)^{t_B-1}/t_B + \cdots + N_B a X_a (1+r)/t_B} =$$

$$= \frac{N_A t_B [(1+r)^{t_A} + (1+r)^{t_A-1} + \cdots + (1+r)]}{N_B t_A [(1+r)^{t_B} + (1+r)^{t_B-1} + \cdots + (1+r)]}; \qquad (23)$$

and if we set $t_A = t_B$ in this expression, we once again have $X_{AB} = N_A/N_B$.

In addition to the directly expended or 'current' labour, let there now be additionally expended in the production of A a certain amount of capital; this capital good is itself the product of a certain amount of current labour assisted by a certain amount of new capital good; ascending ever higher and higher to 'production goods of higher orders' (the *Productivgüter höherer Ordnung* of the theoreticians of marginal utility), let us finally arrive at a capital good (or capital goods) produced solely by current labour. In that case, as we have shown when describing Smith's theory, the total sum of the production costs of a unit of product A (in the Ricardian sense, i.e. including profit) will be given by

$$X_A = n_A a X_a (1+r)^{t_A} + n_1 a X_A (1+r)^{t_A+t_1} + n_2 a X_A (1+r)^{t_A+t_1+t_2}$$
$$+ \cdots + n_m a X_a (1+r)^{t_A+t_1+t_2+\cdots+t_m}, \quad (24)$$

where n_A, n_1, n_2 and so on are the amounts of current labour expended on the production of product A and of the capital goods (K_1, K_2, K_3, ...) used in the production of product A; t_A, t_1, t_2 and so on denote the 'production period' of the product A and of capital goods K_1, K_2, K_3, ... If, in the interests of brevity, we employ the notations $t_A+t_1 = t_{A1}$, $t_A+t_1+t_2 = t_{A2}$ and so on, we have:

$$X_A = n_A a X_a (1+r)^{t_A} + n_1 a X_a (1+r)^{t_{A1}} + n_2 a X_a (1+r)^{t_{A2}}$$
$$+ \cdots + n_m a X_a (1+r)^{t_{Am}} \quad (25)$$

where
$$t_{Am} > t_{A(m-1)} > t_{A(m-2)} > \cdots > t_{A2} > t_{A1} > t_A,$$

correspondingly for increasingly long periods of time separating the times at which the amounts of labour n_m, n_{m-1}, ... n_1, n_A are expended from the time at which the finished product A is delivered to the market.

If we assume that in our formula terms having the same powers have already been summed (so that, for example, $n_1 a X_a (1+r)^{t_1} = m_1 a X_a \times (1+r)^{t_1} + m_2 a X_a (1+r)^{t_1} + \cdots + m_m a X_a (1+r)^{t_1}$), we may also employ it for cases in which any number of different forms of capital goods are *directly* involved in the production of the product A.

This formula serves equally to express the case in which the labour n_1, n_2 and so on preliminarily expended is involved in production of A in the form of machines, tools and 'auxiliary materials' created by it, and to express the case in which the product A itself passes successively through different stages of processing (in this case t_A, t_1, t_2, ... will denote the periods of the separate stages of processing; n_A, n_1, n_2 ... will denote the amounts of labour used in each stage).

The *structure* of the formula will not be altered if, instead of assuming that the amounts $n_A a X_a$, $n_1 a X_a$ and so on are advanced simultaneously at the beginning of the corresponding production processes A, K_1, ... and so on, we assume that they are advanced in parts during the production period; the only difference from equation (25) will be that the term $n_A a X_a (1+r)^{t_A}$ will be replaced by a sum:

$$m_A (1+r)^{t_A} + m_{A1} (1+r)^{t_{A1}} + m_{A2} (1+r)^{t_{A2}} + \cdots + m_{AV} (1+r)^{t_{AV}}, \quad (26)$$

where $m_A + m_{A1} + m_{A2} + \cdots + m_{AV} = n_A$ and $t_A > t_{A1} > t_{A2} > \cdots > t_{AV} > 0$; the term $n_1 a X_a (1+r)^{t_{A1}}$ will be replaced by a sum:

$$m_1 a X_a (1+r)^{t_{A1}} + m_2 a X_a (1+r)^{t_{A11}} + m_3 a X_a (1+r)^{t_{A12}} + \cdots + m_W a X_a (1+r)^{t_{A1W}}$$
$$(27)$$

where $m_1 + m_2 + \cdots + m_W = n_1$, and $t_{A1} > t_{A11} > t_{A12} > \cdots > t_A$, and so on. (Compare with the case considered earlier [p. 54].) Consequently a formula of the type

$$X_A = n_A a X_a (1+r)^{t_A} + n_1 a X_a (1+r)^{t_{A1}} + \cdots + n_m a X_a (1+r)^{t_{Am}} \quad (25)$$

in which n_A, n_1, n_2, ..., t_A, t_{A1}, t_{A2}, ... can be taken to stand for any magnitudes, will also serve us in this case to express the connection between the price of the product and its production costs.

Accordingly, having selected a formula for the production costs of any product B, we obtain

$$X_{AB} = \frac{n_A(1+r)^{t_A} + n_1(1+r)^{t_{A1}} + \cdots + n_m(1+r)^{t_{Am}}}{m_B(1+r)^{t_B} + m_1(1+r)^{t_{B1}} + \cdots + n_p(1+r)^{t_{Bp}}} \quad (28)$$

as an expression of the exchange ratio X_{AB}, i.e. as an expression of the value of product A in terms of B.

Let the number of terms having different indices be equal both in the numerator and in the denominator, so that $m = p$ and let:

$$t_A = t_B; \quad t_{A1} = t_{B1}; \quad \ldots; \quad t_{Am} = t_{Bp}. \quad (29)$$

In that case

$$X_{AB} = \frac{n_A(1+r)^{t_A} + n_1(1+r)^{t_{A1}} + \cdots + n_m(1+r)^{t_{Am}}}{m_B(1+r)^{t_A} + m_1(1+r)^{t_{A1}} + \cdots + m_m(1+r)^{t_{Am}}}. \quad (30)$$

Let us further have:

$$\frac{n_A}{m_B} = \frac{n_1}{m_1} = \frac{n_2}{m_2} = \cdots = \frac{n_m}{m_m} = R. \quad (31)$$

We shall then have $n_A = m_B R, \ldots, n_k = m_k R$ and

$$X_{AB} = \frac{R[m_B(1+r)^{t_A} + m_1(1+r)^{t_{A1}} + \cdots + m_m(1+r)^{t_{Am}}]}{m_B(1+r)^{t_A} + m_1(1+r)^{t_{A1}} + \cdots + m_m(1+r)^{t_{Am}}} =$$

$$= R = \frac{n_A + n_1 + n_2 + \cdots + n_m}{m_B + m_1 + m_2 + \cdots + m_m}, \quad (32)$$

i.e. in this case the value of product A in terms of B once again will not depend on the level of r, but only on the amount of labour expended on the production of products A and B.

The expression usually given to assumptions (29) and (31) made to obtain this result is that 'the capital goods used up in the branches A and B are of *identical organic composition*'. We should take this vague expression to mean (1) that the turnover periods of the different portions of the capital expended in the production of B and of that expended in the production of A are the same, i.e. that it is impossible to find in the production of A a turnover period which could not be found in the production of B *and vice versa*; (2) that the ratios of the portions of capital with correspondingly equal turnover periods in both branches of production are equal. Any attempt to give a briefer definition of the conditions under which value is equal simply to the ratio of the amount of labour expended on the production of a unit of both products renders the definition less *general* than is required and makes it necessary to supplement it by a number of qualifications and special rules, which is the approach followed by Ricardo.[1] Now let t_A not be equal to t_B in the simplest formula (equation (21) on p. 53) expressing the exchange value of the commodities A and B produced by the same current labour as a function of their production costs. Let, for example, $t_A > t_B$, in which case we have $(1+r)^{t_A} > (1+r)^{t_B}$ and in consequence of this:

$$\frac{N_A a X_a (1+r)^{t_A}}{N_B a X_a (1+r)^{t_B}} > \frac{N_A}{N_B} \quad \text{and} \quad X_{AB} > \frac{N_A}{N_B}, \tag{33}$$

i.e. the value of A in terms of B will be greater than the ratio of their 'labour values' (the amounts of labour used in their production).

It may readily be appreciated from the formula that when t_A and t_B are invariable this difference will be greater, the greater is the magnitude of r. Thus, in this case, the magnitude of X_{AB} is a function not only of N_A and N_B, but also of the level of r and, consequently, cannot be determined independently of it. The same will hold for any X_{MN}:

$$X_{MN} = \frac{n_M (1+r)^{t_M} + n_1 (1+r)^{t_{M1}} + \cdots + n_k (1+r)^{t_{Mk}}}{m_N (1+r)^{t_N} + m_1 (1+r)^{t_{N1}} + \cdots + m_p (1+r)^{t_{Np}}} \tag{34}$$

since (as has been shown above) the second part of the equality cannot be expanded into

$$R \cdot \frac{m_M (1+r)^{t_M} + m_1 (1+r)^{t_{M1}} + \cdots + m_k (1+r)^{t_{Mk}}}{m_M (1+r)^{t_M} + m_1 (1+r)^{t_{M1}} + \cdots + m_k (1+r)^{t_{Mk}}} \tag{35}$$

[1] In referring to the conditions by virtue of which products are exchanged in the market *other than in proportion* to the amounts of labour expended on their production, Ricardo first considers the division of capital in *different* proportions into fixed and 'circulating' capital, and then adds those cases in which both commodities are produced by 'current' labour, but more time is needed for the production of one than for the production of the other. 'This case', states Ricardo, 'appears to differ from the last, but is, in fact, the same'; finally, all this is qualified by the statement: 'It is hardly necessary to say, that commodities which have the same quantity of labour bestowed on their production, will differ in exchangeable value, if they cannot be brought to market in the same time' (Ricardo, *Principles*, Ch. 1, Section IV, p. 37 of the Sraffa edition).

2. Ricardo's theory of value

where R is a quantity that is independent of r. Ricardo examines various special cases that are relevant here (see *Principles*, Ch. 1). Note that to convert from our formulas to the Ricardian examples we first have to introduce the condition of the 'durability' of the capital goods $K_1, K_2, \ldots$, in which case we obtain equation (25) (a simplification of (24))

$$X_A = n_A a X_a (1+r)^{t_A} + n_1 a X_a (1+r)^{t_{A1}} + \cdots + n_m a X_a (1+r)^{t_{Am}}. \quad (25)$$

Thus, in all cases when the organic composition of the capital goods used in the production of A and B is not the same, the exchange ratio X_{AB} of the products A and B cannot be determined independently of the level of r; in this case

$$X_{AB} = f(n_A, n_1, n_2, \ldots; m_B, m_1, m_2, \ldots; t_A, t_{A1}, t_{A2}, \ldots; t_B, t_{B1}, t_{B2}, \ldots; r) \quad (37)$$

from which, if $n_A, n_1, \ldots, m_B, m_1, \ldots, t_A, t_{A1}, \ldots, t_B$ and $t_{B1}, \ldots$ have been adopted as quantities dependent on the technical conditions of production of the products A and B, we obtain $X_{AB} = f(r)$, where X_{AB} will be a determined quantity when r is given.

How may the required magnitude of r be determined? Is it possible to use our 'production cost equations' (see p. 55) for its determination? Let us write them in the form:

$$\left.\begin{array}{l} X_A = a X_a [n_A (1+r)^{t_A} + n_1 (1+r)^{t_{A1}} + \cdots + n_m (1+r)^{t_{Am}}] \\ X_B = a X_a [m_B (1+r)^{t_B} + m_1 (1+r)^{t_{B1}} + \cdots + m_p (1+r)^{t_{Bp}}]. \end{array}\right\} \quad (38)$$

If we assume, as previously, that the quantities $n_A, n_1, \ldots, m_B, m_1, \ldots, t_A, t_{A1}, \ldots, t_B, t_{B1}, \ldots$ are constants, it is possible to write the expression in square brackets in the form $f_A(r), f_B(r) \ldots$ where $f_A'(r) > 0, f_B'(r) > 0,$ $\ldots$ (i.e. when r increases, $f_A(r), f_B(r), \ldots$ is also increased, and *vice versa*). We then have from the equations for A and B

$$\frac{X_A}{a X_a} = f_A(r); \qquad \frac{X_B}{a X_a} = f_B(r), \text{ and so on.} \quad (39)$$

It is evident from these equations that when $X_A/aX_a, X_B/aX_a, \ldots$ increase, r also increases by virtue of $\mathrm{d}f_A(r)/\mathrm{d}r > 0$; $\mathrm{d}f_B(r)/\mathrm{d}r > 0$. Consequently, when $X_A, X_B, \ldots$ remain unchanged, r will be greater the less is aX_a and *vice versa*; *i.e. a reciprocal relationship will exist between the profit rate and the level of wages*.[1]

---

[1] Too much importance is often attached to this Ricardian hypothesis. Ricardo's main contribution to the theory of profit does not lie here, but in his establishment of the laws governing the *absolute* level of profit.

Nevertheless, this analysis does not give us the magnitude of r; in the equations

$$\left.\begin{aligned} X_A &= aX_a \cdot f_A(r) \\ X_B &= aX_a \cdot f_B(r) \end{aligned}\right\} \tag{40}$$
$$\cdots$$

and in the equations derived from them:

$$X_{AB} = \frac{f_A(r)}{f_B(r)}; \qquad X_{AC} = \frac{f_A(r)}{f_B(r)}; \ldots \tag{41}$$

r will be a determined quantity if the magnitude $X_{AB}, X_{AC}, \ldots$ are given. *However, without proceeding from production conditions, we have no other* equations for the determination of X_{AB} and X_{AC} apart from the same equations (41), and the same equation cannot serve for the determination of two unknowns. Thus, we are apparently trapped in a logical circle: profit must be known in order to determine value, but profit itself is dependent on value. There would appear to be no way out of this circle other than to relate value or profit to conditions lying *outside the sphere of production*. As we have seen, Adam Smith took this way out, when he related the profit rate to the demand and supply of capital. To proceed in this manner is, however, to acknowledge the untenability of the theory of production costs itself.[1]

Ricardo's immortal contribution was his brilliant solution of this seemingly insoluble problem. Let us take a series of 'production cost equations' expressing the connection between price and production cost for the commodities $A, B, C, \ldots$

$$\left.\begin{aligned} X_A &= aX_a[n_A(1+r)^{t_A} + n_1(1+r)^{t_{A1}} + n_2(1+r)^{t_{A2}} + \cdots + n_m(1+r)^{t_{Am}}] \\ X_B &= aX_a[m_B(1+r)^{t_B} + m_1(1+r)^{t_{B1}} + m_2(1+r)^{t_{B2}} + \cdots + m_p(1+r)^{t_{Bp}}] \end{aligned}\right\}$$
$$\cdots \tag{42}$$

Each new equation incorporates the unknowns X_a and r as in the preceding equations, and additionally a further new unknown X with the appropriate index. Therefore, if the number of equations is n, then the number of unknowns is $(n+2)$. However, no more than n unknowns may be eliminated with n equations. When we arrive at the product N taken by us as the unit of value (e.g. silver), we shall have:

$$1 = aX_a[P_N(1+r)^{t_N} + P_1(1+r)^{t_{N1}} + P_2(1+r)^{t_{N2}} + \cdots + P_S(1+r)^{t_{NS}}]. \tag{43}$$

---

[1] Compare Thünen's criticisms of Smith (J. H. von Thünen *Le salaire naturel et son rapport au taux l'intérêt*, Paris, 1857).

This equation does not contain a new unknown. If we add to it the n former equations, we shall have $(n+1)$ equations with $(n+2)$ unknowns. The number of equations will still be inadequate, and the question of the level of the profit rate will apparently remain unsolved.

It is to Ricardo's credit that he was the first to note that there is one production equation by means of which we may determine the magnitude of r *directly* (i.e. without having recourse for assistance to the other equations). This equation gives us the production conditions of the product a to which in the final analysis the expenditure in all the products A, B, C, ... is reduced. Let us take the 'production costs' equation for this product a compiled in the same way as we compiled the equations for the other products:

$$X_a = aX_a[N_a(1+r)^{t_a} + N_1(1+r)^{t_{a1}} + \cdots + N_q(1+r)^{t_{aq}}] \qquad (44)$$

from which:

$$a[N_a(1+r)^{t_a} + N_1(1+r)^{t_{a1}} + \cdots + N_q(1+r)^{t_{aq}}] - 1 = 0 \qquad (45)$$

and if we determine r from this equation, we have:

$$r = F(N_a, N_1, N_2, \ldots, N_q; t_a, t_{a1}, t_{a2}, \ldots, t_{aq}; a). \qquad (46)$$

But since $N_a, N_1, \ldots; t_a, t_{a1}, \ldots$ and a are given quantities dependent on the technical conditions of production of the product a (i.e. the product forming the essential means of existence of the worker), r is also a given magnitude, i.e. is independent of the economic circumstances.

If we now insert the magnitude of r found by us in the production cost equations (42) and so on (on the basis of the law of the equality of profit rates in different branches of industry), we shall obtain $X_A, X_B, \ldots$ and correspondingly $X_{AB}, X_{AC}, \ldots$ as functions of the same *given* quantities $N, n, m, \ldots$ (with the appropriate indices), t's ... (with the appropriate indices) and of the quantity a. Before proceeding to a general analysis of the expression found by us for the magnitude of r, let us consider whether the solution of the problem remains the same if, instead of taking one product (a) consumed by the workers (e.g. corn, as is done by Ricardo) we take several such products in accordance with reality.[1]

Let $\alpha, \beta, \gamma, \ldots$ be products consumed by the workers. Let the daily consumption of a single worker be a for the product α, b for the product β

---

[1] Ricardo himself makes a stipulation along these lines (after he has established his law of profit). He states 'The effects produced on profits would have been the same, or nearly the same, if there had been any rise in the price of those other necessaries, besides food, on which the wages of labour are expended' (Ricardo, *Principles*, Ch. 6, p. 118 of the Sraffa edition).

and c for the product γ; if we now take the production costs equation for (α), we obtain:

$$X_\alpha = N_\alpha(aX_\alpha + bX_\beta + cX_\gamma \ldots)$$
$$(1+r)^{t_\alpha} + N_{\alpha 1}(aX_\alpha + bX_\beta + cX_\gamma \ldots)(1+r)^{t_{\alpha 1}} + \cdots \quad (47)$$

Clearly this equation does not make it possible to determine r directly as in the preceding case, but if we add to this equation the production costs equation for β, γ, ..., we obtain the equation system:

$$\left.\begin{aligned}
X_\beta &= N_\beta(aX_\alpha + bX_\beta + cX_\gamma \ldots) \\
&\quad (1+r)^{t_\beta} + N_{\beta 1}(aX_\alpha + bX_\beta + cX_\gamma \ldots)(1+r)^{t_{\beta 1}} + \cdots \\
X_\gamma &= N_\gamma(aX_\alpha + bX_\beta + cX_\gamma \ldots) \\
&\quad (1+r)^{t_\gamma} + N_{\gamma 1}(aX_\beta + bX_\beta + cX_\gamma \ldots)(1+r)^{t_{\gamma 1}} + \cdots
\end{aligned}\right\} \quad (48)$$

. . .

Let us multiply both parts of equation (47) by a, both parts of the following by b, of the next by c and so on and then add all our equations term by term. We shall obtain:

$$\begin{aligned}
(aX_\alpha + bX_\beta + cX_\gamma \ldots) &= aN_\alpha(aX_\alpha + bX_\beta + cX_\gamma \ldots)(1+r)^{t_\alpha} \\
&\quad + aN_{\alpha 1}(aX_\alpha + bX_\beta + cX_\gamma \ldots)(1+r)^{t_{\alpha 1}} + \cdots + \\
&\quad + bN_\beta(aX_\alpha + bX_\beta + cX_\gamma \ldots)(1+r)^{t_\beta} \\
&\quad + bN_{\beta 1}(aX_\alpha + bX_\beta + cX_\gamma \ldots)(1+r)^{t_{\beta 1}} + \cdots + \\
&\quad + cN_\gamma(aX_\alpha + bX_\beta + cX_\gamma \ldots)(1+r)^{t_\gamma} \\
&\quad + cN_{\gamma 1}(aX_\alpha + bX_\beta + cX_\gamma \ldots)(1+r)^{t_{\gamma 1}} + \cdots
\end{aligned} \quad (49)$$

Having divided both sides of the equation by $(aX_\alpha + bX_\beta + cX_\gamma, \ldots)$ we shall obtain:

$$1 = aN_\alpha(1+r)^{t_\alpha} + aN_{\alpha 1}(1+r)^{t_{\alpha 1}} + \cdots + bN_\beta(1+r)^{t_\beta} +$$
$$bN_{\beta 1}(1+r)^{t_{\beta 1}} + \cdots + cN_\gamma(1+r)^{t_\gamma} + cN_{\gamma 1}(1+r)^{t_{\gamma 1}} + \cdots \quad (50)$$

Consequently:

$$r = F(N_\alpha, N_{\alpha 1}, \ldots; N_\beta, N_{\beta 1}, \ldots; N_\gamma, N_{\gamma 1}, \ldots;$$
$$a, b, c, \ldots; t_\alpha, t_{\alpha 1}, \ldots; t_\beta, t_{\beta 1}, \ldots; \quad (51)$$
$$t_\gamma, t_{\gamma 1}, \ldots; \ldots).$$

Therefore, our system of equations (47), (48) of the 'production costs' of products consumed by the workers still yields r as a function of the same given quantities.[1] Consequently we may establish that the *level of*

---

[1] If the number of products consumed by the workers is n, we shall have n equations in which we have $(n+1)$ unknowns; $(X_\alpha, X_\beta, X_\gamma, \ldots)$ yielding n unknowns, to which the unknown r is added.

the profit rate r is determined by the production costs of products consumed by the workers. (There is no need for us to repeat the qualification made by Ricardo 'on that land or with that capital which yields no rent',[1] since it has already earlier been proposed to exclude rent from our investigation.) Production costs in this case should be understood as '*only costs in the "objective sense"*' (similar to what was denoted by Rodbertus by the term *Kosten des Gutes* [cost of the good] in contrast with *Auslagen des Unternehmers* [expenditure of the entrepreneurs] or *Kosten des Betriebs* [cost of running the enterprise],[2] namely *the quantity of goods used in production, and the period of reproduction* (i.e. the time between the moment or moments of expenditure of 'production goods' and the time at which the ready product appears on the market).

If we assume a, b, c, ... to be constants (which, if the 'iron law of wages' prevails, amounts to the assumption that the minimum of means of subsistence of the worker is invariable), we obtain r exclusively as a function of the *quantities of labour and time* N_α, $N_{\alpha 1}$, ...; N_β, $N_{\beta 1}$, ...; N_γ, $N_{\gamma 1}$, ...; t_α, $t_{\alpha 1}$, ...; t_β, $t_{\beta 1}$, ...; t_γ, $t_{\gamma 1}$, ...; ...; corresponding to industries, α, β, γ, ... making products consumed by the workers. Once these quanties are given, the magnitude of r, i.e. the profit rate, is a fully defined quantity.

Consequently, Ricardo succeeded in finding a solution to the problem. Our formulas of 'production costs' have now taken the general form:

$$\left.\begin{aligned}
X_A = F(n_A, n_1, n_2, \ldots, t_A, t_{A1}, \ldots; N_\alpha, N_{\alpha 1}, \ldots, \\
t_\alpha, t_{\alpha 1}, \ldots; N_\beta, N_{\beta 1}, \ldots, t_\beta, t_{\beta 1}, \ldots; \ldots) \\
X_B = F(m_B, m_1, m_2 \ldots, t_B, t_{B1}, \ldots; N_\alpha, N_{\alpha 1}, \ldots, \\
t_\alpha, t_{\alpha 1}, \ldots; N_\beta, N_{\beta 1}, \ldots, t_\beta, t_{\beta 1}, \ldots; \ldots)
\end{aligned}\right\} \quad (52)$$

where the element of 'price' does not appear at all in the second part of the equation. To level at Ricardo's theory the hackneyed reproach that it 'defines price in terms of price' is to manifest a complete lack of understanding of the writings of this very great theoretical economist.

The *starting point* for Ricardo's analysis was provided by the present-day *capitalist system* based on the use of *hired human labour*; it would, however, be extremely erroneous to imagine that the *conclusions* at which he arrived have a bearing only on the present time. Zhukovsky has quite correctly understood and explained in his book the importance of Ricardo's theoretical conclusions.[3] Ricardo's theory of rent may serve as an

[1] Ricardo, *Principles*, Ch. 6, p. 126 of the Sraffa edition.
[2] See C. Rodbertus, *Zur Erkenntniss unserer staatswirthschaftlichen Zustände*, 1842, pp. 25–6.
[3] *History of 19th Century Political Theories* (Vol. 1, pp. 388–9). Zhukovsky states that 'Ricardo deals with the question of distribution only in the sense of the division of separate

example: the movement of individuals from more fertile to less fertile areas of land is taken as the starting point, but the theory retains its significance even if the opposite assumptions are made. Ricardo subsequently clarifies the laws of rent only in land rent and rent from mines, but this does not prevent the laws established by him from being of general significance for all cases to which the conditions of the origin of rent stated by him apply. (See, in this respect, Zhukovsky, *History . . .*, p. 318.) In our equations for 'production costs' (see equation (25), p. 54), let us set the magnitudes $an_A, an_1, an_2, \ldots, am_B, am_1, am_2, \ldots$ to be respectively $A_A, A_{A1}, A_{A2}, \ldots, A_B, A_{B1}, A_{B2}, \ldots$: in this case $A_A, A_{A1}, \ldots, A_B, A_{B1}, \ldots$ will denote the quantity of some good α to the expenditure of which we may, in the final analysis, reduce the production costs of the products $A, B, \ldots$ Having effected such a transformation in the 'production costs' equation of the product α, we have:

$$X_\alpha = A_\alpha X_\alpha (1+r)^{t_\alpha} + A_{\alpha 1} X_\alpha (1+r)^{t_{\alpha 1}} + \cdots \qquad (53)$$

Shortening as necessary and solving the equation with respect to r, we shall have:

$$r = F(A_\alpha, A_{\alpha 1}, \ldots, t_\alpha, t_{\alpha 1}, \ldots). \qquad (54)$$

Since the periods of production $t_\alpha, t_{\alpha 1}, \ldots$ are always finite, it follows that when

$$A_\alpha + A_{\alpha 1} + A_{\alpha 2} + \cdots < 1, \qquad (55)$$

we have $r > 0$.

Equation (54) does not contain the quantities $n_\alpha, n_{\alpha 1}, \ldots$, i.e. the quantity of labour used in the production of the product α, and it yields r as a function of the *production period* and the *quantity of the good α* expended in production.

Equation (54) shows that whenever a known quantity of some product α has been used up in the production of α and we can obtain a *larger* quantity *of the same* product within some finite period of time as a result of the production process, the profit rate in the given branch of industry will be a fully-determined quantity *greater than zero, irrespective of the price of the product α*. If the production costs of the other goods, $A, B, C, \ldots$ are

---

parts of a product between the three elements of price–rent, past labour and current labour *in the sense of elements of price* (p. 388).

It is a matter of indifference for Ricardo's theory whether these elements correspond in a given society to individual classes and persons or not, since 'by worker, rentier and capitalist he always understands more or less abstract fictitious persons'. However, 'Not merely does this not do any harm to the formulation of the problem of distribution given by Ricardo but, on the contrary, it is an indication of the theoretical, philosophical nature of this formulation, which ensures that Ricardo's deductions, should they be correct, have the nature of general laws' (p. 389).

2. Ricardo's theory of value

reduced *in the final analysis* to the same product α, the same profit rate should also be established in these branches under conditions of free mobility from one branch of production to another (irrespective of what the ratios $X_{A\alpha}$, $X_{B\alpha}$, ... will be). The essence of the production process by means of which a 'production good' α yields as a result the products $A, B, C, \ldots$ and new quantities of the same good α is a matter of complete indifference for determination of the rate of profit. Whether the potential energy incorporated in the production good α is released and used in production in the form of *human labour*, as happens at present, or by means of some other process (*not involving the participation of human labour*) is a matter of indifference; whenever we have:

$$1 = A_\alpha(1+r)^{t_\alpha} + A_{\alpha 1}(1+r)^{t_{\alpha 1}} + \cdots \tag{56}$$

on condition that

$$A_\alpha + A_{\alpha 1} + \cdots < 1, \tag{55}$$

the profit r will be a fully-defined quantity and greater than zero. For example, suppose some production good β, to which the production costs of all the economic goods $A, B, C, \ldots$ may be ultimately reduced, be utilised in production by means of the conversion of its potential energy into the work of some living creatures *other than man*. On the basis of the conditions of production we can have and we shall have all the conditions needed for the occurrence of a profit. In this case the profit rate will be a fully-defined magnitude greater than zero, despite the fact that no unit of *human* labour was used in production.[1]

Finally, it is theoretically possible to imagine a case in which all products are produced exclusively by the work of machines, so that no unit of *living labour* (whether human or of any other kind) participates in production, and nevertheless an industrial profit may occur in this case under certain conditions; this is a profit which will not differ essentially in any way from the profit obtained by present-day capitalists using hired workers in production.

Suppose that a machine M is able, without the participation of human labour, and using natural forces as a motor, to produce machines of the following orders: $M_1, M_2, M_3, \ldots$; let these machines in their turn singly or in combination automatically produce machines of an even higher order $M'_1, M'_2, M'_3, \ldots$ until we ultimately arrive at machines $M_A, M_B, M_C, \ldots$ which directly produce the consumer products $A, B, C, \ldots$

[1] The quantities A_β, $A_{\beta 1}$, ... are determined in a completely similar manner to the determination of production costs when human labour is used: $A_\beta = N_\beta b$, $A_{\beta 1} = N_1 b$, $A_{\beta 2} = N_2 b, \ldots$, where $N_\beta, N_1, N_2, \ldots$ are the quantities of living labour (in any unit), and b is the quantity of product β which must be expended for the production of one unit of labour.

In this case the production costs of these products $A, B, C, \ldots$ may always be reduced in the final analysis to the number (or parts) of machines M consumed in the production of the products $A, B, C, \ldots$

Suppose also that among the machines directly or indirectly produced by the machine M, there is the machine M itself, i.e., in other words, let the machine M be *capable of reproduction*. In this case we shall have

$$
\left.
\begin{aligned}
X_A &= n'_M X_M (1+r)^{t_A} + n''_M X_M (1+r)^{t_{A1}} \cdots \\
&\;\;\vdots \\
X_M &= N'_M X_M (1+r)^{t_M} + N''_M X_M (1+r)^{t_{M1}} \cdots
\end{aligned}
\right\}
\tag{57}
$$

where $n'_M, n''_M, \ldots, N'_M, N''_M, \ldots$ will denote the number of machines M (or parts of the machine M, if $n'_M, n''_M, \ldots$ are less than unity) used up in the production of units of the products $A, B, C, \ldots, M, \ldots$ If $N'_M + N''_M + \ldots < 1$ in the equation for M, *then r will be greater than zero and a fully-defined quantity, provided that the quantities $N'_M, N''_M, \ldots, t_M, t_{M1}, \ldots$ are given.*

We have therefore seen, proceeding from Ricardo's analysis, that the origin of industrial profit does not stand in any 'special' relationship to the human labour used in production. Profit may equally well occur in other production processes provided that they satisfy the quite definite conditions stated above. Whether or not such modes of production are capable of existing in the present state of technical knowledge is not a subject for political economy.

Let us assume that the production costs of the economic goods, $A, B, C, \ldots$ may be reduced in the final analysis to the expenditure of the production good α, whose production costs are themselves determined by the formula:

$$
X_\alpha = A_\alpha X_\alpha (1+r)^{t_\alpha} + A_{\alpha 1} X_\alpha (1+r)^{t_{\alpha 1}} \ldots
\tag{58}
$$

Let us assume that by using a different production process (e.g. by using the work of *animals* in place of *human* labour) we can reduce the production costs of the goods $A, B, C, \ldots$ to the expenditure of a production good β, whose production costs are themselves determined by the formula:

$$
X_\beta = A_\beta X_\beta (1+r)^{t_\beta} + A_{\beta 1} X_\beta (1+r)^{t_{\beta 1}} \ldots
\tag{59}
$$

Let us assume that by using a further production process (e.g. exclusively the work of machines employing natural forces as a motor) we shall have correspondingly:

$$
X_M = A_M X_M (1+r)^{t_M} + A_{M1} X_M (1+r)^{t_{M1}} + \cdots
\tag{60}
$$

Let r, determined from equation (58), be r_α and let r from equation (59) be denoted by r_β and so on. Which of the possible production processes will in reality be used? Obviously, the one which yields the greatest value for r (this follows directly from the hypothesis that an economic subject tends to pursue the greatest advantage). Consequently, for any given production process *actually* to determine the profit rate, it is still insufficient that it *could in general* serve as a source of profit, and it is further necessary that it should yield a *higher profit* rate than all other possible processes. Consequently, for example, if the present state of technology could realise the hypothesis made above of production of all commodities exclusively by machines capable of reproducing themselves, the condition $A_M + A_{M1} + \cdots < 1$ would still be inadequate for the rate of profit in fact to be defined by the equation

$$1 = A_M(1+r)^{t_M} + A_{M1}(1+r)^{t_{M1}} \ldots \tag{61}$$

from which

$$r_M = f(A_M, A_{M1}, \ldots, t_M, t_{M1}, \ldots); \tag{62}$$

it would further be necessary for r_M to be greater than the profit rate r_α established when human labour is used in production. We have previously assumed for simplicity that there is only one series of production costs equations corresponding to each production good α, β, γ, ..., to the expenditure of which the production costs of each product A, B, C, ... (including the products α, β, γ, ... themselves) may be reduced:

$$\left.\begin{aligned}
X_A &= A_A X_\alpha(1+r)^{t_A} + A_{A1}X_\alpha(1+r)^{t_{A1}} + \cdots \\
X_B &= A_B X_\alpha(1+r)^{t_B} + A_{B1}X_\alpha(1+r)^{t_{B1}} + \cdots \\
&\vdots \\
X_\alpha &= A_\alpha X_\alpha(1+r)^{t_\alpha} + A_{\alpha1}X_\alpha(1+r)^{t_{\alpha1}} + \cdots
\end{aligned}\right\} \tag{63}$$

In reality, however, there may undoubtedly be several equations systems corresponding to each of them; thus, in addition to the system (63), it is also possible to have any system (64) for the same production good α.

$$\left.\begin{aligned}
X_A &= A'_A X_\alpha(1+r)^{t_A'} + A'_{A'} X_\alpha(1+r)^{t'_{A'}} + \cdots \\
X_B &= A'_B X_\alpha(1+r)^{t'_B} + A'_{B'} X_\alpha(1+r)^{t'_{A'}} + \cdots \\
&\vdots \\
X_\alpha &= A'_\alpha X_\alpha(1+r)^{t'_\alpha} + A'_{\alpha'}X_\alpha(1+r)^{t'_{\alpha'}} + \cdots
\end{aligned}\right\} \tag{64}$$

Thus, for example, let the product α be a product consumed by the workers and at the same time a product consumed by some other living creatures to whose work it is also possible to reduce the production costs of each of the products $A, B, C, \ldots$, so that $A_A = n_1a$, $A_{A1} = n_2a$, $\ldots, A_B = m_1a$, $A_{B1} = m_2a, \ldots, A_A' = n_1'a'$, $A_{A1}' = n_2'a', \ldots, A_B' = m_1'a'$, $A_{B1}' = m_2'a'$, where $n_1, n_2, \ldots, m_1, m_2, \ldots$ are the *quantities of human work* used in production; $n_1', n_2', \ldots, m_1', m_2', \ldots$ are the *quantities of the work of animals* capable of being used instead of people in the productions A, $B, \ldots$; a is the amount of the product α per unit of work consumed by a *man*; a' is the amount of the product consumed per unit of work completed by an *animal*.

The systems (63), (64), and so on will correspond to *different production processes* by means of which the potential energy of a production good α is used in the production $A, B, C, \ldots$ There can be assumed to be any number of such processes corresponding to each of the production goods $\alpha, \beta, \ldots$

But in reality one out of all these equation systems will be in force, namely the one which will yield the greatest value for r (determined from the equation for α). This is because no one will begin to use modes of production which yield a low-profit rate if it is possible to use a mode determining a higher rate.

Now let us assume that the production costs of the products A, B, C, $D, \ldots, L$ may be reduced to the expenditure of the product D; let the production good D be the *only good* to which the production costs of all the products $A, \ldots, L$ (including D itself) may be reduced. The 'production costs' equation for D from the foregoing gives us a fully determined magnitude of r. From the equation

$$X_D = A_D X_D (1+r)^{t_D} + A_{D1} X_D (1+r)^{t_{D1}} + \cdots \tag{65}$$

we have

$$r_D = f_D(A_D, A_{D1}, \ldots; t_D, t_{D1}, \ldots); \tag{66}$$

the same profit rate is also established in the productions $A, B, \ldots, L$. Now let us assume that the production costs of the remainder of the products $M, N, \ldots, P$, cannot be reduced to the product D.[1] Let the only product to which they may be reduced be N,[2] in which case the production costs equation of the product N:

$$X_N = A_N X_N (1+r)^{t_N} + A_{N1} X_N (1+r)^{t_{N1}} + \cdots \tag{67}$$

still yields a fully-determined quantity for r:

$$r_N = f_N(A_N, A_{N1}, \ldots, t_N, t_{N1}, \ldots). \tag{68}$$

[1] For example, let D be a product consumed by animals; in that case only the production costs of commodities producible by the labour of animals may be reduced to the product D, since if the products $M, N, \ldots, P$ may be produced only by human labour, their production costs can no longer be expressed in terms of D.

[2] If products $M, N, \ldots, P$ are products of human labour, N should be understood as the product consumed by the workers.

This profit level is also established in the branches of production M, $N, \ldots, P$.

Therefore, we shall have one rate of profit r_D for one part of the production $A, B, \ldots, L$, and another rate r_N for the other part $M, N, \ldots, P$.

Let $r_D > r_N$; in that case producers will begin to forsake the branches $M, N, \ldots, B$ and transfer to the branches $A, B, C, \ldots, L$. The price of the products $A, B, C \ldots, L$ will begin to fall (owing to the excess of supply over demand), but since the profit rate determined from the equations

$$
\left.
\begin{aligned}
r_D &= f_D(A_D, A_{D1}, \ldots, t_D, t_{D1}, \ldots) \\
r_N &= f_N(A_N, A_{N1}, \ldots, t_N, t_{N1}, \ldots)
\end{aligned}
\right\}
\tag{69}
$$

is not dependent on X_D and X_N, and consequently is not dependent on $X_{DN} = X_D/X_N$, the profit level r_D will continue to remain above r_N however much capital may be 'poured' from the branches $M, N, \ldots, P$ into the branches $A, B, \ldots, L$. However much value the product D may lose owing to the excess of supply, it will nevertheless be more advantageous to entrepreneurs to lay out capital in the production of D than in production of the product N (or any other product from among $M, N, \ldots, P$), which is very costly, since the entrepreneur will receive a larger sum *per unit of value expended in unit time in* the production of D than *per unit of value* in the production of N. The reason for this is that a drop in the price of the finished product D will invariably be matched by a proportionate drop in its production costs, since these costs are reduced to the product D itself.

Whatever quantities we insert for X_D in equation D we obtain the same magnitude for the rate of profit r_D (the amount of profit per unit of value expended in unit time). Consequently, there is apparently no natural limit to the movement of capitalists from the branches $M, \ldots, P$ into the branches $A, \ldots, L$ apart from complete cessation of the production of $M, \ldots, P$. Such a conclusion would be correct if, when $r_D > r_N$, economic expectation always led producers to transfer from the branch N to D. In fact, the hypothesis that producers tend to transfer from branches with a low *rate* of profit to branches with a high rate holds only for cases in which all the quantities entering into the economic calculation of the entrepreneurs have a *finite* value. Since this latter condition does in fact hold in most instances, the foregoing hypothesis is in general found to be correct in practice, but if adopted as the basis of abstract analysis it may lead to false conclusions. Let us assume that an entrepreneur previously expended N units of value (in an arbitrary unit) in production of A, so that in a unit of time we have $N(1+r_A) - N$ units of profit, and in T units of time we have $N(1+r_A)^T - N$ units of profit; were he to place this amount of value in production B, he would have $N(1+r_B)^T - N$. If $r_B > r_A$, we have in general

$$N(1+r_B)^T - N > N(1+r_A)^T - N \qquad (70)$$

from which

$$N[(1+r_B)^T - (1+r_A)^T] > 0. \qquad (71)$$

The situation will, however, be different if one of the factors in the first part of the inequality disappears. For example, let the price of product B fall to nothing owing to excess of supply (assuming as the unit of value the value of any of the products produced by expenditure of the product A), in which case, however much of product B is produced, N will also be zero, and consequently so will the entire expression

$$N[(1+r_B)^T - (1+r_A)^T] = 0, \qquad (72)$$

i.e. all motive for the movement of producers from A to B is destroyed. Therefore, when the value of product B (and of others produced by its means), expressed in terms of product A (or by some other commodity produced by its means), falls to zero, the incentive for conversion from A to B will cease, despite the fact that the *rate* of profit continues to remain higher in B than in A (since the rate is not dependent on price). Consequently, when different constant profit rates exist in different branches of production, a balance will be established either when products yielding a high profit rate pass into the realm of *free goods* or when the production of products with a low rate of profit is discontinued. What is actually produced in such a specific case is a question of fact and is dependent on the form of $f_A(D_A), f_B(D_B), \ldots, f_M(D_M), f_N(D_N), \ldots$ expressing the price of products $A, B, \ldots$ as a function of their sale: $D_A, D_B, \ldots$ The smaller is the group represented by the goods $A, \ldots, L$ (by comparison with the group $M, \ldots, P$) and the smaller is the demand for these goods (i.e. the smaller is the quantity of these goods which *completely* satisfies the demand for them), the greater is the probability that they will become 'free' goods before all capital leaves the branches $M, \ldots, P$ (and *vice versa*). Therefore, even were there actually to exist at present some exceptional production processes which were able *without the participation of human labour* to reproduce their real production costs *in natura* (and not in the form of equivalent value) and consequently to determine an *independent* level of profit unrelated to the production costs of the means of subsistence of the workers, the only result of such a situation, in view of the limited nature of the demands which these processes could satisfy, would be to render these products completely valueless and to transfer them to

2. Ricardo's theory of value

the realm of free (non-economic) goods. There is, therefore, no foundation for any of the references to various 'natural' processes (such as the breeding of animals and yields which do not necessitate human tending of the plants etc.) as independent sources of 'profit on capital'.[1]

Let us now present our 'production costs' formulas in a more general form (more general than the formula $X_A = A_A X_a (1+r)^{t_A} + A_{A1} X_a \times (1+r)^{t_{A1}} + \cdots$), namely let us set:

$$A_A X_\alpha = P_A; \qquad A_{A1} X_\alpha = P_{A1}; \qquad \cdots \qquad (73)$$

in which case we obtain:

$$X_A = P_A (1+r)^{t_A} + P_{A1} (1+r)^{t_{A1}} + \cdots \qquad (74)$$

where P_A, P_{A1}, ... will directly denote the number of units of value expended in production or, in other words, will denote the real production costs expressed in a common unit of value with the finished product.[2] Equation (74) is the most general expression of the connection between the price of a product and production costs, and therefore it enables us to extend our analysis beyond *present-day* forms of production.

Let us imagine* a situation in which manpower is withdrawn from market circulation (for whatever reason: without or by means of legislation) so that it is impossible to buy or sell human labour on the *market*. In that case, obviously, it will no longer be possible to reduce the real *production costs* of products to the *expenditure of products* (the means of subsistence of the workers): human labour will be the last level to which they can all be reduced. Let the value of a unit of labour expressed in the same common measurement unit in which the values of the finished

---

[1] See pp. 77-78 for the characteristics distinguishing 'profit on capital', as a special form of income, from other forms of 'income from ownership'.

[2] This formula may be derived directly from the definition of the concept of 'profit' as the difference between the value expended in production and the value obtained as a result of production:

$$A_A = P_A + Z + P_{A1} + Z_1 + \cdots$$

where the sums of the profits are replaced by expressions corresponding to them in terms of the rate of profit r.

* *Ed. note.* In this passage Dmitriev argues that if labour ceased to be a commodity (i.e. if it were 'withdrawn from market circulation') all other commodities would exchange at prices equal to their direct and indirect labour contents (*labour values*). Obviously Dmitriev needs an additional assumption, that labourers as free (i.e. non-hired) producers should not be able to rent capital goods from capitalists (or from each other) and sell capital goods to capitalists (or to each other); for otherwise there would be no reason why relative prices should be different, whether workers are hired by capitalists or machines are hired by workers. If we add this assumption then we must be either in a world without capital goods or in a world without capitalists (including the State among capitalists). In either case there would be no profit, hence relative prices could conceivably be equal to relative values. However, under this necessary additional assumption Dmitriev's proposition seems somewhat trivial.

products X_A, X_B, ... are expressed be K. In that case, if the quantity of labour used (directly and indirectly) in the production of a unit of the products A, B, ... is expressed by M_A, M_{A1}, ..., M_B, M_{B1}, ..., we shall have a series of equations:

$$
\left.
\begin{aligned}
X_A &= M_AK(1+r)^{t_A} + M_{A1}K(1+r)^{t_{A1}} + \cdots \\
X_B &= M_BK(1+r)^{t_B} + M_{B1}K(1+r)^{t_{B1}} + \cdots
\end{aligned}
\right\}
\tag{75}
$$
...

The unknowns in the equations for X_A, X_B, ... will be K and r. Having regard to the fact that we shall have one equation in the equation system (75) (for the commodity used as a measure of value, i.e. a commodity whose value is taken to be unity):

$$
1 = M_pK(1+r)^{t_p} + M_{p1}K(1+r)^{t_{p1}} + \cdots
\tag{76}
$$

which does not add a new unknown, we shall therefore have a total of n equations with $(n+1)$ unknowns. In our previous analysis we excluded the superfluous $(n+1)$ unknown by means of the equation:

$$
X_\alpha = A_\alpha X_\alpha(1+r)^{t_\alpha} + A_{\alpha1}X_\alpha(1+r)^{t_{\alpha1}} + \cdots
\tag{53}
$$

which directly yielded us r as a function of the known quantities. It is natural to consider whether it is also possible to find a similar equation in the system (75). Clearly this is not possible; for this to be possible one would have to obtain, as a result of production, the same 'production good' to which all real production costs could be reduced. But this is impossible, because *production costs will always consist of labour* (since labour cannot be bought by the price of its means of subsistence), *and the result of production will always be a product*, and not labour. Therefore the production cost equation for product α will be *included in labour* (since labour cannot be bought by the price of the means of its subsistence), *and the result of production will always be a product*, and not labour. Consequently, the production costs equation for the product α will be:

$$
X_\alpha = M_\alpha K(1+r)^{t_\alpha} + M_{\alpha1}K(1+r)^{t_{\alpha1}} + \cdots
\tag{77}
$$

where X_α, K and r are unknowns. If we take the value of the product α to be the unit of value (i.e. if we take the commodity α to be the commodity used as a measuring unit), the equation becomes:

$$
1 = M_\alpha K(1+r)^{t_\alpha} + M_{\alpha1}K(1+r)^{t_{\alpha1}} + \cdots
\tag{78}
$$

In order to determine r from this, K would have to be a known quantity. However, for K to be known, r would have to be known. Therefore, the question *apparently* remains unresolved, at least within the limits of the data of *production* conditions (expressed by the production costs equation). This is, however, only apparent. In reality, the quantity K, expressing the equivalent ratio of product α and labour, *cannot be determined on the market*, by virtue of the assumption made at the beginning of the present analysis (since labour has been removed from market exchange). It follows therefore that the *only* process by means of which the two different goods (the product α and labour) may replace each other in equivalent quantities will be the *process of production* of product α.

Every man who has in his possession some quantity of units of labour *has no means of replacing them by the product α other than by expending his labour in the production of the product* (he cannot sell his labour on the market). The coefficient K cannot therefore remain *undetermined*, but will have a quite precise (and *unique*) value determined by the conditions of production of product α. If N units of labour are capable of producing S units of the product α, it follows that $K = S/N$.[1] Consequently, we shall have $M_\alpha K + M_{\alpha 1} K \ldots = 1$ in our equation (78), from which the only value for r satisfying this equation will be $r = 0$. Therefore despite the apparent inadequacy of equation system (75), we obtain a *fully determined magnitude for r* which, by the law of the equality of the profit level in all industries, is also established in the industries $A, B, \ldots$

Setting $r = 0$ in the system (75), we obtain:

$$\left. \begin{aligned} X_A &= M_A K + M_{A1} K + \cdots \\ X_B &= M_B K + M_{B1} K + \cdots \end{aligned} \right\} \tag{79}$$

$$\cdots$$

From this

$$X_{AB} = \frac{X_A}{X_B} = \frac{M_A + M_{A1} + \cdots}{M_B + M_{B1} + \cdots}, \quad \text{and so on,} \tag{80}$$

i.e. *the exchange ratio of commodities will be determined exclusively by the quantity of labour used in their production, irrespective of the time that will have elapsed between the time labour was expended and the time when the finished product was obtained.*[2] Therefore, the law of 'labour value' would *always* hold were human labour to be withdrawn from circulation in the market (whereas in the present state of affairs it holds only for products produced by capital goods of the same organic composition, as is noted and *emphasised* by Ricardo).

---

[1] $N \cdot K = S \cdot X_\alpha$, from which $K/X_\alpha = S/N$ and, since $X_\alpha = 1$ (because we have taken the product α as the commodity used as a unit of measure), we have: $K = S/N$.

[2] In the absence of hired labour, the introduction of capital goods (*capitale tecnico*) will not therefore serve to infringe the 'labour theory of value' (see, in this respect, the remarks by A. Loria, *Analisi della proprietà capitalista*, 1889. Loria does not directly assume the absence of hired labour, but this stems indirectly from the other conventional assumptions which he makes, such as free land (*terra libera*)).

The same conclusion may be arrived at by a different route. For there to be equilibrium in the sphere of production it is essential that entrepreneurs should be identically rewarded in all branches of industry. This condition is satisfied if equal amounts *of value expended in equal periods of time* yield *equal amounts of value* in all branches of production. Let us assume that we have two industries A and B; let the process of production of product A require t units of time for its completion and let the process for B require nt units of time. Let us assume that when N units of labour have been expended we obtain M_A units of the product A or M_B units of the product B.

Let K_N, X_A and X_B respectively denote the value of a unit of labour and of units of the products A and B expressed in some arbitrary but *common* unit. In that case the amount of value *expended* in the productions A and B will equal $K_N N$; the amount of value *obtained* in the production of B on completion of the production process, i.e. after nt units of time (from the expenditure of labour) will equal $X_B M_B$. For equilibrium to exist between sectors A and B it is essential that the value of the total quantity of the product obtained in sector A *over the same period of time* should also equal $X_B M_B$ (since otherwise there would be infringement of the condition that equal quantities of value yield equal quantities of value in all branches in equal periods of time).[1] In order now to determine the value of one unit of the product A, it is necessary to divide $X_B M_B$ by y, the number of units of the product A obtained in sector A for N units of labour expended in nt units of time. The question which arises is how large y will be in the absence of hired labour? It is not difficult to see that in this case (in contrast to what is observed under present-day conditions) $X_A M_A$ units of value obtained in the production of A at the end of t units of time cannot be exchanged in the market for an equivalent quantity of labour (which, when $r > 0$, is always greater than N, i.e. is greater than the quantity of labour expended in the production of M_A units of product A). Therefore, N units of labour will yield as many units of the product in the production of A in nt units of time as will be yielded in t units of time, i.e. M_A since the production process for A cannot be repeated without the expenditure in production of N *further new* units of labour.

Hence, for sectors A and B to be in equilibrium, the value of a unit of product A should equal:

$$\frac{X_B M_B}{M_A} = X_A \quad \text{from which} \quad \frac{X_A}{X_B} = \frac{M_B}{M_A} \tag{81}$$

[1] By virtue of the law of the 'equality of profit rates' already established by Adam Smith.

and since the quantities of labour needed for a unit of product A and of product B are respectively

$$N_A = \frac{N}{M_A} \quad \text{and} \quad N_B = \frac{N}{M_B}, \tag{82}$$

we have:

$$\frac{N_A}{N_B} = \frac{N \cdot M_B}{M_A \cdot N} = \frac{M_B}{M_A}, \quad \text{from which} \quad \frac{X_A}{X_B} = \frac{N_A}{N_B}, \tag{83}$$

i.e. the relation between the values of units of products A and B, expressed in any common unit, should be equal to the relation between the quantities of labour used in their production, irrespective of the length of the production processes of A and B.

Let us now proceed from this general analysis of the conditions affecting the appearance and rate of profit to the present state of affairs. Hardly anyone will dispute[1] that the *only* process determining the level of profit at the *present time* is the process of production of the means of subsistence of the workers (*capitale alimento*[2]). Let us consider this special case of the existence of profit on capital in greater detail. Take the production costs equation of the means of subsistence a of the workers:

$$X_a = n_a a X_a (1+r)^{t_a} + n_{a1} a X_a (1+r)^{t_{a1}} + \cdots \tag{84}$$

which, when shortened, yields

$$1 = n_a a (1+r)^{t_a} + n_{a1} a (1+r)^{t_{a1}} + \cdots \tag{85}$$

from which

$$r = F_a(t_a, t_{a1}, \ldots; n_a, n_{a1}, \ldots; a). \tag{86}$$

It is evident from equation (85) that the derivatives of F_a with respect to the variables $t_{a1}, t_a, \ldots, n_a, n_{a1}, \ldots, a$ will all be negative. This means that the quantity r will be smaller: (1) the greater is the labour expended on production of a unit of a subsistence product of the workers, (2) the greater is the time elapsing between the moment that the labour is expended and the time when the finished product is obtained, (3) the greater is the amount of the consumer product of the workers consumed per unit of work.

In Ricardo's opinion, the most important factor affecting an increase

---

[1] Although discussion of this question is not within the competence of political economy.
[2] The terminology of Loria; see his *Analisi della proprietà capitalista*, 1889.

in the quantity of labour expended on the production of a unit of a product consumed by the workers is the need to go over to the cultivation of less fertile land as the population increases. This point can be largely nullified by improvement in the techniques of land cultivation and, in particular, by the acceleration of production processes.

The quantity denoting the amount of the product consumed per unit of work, when the iron law of wages prevails,[1] will be dependent on the level of needs of the worker and will increase together with them. If we imagine a situation in which the iron law of wages does not hold, the quantity a will in general be determined by the actual struggle of the mutually opposed interests of the capitalists striving to establish the greatest possible value for r and therefore striving to reduce the quantity a to the minimum possible, and of the workers striving conversely to raise a to the greatest possible value. The level of a at which equilibrium is established is a question of fact and is dependent on the strength of the contending parties. In this state of affairs investigation of the conditions affecting the level of a falls outside the scope of political economy and within that of other disciplines; in this case also, as when the iron law of wages prevails and a is determined by the physiological needs of the worker's body, political economy should take the quantity a to be given in its analysis. To proceed in any other way would be to offend against the requirements of correct methodology, by virtue of which every science should have its own special subject and corresponding strictly defined limits.

At all events we invariably have two limits for a: a lower limit, which will be the quantity a established when the iron law of wages (determined

---

[1] The action of this law is manifested only over long periods of time; for short periods, for which the *number of workers is a constant*, the relationship between the level of wages and the supply of *labour* will sometimes be completely the opposite; when wages rise the supply of labour may not only not increase, but may even decrease. In fact, if we take the number of *workers* to be invariable, we obtain the following curve for variation of the supply of labour as a function of the wage rate:

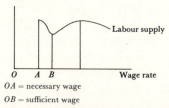

OA = necessary wage
OB = sufficient wage

Figure 1.1

Clearly when the wages rate rises from OA to OB not only will the supply of labour not increase, but on the contrary it will fall. A detailed and thorough analysis of the 'labour supply curve' (and also of the prototype curves from which it is derived) is to be found in W. Launhardt: *Mathematische Begründung der Volkswirthschaftslehre*, Leipzig, 1885, pp. 94–5 and also p. 90 [the figure is from Launhardt, p. 95].

by the physiological needs of the worker's body) prevails, and an upper limit, which will be the total quantity of the product produced per unit of work.

A question which arises is whether it is possible to find a value for *a* between these limits which, even if only in some hypothetical ideal system, would be *simultaneously the most advantageous both for the capitalist employers and for the workers* and consequently would be determined by an *economic* factor.

We know that this is a problem which the celebrated economist J. H. von Thünen, one of the first economists to decide to apply higher mathematical analysis to economic problems, set himself. Thünen refers to the wages which satisfy such conditions as 'natural wages' (in contrast to the wages established by the struggle of the mutually opposed interests of capitalists and workers). Thünen concludes as a result of his study that it is possible to achieve complete harmony of the interests of capitalists and workers under certain ideal conditions; Thünen defined the level of wages most advantageous both to the capitalists and to the workers by the formula $\sqrt{(ap)}$, where *a* are the means of subsistence necessary to the worker in a unit of time and *p* is the entire production of the worker in the same unit of time.

Unfortunately, despite its apparent rigour, Thünen's research suffers from many omissions, each of which is sufficient in itself (owing to the very nature of the study) to make his conclusion unconvincing. We shall not here make a detailed analysis of Thünen's work (see the criticism of Thünen's theory in Launhardt)[1] but shall confine ourselves to an indication of his principal error (thanks to which alone he was able to obtain a *definite* answer to the problem which he had set himself), which is of general fundamental (methodological) importance. We refer to Thünen's incorrect use of *maximum formulas*. There is no doubt that the techniques made available by higher mathematics for determination of the value of a variable which maximises a

[1] See Launhardt, 1885, p. 150. 'This doctrine is erroneous. By contenting themselves with the necessary wages, the workers employed in the factory incur a privation which cannot be measured by the number of days during which they are subject to this privation but by the magnitude of this privation which is equal to y for each day. The magnitude of the privation is therefore equal to $na(a+y)$; if this is divided by the profit of the firm one obtains $[1/(a+y)-1]/q$; this expression is greatest for $y=0$. And this cannot be otherwise if one considers the question of the wage rate from the viewpoint of the entrepreneur, since the entrepreneurial profit will be greater the smaller the wage.'

Launhardt's correction would be right if people did strive under the influence of economic calculation to the *highest level of income on their capital*; in fact this occurs *only* when capital is a constant or a *variable independent of the rate of interest*. We are not justified in assuming either case on the basis of the main assumptions made by Thünen. And that is why the aspiration of people toward the greatest well being may be regarded as satisfied (and consequently a balance of interests as established) *only when the total sum of income on capital is greatest*. The maximum formula given by Launhardt does not satisfy this requirement.

function ought to find extremely important application in political economy, which studies the actions of individuals under the influence of their striving for the *greatest advantage*. Nevertheless, great care ought to be taken to ensure that the differential formulas which serve to determine the value of a variable corresponding to the maximum of a function should not be applied purely mechanically to economic problems. Under the influence of the pursuit of the greatest benefit every economic subject in fact strives (in as far as this is dependent on his will) to impart to all variables on which his net income depends, values such that the *total sum* of this net income should be *greatest*, but from this it does not at all follow that the same may be accepted in relation to any partial income (*revenue partiel*) of the subject. A value of the variable which yields the maximum value for some one partial income of the subject may completely fail to correspond to the maximum value of his *total* income and, consequently, may contradict the basic striving of every economic subject toward the greatest benefit. The sole exception is the case in which a given *partial* income does not stand in any functional relationship to the other parts of the total income.

The differential equation $d\{[(p-a-y)y]/[q(y+a)]\} = 0$ from which Thünen determines the most advantageous level of wages $(a+y)$ for a hired worker obviously contradicts this basic methodological rule: in fact, given the conventional assumptions which Thünen makes in order to present the worker as completely free of the effect of the 'iron law of wages', the formula $[(p-a-y)y]/[q(y+a)]$ expresses only a part of the worker's *total income*[1] and moreover a part which cannot be accepted as an independent variable relative to the remaining income (since the income from previously accumulated capital is also a function of the variable y).

It was only thanks to the methodological error that Thünen was able to obtain a *definite* answer to the task which he has set himself. Had he based his analysis on an expression of the worker's *total income*, and not on an arbitrarily selected part of it, he would have found that the question which he had formulated did not have and could not have any *definite* solution since, given the assumptions made by him, the sum of total income is a quantity independent of y and consequently also of $(a+y)$ (despite the fact that *taken separately* each of the parts of the total income is a function of the variable y), so that in such a hypothetical state of affairs the amount of wages would be a matter of complete indifference both for the workers and for their employers.

---

[1] This formula would express the *total sum* of the worker's income only if the worker *had no previously accumulated savings at all*, but under such conditions it would obviously also not be possible to refer to any 'natural' wages.

2. Ricardo's theory of value

Now let us turn to our equation (85), which defines the quantity r under present conditions:

$$1 = n_a a(1+r)^{t_a} + n_{a1} a(1+r)^{t_{a1}} + \cdots \qquad (85)$$

Setting in it $n_a a + n_{a1} + \cdots = 1$, we have $r = 0$. With this state of affairs any extraction of profit from capital becomes impossible and, in consequence of this, any capitalist production (i.e. with hired workers) should cease (in fact it would cease even before r became zero). This at least is how it would be if the conventional assumptions made by us at the beginning of our analysis of the phenomenon of profit on capital were in fact to hold. But since in fact these conventional assumptions are realised only in exceptional cases, the incentive to continue production and exchange would still remain in force for some of the entrepreneurs even when $r = 0$. The point is that *profit on capital* is not the only form of income yielded by capital. Following Ricardo, we take *profit on capital* to mean only one quite definite form of income regulated by its own precisely defined laws. The characteristic distinguishing this form of income from the group of remaining (rent-like) incomes governed by their own laws is that the 'profit on capital' is obtained by virtue of the mere possession of capital, whereas all other forms of income connected with capital are obtained by virtue of the various *advantages* of some capitalists over others. These advantages may relate both to the sphere of production and to the sphere of sale (exchange) and even to the sphere of consumption; they may be either temporary or permanent (the former correspond to what are known as incomes depending on the general conditions of markets [*kon"yunktural'nyye dokhody*], and the latter to rent-like incomes in the strict sense). However they may be expressed, the incomes produced by them are subject to their own definite laws *which have nothing in common with the laws governing the origin and level of the 'profit on capital'*. It would be not merely unscientific but impossible to study these two groups of incomes together,[1] since the difference existing between them is not merely superficial but *fundamental*. The actual classification of incomes (into profit on capital and rent-like incomes) cannot present the slightest difficulty: all that needs to be done to decide to which group a given income belongs in each specific case is to consider whether this income would be possible if all the capitalist entrepreneurs were placed under *completely identical conditions* both in relation to production and in relation to sale and consumption. Such a conventional assumption excludes all possibility of the occurrence of rent-like profits and the only possible

[1] For this reason the extension of the concept of 'rent' (made by Rodbertus) to 'all income which any person obtains without personal labour, solely on the basis of some possessions' is highly irrational. (C. Rodbertus, *Zur Erkenntniss*, 1842, p. 64; *Zur Beleuchtung der socialen Frage*, Berlin, 1875, Vol. I, p. 32.)

income from capital will be 'profits on capital' in the strictly scientific sense (i.e. understood as a quite definite form of income governed by its own unique laws). This is the approach which we have previously used in our analysis of the 'profit on capital'. Given such an assumption, all possibility of the extraction of income from capital is eliminated when $r = 0$ (since all the conditions for the development of rent-like income have thus been excluded beforehand and 'profit on capital' is the *only* possible income from capital).

We still have to consider whether or not our conclusion will be modified if, instead of calculating income in exchange units, we calculate it (as is in fact done by every economic subject) in its *use value*.* For this purpose we must calculate the sum of the use value (utility) represented to a given individual by the product expended by him in production and to subtract this sum from the sum of the use value represented to the same individual by the finished product of the production. If, in the interests of simplicity, the actual period of production is taken as the unit of time, the profit rate r may be arrived at by dividing the difference obtained by us by the sum of the use value expended.

Let the use value of a unit of the product α be K. In this case, under the production conditions we have assumed we shall have for the determination of r:

$$K = n_a a K (1+r)^{t_\alpha} + n_{a1} a K (1+r)^{t_{\alpha 1}} + \cdots$$

$$\text{or} \quad 1 = n_a a (1+r)^{t_\alpha} + n_{a1} a (1+r)^{t_{\alpha 1}} + \cdots \quad (87)$$

from which $r = 0$ when $n_a a + n_{a1} a + \cdots = 1$. But this will be so only while we assume that the *use of a unit of the given product is a constant for the given individual*, at least within the effective limits of economic calculation. In fact, however, this is not so: the use value of a unit of a given product for a given individual is a *function of time*. It was on this basis that Böhm-Bawerk attempted to construct an independent theory of profit on capital (i.e. independent of production conditions) in his work *Kapital*

---

* *Ed. note.* It is difficult to think what Dmitriev seeks in this passage (up to the end of Section 2 of the First Essay) by calculating income (and inputs) in terms of 'use value', unless he has in mind a situation of equal marginal and average (cardinal) utility of commodities, *and* admits the interpersonal additivity of utility levels. The weakest point of his analysis is his criticism of Böhm-Bawerk, on the ground that it is sufficient 'to postulate that all people "overvalue" present goods by comparison with future goods to an *equal degree* for this overvaluation to cease' to be a source of income'. In modern terminology 'overvaluation' of this kind does not require a rate of substitution between present and future consumption equal to $(1+r)$, where r is the interest rate, whatever the relation between present consumption c_0 and consumption at a future date c_1; 'overvaluation' would be interpreted as $(1+r) > 1$ for $c_0 = c_1$. Even if economic agents had the same rate of 'overvaluation', or more generally if they had identical time preference functions, as long as their relative endowments of dated consumption differ there would be a positive mutual gain from exchange.

und Kapitalzins. He states: 'Present goods are generally of greater value than future goods of the same sort and number. This proposition is the kernel and centre of the theory of interest, which I have to propose' (*Positive Theorie*, 1889, p. 248).[1]

It is not difficult to demonstrate that although Böhm-Bawerk wished to indicate the source of 'profit on capital' he in fact indicated only a new source of *rent-like* (differential) *income*. In fact, we only have to postulate that all people 'overvalue' present goods by comparison with future goods *to an equal degree* for this overvaluation to cease to be a source of income.

In fact, let us assume that an individual A gives an individual B a sum of 100 roubles to be returned with interest a year later. Let the ratio of the usefulness of one rouble at the present time to the usefulness of one rouble after a year be $2:1$, denoting these usefulnesses by K_p and K_f and we have $K_p:K_f = 2:1$, from which $K_f = \frac{1}{2}K_p$; if B agrees to give A 200 roubles at the end of a year, his income from this operation expressed in use value is:

$$100K_p - 200K_f = 100K_p - 200 \cdot \tfrac{1}{2}K_p = 100K_p - 100K_p = 0. \quad (88)$$

Were he to return more than 200 roubles at the end of a year, his income would be expressed by a negative quantity: therefore 200 will be the highest sum which B may in general return to the creditor A. Let us consider what will be A's income at this highest sum of 200 roubles which B may return to him. Since we assume that neither of the contracting parties A and B has an advantage over the other in the sphere of consumption, the coefficients K_p and K_f will be the same for both. Consequently, the benefit obtained from the operation by contracting party A will also be expressed by $100K_p - 200K_f = 100K_p - 100K_p = 0$.

A transaction between A and B under conditions which exclude the

[1] Böhm-Bawerk notes three main 'overvaluations' of goods in hand. It is only the second of these three bases (the difference in the use value of goods in hand and future goods) that is an essentially new factor capable of providing a basis for the construction of an independent theory 'of the origin of profit on capital'. Böhm-Bawerk gives the following formulation of the second basis (*Zweiter Grund*): 'We underestimate systematically our future needs and the means for their satisfaction' (p. 266). '. . . The existence of this fact is beyond doubt. It is more difficult to say why the fact exists' (p. 267). Böhm-Bawerk subsequently indicates three bases for this fact. 'It seems to me that a first reason stems from the fragmentary character of the idea we have about the future state of our needs' (p. 268). '. . . While this reason seems to amount to erroneous estimation, a second reason seems to stem from an erroneous decision. I believe that it occurs frequently that somebody who is faced with a choice between a present and a future pleasure or pain decides in favour of the lesser present pleasure although he knows exactly and is aware at the moment of his choice that the future disadvantage is greater and hence that his choice is disadvantageous for his wellbeing as a whole' (p. 268). '. . . Finally as a third reason, the consideration of the short duration and insecurity of our life seems also, to me, to be important' (p. 269).

possibility of the development of rent does not therefore give any advantage to either of the contracting parties; it is further not difficult to prove that *under such conditions an advantage will be completely impossible* provided, of course, that the contracting parties are guided in their actions by correct economic calculus.

In fact, correct economic calculus is incompatible with any *economically purposeless* acts (i.e. acts as a result of which the benefits do not exceed the sacrifices), even when a given act does not entail any risk (since every act invariably entails some expenditure of energy, which could be otherwise used on something else with greater benefit or satisfaction). But every transfer of value to other hands *always* entails some risk. There is no point in incurring this risk if the transaction is *unprofitable*, and therefore the very transfer of value to other hands under such conditions is opposed to the economic calculation of a contracting party acting in good faith. Consequently, under conditions which exclude the possibility of the occurrence of rent, no overvaluation of goods in hand can provide an independent source of profit on capital. Therefore, if production conditions are such as we have assumed at the beginning of this section, profit on capital cannot arise whatever the units in which the balance of the economic operation is calculated (units of exchange or use).

All the foregoing is fully applied in the theory in which Launhardt attempted several years before the appearance of the second volume of *Kapital und Kapitalzins* (in which Böhm-Bawerk's own views are set out) to construct a theory of profit on capital on the same basis as Böhm-Bawerk.[1]

Although the 'overvaluation' of goods in hand by comparison with future goods, which is noted by Böhm-Bawerk, does not contribute anything new to the theory of the development of profit and the level of profit, it is a significant factor under the *given* conditions of production in the question of the accumulation of capital. (For a detailed analysis of this question see Launhardt, 1885, pp. 67–9).

3. THE THEORY OF MONOPOLY PRICES

Ricardo pays hardly any attention to the laws determining the price of scarce products. Nor is any clear distinction to be found in his writings between scarce products in the true sense and monopoly products (the

---

[1] Compare Launhardt, 1885. '. . . an enjoyment is the less appreciated the more distant the future when it can be had . . .' (p. 5). 'The secure prospect of an enjoyment in the future is thought to be of lesser value than the same enjoyment in the present . . .' (p. 6). This hypothesis is subsequently related to interest: 'Interest is the compensation for waiting for an enjoyment or for the temporary renunciation of an enjoyment . . .' (p. 7).

3. The theory of monopoly prices

quantity of which is arbitrarily limited by the individual in whose hands the production of this product is exclusively concentrated).

We shall consider the first case in passing when we analyse the laws determining the price of products whose production is under the influence of unlimited free competition. The second case, which is of interest in its own right, we shall consider straight away. It will be seen subsequently that it is impossible to proceed to a scientific criticism of the theory of competition unless this problem is correctly solved.

How should a monopolist, motivated by the desire to achieve the greatest advantage, decide how much to produce?

Adam Smith stated that a monopolist will restrict supply so as to obtain for his goods the highest price the consumer will agree to pay. It is not difficult to see that to proceed in this manner would not be in accordance with the aspiration for the greatest advantage; a large price does not in fact ensure an even greater advantage and would do so only if the price and the amount sold were to be independent variables. However, this is not so in practice, and price is invariably a function of the quantity sold.

If we denote the amount sold in a unit of time by D and the price by p, we shall have $p = f(D)$; now let the production costs of each *unit* be u; except for the category of products which we shall consider in the next section, this quantity is independent of the amount produced and may be taken by us to be a constant. In this case the total profit of the monopolist in a unit of time will be given by

$$D \cdot f(D) - D \cdot u \tag{89}$$

If the quantity D is determined by a single individual (the monopolist) motivated by correct economic calculation, he will so determine it that the value of the expression $[D \cdot f(D) - Du]$ will be as large as possible. This quantity D is determined from the equation:

$$\mathrm{d}[D \cdot f(D) - D \cdot u] = 0. \tag{90}$$

Before proceeding with further analysis, let us pause to consider in greater detail the relationship between price and the amount sold (expressed by the function f). An excellent analysis of this question is to be found in Cournot.[1]

Even so, we are able to employ more illustrative mathematical techniques. Instead of taking the various values of D as the abscissa of the

[1] A. Cournot, *Recherches sur les principes mathématiques de la théorie des richesses*, Paris, 1838, Ch. 4; English translation by N. T. Bacon, *Researches into the mathematical principles of the theory of wealth*, New York, 1897.

curve, as is done by Cournot, we can take the product pD as the ordinates; in this case the equation of the curve will be:

$$Y = D \cdot f(D) = F(D). \tag{91}$$

If we set $D = 0$, we have $Y = 0$; by successively increasing D, we finally arrive at a value of D at which Y once again vanishes; this will occur at the value of D for which $f(D) = 0$; since the demand for each product is limited and since no one will pay money for a product which he does not need at all (and there cannot be several prices for one product in the market), the price of the product will vanish at some *finite* value of D,[1] and therefore the form of the curve defined by the equation $Y = F(D)$ will be that shown in Fig. 1.2. If sales D are taken as the abscissae and costs Du as the ordinates, we shall obtain a straight line OA running at an angle to the axis of the abscissae. The vertical distance between the lines ON and OA will denote the net profit corresponding to each scale of production. This distance will be greatest at the point on the curve ON where the tangent to it become parallel to the straight line OA. If this point is C, the quantity yielding the greatest net income will equal the abscissa OB; the price corresponding to this quantity will equal the tangent of the angle ϑ (which will equal BC/OB).

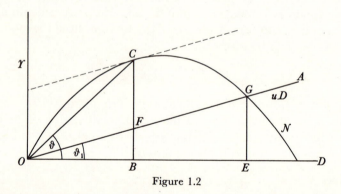

Figure 1.2

Therefore, if the monopolist has a correct understanding of his advantage, this is the price which he will set. Were the production of the given product to be influenced by free competition, the scale of production would be increased until the market price of the product exactly equalled the necessary production costs (this, at least, is what Ricardo's theory asserts; we shall see subsequently whether or not it is correct), which would occur when the amount produced equalled OE; in this case the

[1] For the present this will be taken to be an empirical fact. For the *explanation* of this fact the reader is referred to the third essay, in which there is a detailed analysis of $f(D)$.

price of a unit would equal the tangent of the angle ϑ_1 and would always be less than the tangent of the angle ϑ, as is shown by Figure 1.2.

4. RICARDO'S THEORY OF RENT

We shall not make a detailed analysis of the theory of rent in general at this point, but shall deal with Ricardo's theory of rent only to the extent to which it is an element of his general theory of value (for this reason, for example, we shall not deal at all with the question of the importance, to Ricardo's theory, of *land* rent, of the historical sequence of the occupation of lands of different quality, or with whether rent necessarily swallows an ever-increasing portion of the product produced as population increases: it is not even necessary to understand Ricardo's theory to imagine that it is connected with some sequence or other of the occupation of lands.[1] Although Ricardo does not himself clarify the laws governing rent in a special case of the origin of this kind of income (namely in the case of land rent and rent from mines, see Ricardo, *Principles*, Chs. 2 and 3), this does not prevent his theory from being of general significance for all possible cases of the origin of rent-like incomes.[2] Yu. Zhukovsky states[3] that

'According to Ricardo's theory, the fundamental condition for the origin of rent is in no sense the correct transfer of cultivation from some portions of land to others, but the general law of the *equality of profits*. According to this law the same capital and labour cannot yield different profits in the same production, since competition will hasten to equalise these profits if they can occur. If this law holds not even for different productions, but for the same production, an unavoidable consequence of this should be the subtraction of all differences in profits in favour of the monopolist of the cheap method and in the particular case of the land owner, and it is this which constitutes rent.'

Ricardo himself was well aware of this when he stated that 'If air, water, the elasticity of steam, and the pressure of the atmosphere, were of

[1] See K. McKean, *Manual of social science*, being a condensation of the *Principles of Social Science* of H. C. Carey [Philadelphia and London, 1837, 1838, 2 Vols.], Philadelphia, 1864. Carey states that Ricardo's whole theory rests on the preconception that only fertile soil was initially cultivated when the population was low and there was consequently excess land.

[2] The statement by A. Miklashevsky, that 'the *law* of rent on capital expended in manufacturing industry differs *fundamentally* from the *law of rent in general*' merely proves that this author has not sufficiently understood the concept of a scientific 'law' (he confuses the law itself with the conditions under which its operation is manifested). See A. Miklashevsky, *Den'gi – Opyt' izuchenii osnovnikh polozhenii ekonomicheskoy teorii klassicheskoy shkoly* [Money – An examination of the basic propositions of the classical school of economic theory], pp. 246–7.

[3] Yu. Zhukovsky, *A history of 19th century political theories*, p. 318.

various qualities; if they could be appropriated, and each quality existed only in moderate abundance, they, as well as the land, would afford a rent as the successive qualities were brought into use.' which would be governed by the same laws as land rent.[1]

We shall not repeat Ricardo's theory of rent, which is well known, but shall proceed directly to a close analysis of it (an excellent analysis is to be found in Zhukovsky's book to which reference has been made), and in our analysis we shall make use of the constructions of Auspitz and Lieben (Auspitz and Lieben, *Untersuchungen über die Theorie des Preises*, 1889). Although Auspitz and Lieben were not specially concerned with the theory of rent, their constructions nevertheless provide excellent material for an analysis of this phenomenon because in a *general* analysis of the phenomenon of value they arbitrarily and completely incorrectly give to the curve of production costs the form which is appropriate for branches of production *yielding rent*; this arbitrary assumption, which deprives their own conclusions on the question of value of any generality, enables us to use their constructions for an analysis of the phenomenon of rent.

'Let us construct a system of coordinates [Figure 1.3] where the abscissae denote quantities of the article *A* and where the ordinates denote quantities of money. If we draw the various possible quantities of the yearly product horizontally, and the corresponding cost of production vertically, we obtain a series of points which, connected, present a curve *OA*, which we shall call the curve of total cost of production' (Auspitz and Lieben, p. 6).

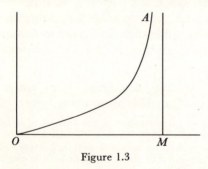

Figure 1.3

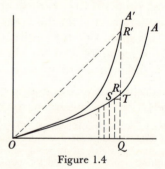

Figure 1.4

This curve *OA* has the following characteristics: (1) its starting point is the origin of coordinates, (2) it is rising, (3) it has an asymptote parallel

---

[1] Ricardo, *Principles*, Ch. 2, p. 75 of the Sraffa edition. Buchanan remarks quite correctly, commenting on Adam Smith, that the excess income obtained by the possessor of any secret in manufacturing industry is, in its essence, rent governed by the same laws as land rent and any other rent. See Buchanan, *Observations . . .*, pp. 39–41.

to the axis of ordinates (this latter assertion is equivalent to the assertion that there is a limit to every production, beyond which it cannot be expanded whatever the expenditure), (4) the curve is convex throughout, i.e. each successive tangent is less inclined to the axis of abscissae than all the preceding tangents. Consequently, an increase in the quantity of the product causes a greater increase of cost, the higher is the annual production of the product to which this increase is added.

In Figure 1.4 let OA be the 'cost curve' of a product A; let OA' be

'the quantity of the article A under consideration actually produced and turned over during one year. We can then imagine it being partitioned into a number of small parts of equal length. Each of these small parts will yield the same revenue since the whole quantity will be sold at one and the same price. The costs of production however are different, for each further part necessitates a greater cost of production than the one which precedes it. If the producers are to be induced to produce the quantity OQ, the revenue from the last part, which we denote by TS, has to be as big as the additional costs necessitated by the production of this last part, for otherwise it could not be produced.'

'On the other hand, if the revenue from this last part were greater than the cost which it causes, the producers would be led to increase their production still further by the free competition prevailing between them. Since we have now assumed a stable situation and OQ represents the appropriate annual quantity, the costs TR necessary for the production of the last part ST which has actually been produced have to be equal to the revenue generated by it. The length TR therefore represents the income generated by the last unit of production ST; but since there exists only one price for the whole quantity OQ produced during the year, and since there is also only one price for the last unit ST of that quantity, the total quantity produced during the year must bear the same proportion to the total revenue generated by it as ST to TR. If we now draw a parallel to the curve SR through the origin, and if the chosen unit into which the quantity annually produced is partitioned is small enough, the curve SR will indicate the direction of the tangent to the cost curve at point R. This parallel cuts the ordinate continued beyond the point R at R', and the length of QR' indicates the total revenue corresponding to the above proportions which the producer must attain to induce him to produce the quantity OQ. If we repeat the same construction for each other quantity to be produced during the year, from the smallest to the biggest, we obtain a series of points which represents a new curve OA'. . . .'

'. . . the ordinates of this curve indicate the quantity of money for which the annually produced quantities shown on the abscissae are

offered. We call this curve, therefore, the curve of total supply'
(Auspitz and Lieben, pp. 12–14).

Consequently, the ordinates of this curve show the sum which
consumers should pay for the amount of the product on the market (the
annual amount or in general the amount in a unit of time) to correspond
to the given abscissa. The sum which consumers agree to pay will, in its
turn, depend on the quantity of the product bought by them; if we take
the quantities purchased as the abscissae and the sum which the
consumers agree to pay for these quantities as the ordinates, we obtain
the total demand curve already used in the preceding analysis. (Auspitz
and Lieben construct this curve in a different manner, deriving it from
the general utility curve, but the form which they take for this curve is

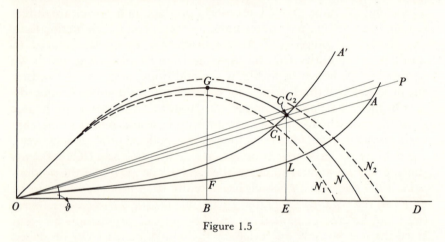

Figure 1.5

quite incorrect and has no data in support of it (cf. Auspitz and Lieben,
pp. 14–16).)

According to Ricardo's theory, when free competition prevails the
scale of production should be established at a level OE (see Figure 1.5)
at which, as the figure shows, the market price paid for a unit of the
product (equal the tangent of the angle ϑ) will equal the production
costs of the last unit of the product to be produced (i.e. the unit produced
with the greatest costs; it is evident from the construction that these costs
will also equal the tangent of the angle ϑ).

The direction of the price line OP (*Preislinie*) is defined by the intersection of the curves OA' and ON, and therefore the price of the product
(which equals the tangent of the angle formed by the line OP and the
axis of abscissae) will also be dependent on the form of *both* curves and
consequently *production conditions alone cannot suffice for its definition*, as is
asserted by Ricardo.

4. Ricardo's theory of rent

Consequently, Ricardo gives us an impeccable analysis of the law governing the value of products when individual portions of these products are produced with different production costs (in particular with different expenditure of labour when production costs may be reduced to labour alone), but this analysis definitely does not prove, as Ricardo assumes, that the value of such products is not ultimately dependent on the conditions of supply and demand and will tend to settle at a level exclusively dependent on production conditions. On the contrary, we have seen that any alteration in the conditions of supply and demand (leading ultimately to an alteration in the sphere of consumption, as we shall see when we analyse the demand curve in the third essay) leads inescapably to an alteration in the price of the product (= value in some product, whose own value is assumed to be constant). This is the case even if all production conditions (which are not dependent on the economic calculation, but only on the state of technology and the availability of the various natural factors of production) have remained unchanged.

All that we have said above concerning the law of value established by Ricardo for products when individual portions of them are produced with *different* production costs is also fully applicable to the theory which states that the value of products is determined by the amount of *socially necessary* labour expended on their production. In fact, by relating value to the amount of *socially necessary* labour, this theory makes *value dependent* (as we have demonstrated in the analysis of Ricardo's theory of rent) *on the condition of supply and demand*[1] (ultimately on the conditions of consumption).

In order to free the definition of the amount of 'socially necessary' labour from the conditions of supply and demand, some advocates of this 'developed' form of the labour theory of value attempt to *equate the amount of socially necessary labour with the average amount* used in the production of a given commodity. To assert this is, however, to deny everything which Ricardo did to clarify the laws governing the value of those products, individual portions of which are produced with different production costs. Ricardo's analysis leaves no doubt that the value of commodity is determined by the quantity of labour expended on its production *not under average but under the most disadvantageous* conditions of its production.

The amount of socially necessary labour could be equated to the *average* amount only in the *exceptional special* case when the sum of positive rent in a given sector was exactly equal to the sum of negative rent (negative rent may rise only in exceptional cases when, owing to various obstacles to the free movement of entrepreneurs from poorly rewarded

[1] Since it is only the conditions of supply and demand which determine how much labour is 'socially necessary' in each specific case.

branches of industry into better rewarded branches, the scale of production is expanded beyond the limit at which the least favourably placed entrepreneurs obtain all the production costs in the price of the product: Ricardo does not analyse this case, since he invariably assumes complete (juridical and actual) mobility of entrepreneurs from one branch of industry to another). Our construction and the corresponding analysis present all the data needed for clarification of the phenomenon of negative rent.

Let us assume that all the *production* conditions and, consequently, the form of the OA curves and of the derived OA' curve remain unchanged, and let us give various positions, denoted by a dashed line, to the ON curve, which is not dependent on production conditions. The point of intersection of the two curves will then assume different positions C_1, C_2, C_3, ..., and by linking these points with O we obtain a series of lines OC_1, OC_2, OC_3, ... The tangents of the angles between them and the axis of abscissae will denote the price established in the market under the influence of free competition for given conditions of *demand*. Clearly by arbitrarily varying the form of the curve ON we may also arbitrarily vary the price of the product, and therefore the assertion that this price is determined by the conditions of production is based merely on a misunderstanding; the price of the product will be affected by all conditions which affect the form of the overall demand curve. Therefore, any change in the sphere of supply which affects the value which consumers place upon a given good, and which consequently affects the sum they will agree to expend in order to acquire it, will affect the price ultimately established in the market. This price will be determined only if the equation of the curve ON is given: $Y = F(D) = Df(D)$, for which the function f expressing the relationship between price and the quantity sold needs to be known. Consequently, in this case, as in the monopoly determination of price, the price cannot be determined independently of the form of the function expressing price as a function of the quantity sold, $p = f(D)$.

We have seen that, on the assumption that both curves are continuous, production will settle down in such a way that the price for a unit of the product in the market will equal the production costs of the last unit produced. The situation will be different if (as is the case in reality) the line OA depicting the increase of production costs as the total amount produced increases is *discontinuous* (at least at some points), i.e. if the tangents to two points infinitely close together on this line form an angle of finite magnitude; in this case, by virtue of the conditions of its construction, the curve OA' will necessarily be *discontinuous*, and the points of discontinuity of the curve OA' will correspond to the points of discontinuity of the original curve OA (Figure 1.6).

For example, let the amount produced be *OE* when the price equals the tangent of the angle *EOH*, and let us now assume that in order to cause the appearance on the market of a larger quantity differing from the quantity *OE* by an infinitely small amount, the price should be immediately increased by some finite amount. In that case the ordinate corresponding to the abscissa larger than *OE* by an infinitely small amount will be larger than the ordinate *EH* by some finite amount, since the curve *OA'* will assume the form *OHJA'*. Obviously, under such conditions, production cannot expand beyond *OE*, since in this case the costs of the last units to be produced (above the amount *OE*) would be greater than the price paid for a unit of the product in the market. It is evident from Figure 1.6 that when production is *OE* the price paid in

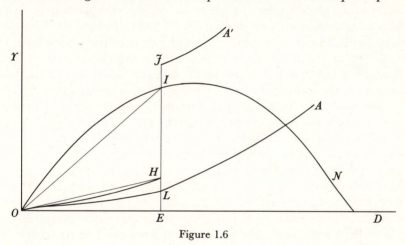

Figure 1.6

the market will be greater than the costs of the last unit produced; it will be greater by as many times as *EI* is greater than *EH* (since the market price of a unit of the product will equal the tangent of the angle *EÔI*, and the production costs of the last unit produced will equal the tangent of the angle *EÔH*). Consequently, the law which states that the price of a product, individual units of which are produced with different production costs, will equal the production cost of the part of the product produced under the most disadvantageous conditions, holds only when $\Phi(Q)$, expressing the production costs of the last unit of the product to be produced as a function of the total quantity produced, is a *continuous* function (i.e. when every infinitely small increment to the amount is matched by an infinitely small increase in the production costs of the last unit to be produced).

In reality we frequently encounter instances of the discontinuity of $\Phi(Q)$ both in agriculture and in the manufacturing industry. This occurs especially in manufacturing industry: here it is only in rare instances that slow gradation of an increasingly less efficient mode of production may be observed. It is only when rent arises *solely* from a difference in the distance between production points and the market (the case investigated in detail by Thünen) that the curve OA' can in fact be taken to be continuous and that, consequently, the Ricardian law of the price of products which yield rent is fully applicable.

Let us return to our original construction (Figure 1.5). The segment CL will express the total sum of rent yielded by OE units of the product; the distribution of this sum between the individual producers has no bearing whatsoever on the amount of the rent.

The only important factor is whether the production of the given product takes place under the influence of free competition or in the monopoly possession of a single individual. In the latter case the scale of production will be determined (in accordance with the principles in the preceding paragraph) by the abscissa OB, for which we have tangents to the curves ON and OA at the points G and F which are parallel and consequently the distance between these curves (expressing gross revenue and *actual* total costs incurred in the production of OB units) is greatest. Clearly OB will always be smaller than OE; also FG is invariably greater than CL, i.e. the sum paid by the consumer *over and above* the actual production cost will be greater in the case of monopoly than under the influence of free competition.

As is shown by Figure 1.5, the magnitude of CL will be smaller, the less is the curvature of the curve OA. If the curve OA is ultimately converted into a straight line, *the curve OA' will also be converted into a straight line*, by virtue of the conditions of its construction from the original curve OA, and it will merge with OA. This will happen *when* total production costs become proportional to the quantity produced, i.e. *when all units of the product are produced with the same costs*. In this case rent will vanish (since the vertical distance between the curves OA and OA' will be zero). The next chapter will be devoted to an investigation of this case. We have just shown that production costs cannot be recognised as the sole regulator of value for a product when price includes rent, and that evey change in the sphere of demand (independently of production conditions) alters the price of such a product even if no changes have occurred in production conditions. This objection to the theory of production costs is not applicable when the production costs curve becomes a straight line. In fact, let the straight line OA be the production costs line and let the curve ON remain the demand curve. In this case, as is asserted by Ricardo, given that free competition prevails, *production will expand until the price paid in the market is no more than sufficient to cover the essential production costs*. Consequently, the amount produced will be OE (Figure 1.7). The price of a unit of the product will be EC/OE, i.e. will equal the tangent of the angle ϑ.

Now let us assign different positions denoted by a dashed line to the curve ON. Clearly the price will remain permanently equal to the tangent of the angle ϑ; changes in demand conditions do not affect the price

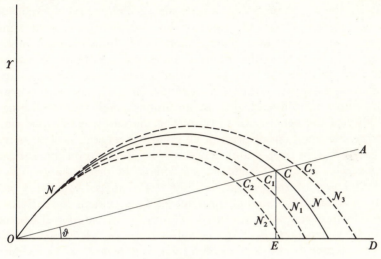

Figure 1.7

until there are changes in production conditions, i.e. until the position of the straight line OA is altered. Consequently, price is *apparently* actually determined in this case *exclusively* by production costs.[1]

And this would be so were the assertion by Ricardo italicised by us above in fact to be correct.

5. RICARDO'S THEORY OF THE VALUE OF INFINITELY REPRO- DUCIBLE GOODS (BY THE APPLICATION OF LABOUR AND CAPITAL UNDER ZERO RENT CONDITIONS)

We have seen that the value of scarce goods, i.e. of goods whose quantity is limited by natural conditions (scarce in the true sense), or artificially as

---

[1] Here and elsewhere in our account of Ricardo's theory of value we invariably refer to the costs of *production* rather than of *reproduction*, since we invariably assume in the interests of simplicity of analysis that no changes occur between the time of manufacture of the product and the time of its sale under the technical conditions of a given branch of industry. This does not, however, mean that Ricardo did not evaluate and take into consideration in his theory the effect of technical progress on the value of *stocks previously produced but still not sold*. On the contrary, only one completely ignorant of Ricardo's work would think that Carey had made a significant correction on this point to Ricardo's theory of value (see the

a result of their production under the monopoly possession of a single economic subject, cannot be determined independently of $F(D)$. Other things being equal, any change in $F(D)$, i.e. in the demand conditions, will also entail a change in the value of the good.

We have further shown that the exclusion of $F(D)$ from the equations of the goods (as essential production costs related to the quantity produced by the function $\Phi(Q)$) is only an apparent, verbal exclusion in Ricardo's theory; in fact the value of these goods cannot be determined independently of the form of $F(D)$ and, other things being equal, any change in $F(D)$ necessarily entails a corresponding change in the value of these goods as in the previous case of scarce goods. We now have to consider the last case, namely the formula for the value of goods which are infinitely reproducible by labour under conditions excluding the possibility of the occurrence of rent. The market price of goods in this category, like the market price of all goods in general, is determined by the 'conditions of supply and demand' (see Ricardo on market prices, *Principles*, Ch. 4), and therefore, if we denote the price of a good by X_A, we shall have, *caeteris paribus*, $X_A = F(D_A)$, where D_A is the 'actual supply' (in Smith's sense) of product A. It is evident by definition of the goods under consideration that D_A may be varied at will between 0 and $+\infty$. What value is in fact established for D_A? Ricardo states that D_A is *ultimately* established as if $F(D_A) = u$, where u stands for the essential production costs of the product A. Direct substitution yields $X_A = F(D_A) = u$. The new expression $X_A = u$ no longer includes $F(D_A)$, and consequently X_A is no longer *directly* dependent on the conditions of 'supply and demand', but for X_A to be *completely* independent of market conditions it is essential that the magnitude of u should also be independent of these conditions.

The whole of this analysis of Ricardo's theory of value has led to the conclusion that Ricardo in fact succeeded in excluding the element of price from production costs and, consequently, in formulating the quantity u independently of demand conditions (this is the *main* difference between Ricardo's theory of value and Smith's theory, which still had to

---

comment by Zalessky, 1893, p. 244. 'It is greatly to Carey's credit and recognised by all that he drew attention to the importance of the costs of reproduction'). Suffice it to refer to Chapter 20 of Ricardo's work, where he states directly that any technical improvement raising the productivity of labour in a given industry will necessarily also have an effect 'on the portion of goods still unconsumed, which were manufactured previously to the improvement; *the value of those goods will be reduced, in as much as they must fall to the level, quantity for quantity, of the goods produced under all the advantages of the improvement*: and the society will, notwithstanding the increased quantity of commodities, notwithstanding its augmented riches, and its augmented means of enjoyment, have a less amount of value. By constantly *increasing the facility of production, we* constantly *diminish the value* of some of the *commodities before produced* ...' (Ricardo, *Principles*, Ch. 20, p. 274 of the Sraffa edition [*emphasis added*]; see also Ch. 6 'On profits').

relate one of the elements of production costs, namely profit, to the conditions of 'supply and demand', namely the supply and demand of capitals). Therefore, provided that the hypothesis $F(D_A) = u$ is correct, we shall have an expression of value, for the kind of goods we are considering, which is independent of market conditions and determined *exclusively* by 'objective' production conditions. On what basis does Ricardo consider it possible to assume $F(D_A) = u$, i.e. assume that the 'actual supply' of a good A produced under free competition without natural limits will expand to the point where the market price barely covers essential costs? Why is it not possible to establish for D_A some quantity D_{Ao} for which we shall have $F(D_{Ao}) > u$, i.e. at which the producers will still make some surplus over and above the essential production costs? Nothing new concerning this question is to be found in Ricardo; he accepts as true the theory of Smith which we have already set out above. Smith and Ricardo reason as follows: if the price of the product in a given industry A exceeds essential production costs, the producers of this industry will receive more profit on their capital than do the producers of other industries. This surplus is the prize which compels the producers of other industries to transfer to the production of A; *as a consequence competition will increase in industry A and the price of product A will fall.* This fall in price will continue until the movement of producers ceases. The influx of new producers will continue until the motive for making the change, i.e. the advantage, disappears. But the advantage will not be destroyed until $F(D_A) = u$, and consequently the fall in the price of the product A will not cease until $F(D_A) = u$, i.e. until the price of the product equals the essential production costs.

There is an undoubted logical omission in this reasoning; the final conclusion holds if the tacit assumption that 'competition lowers prices' also holds.

In fact, why should the movement of new producers into industry A lower the price of product A? After all, whatever part of the net profit earned in the whole industry A was received by each producer, it appears that the price most advantageous for each should be that at which total net profit is greatest.

If we assume that the total sum of the profit in a given industry is 100,000 roubles at the price which yields the maximum net profit (i.e. at a monopoly price), and if we assume that there are 1,000 isolated producers, we obtain a profit of 100 roubles for each. At any price *below* the monopoly price, the total sum of the net profit will be less than 100,000 roubles and, consequently, each of the 1,000 competing producers will have a share of net profit smaller than 100 roubles. But why should 1,000 isolated producers settle on a price less than the monopoly price, despite the fact that this lower price *is far less advantageous for each of them than the monopoly price? And, in general, what is the relationship between the number of competing individuals and price?*

We have sought in vain for a clear answer to these questions in the writings of Smith and Ricardo and their followers. The arbitrary nature of the assumption that the movement of new entrepreneurs into a given industry *A* produces a reduction in the price of the product *A* is concealed in the writings of the classical school. This is done first by a word play; reference is made to the movement of 'capitals' instead of to the movement of 'capitalist entrepreneurs'; this substitution is equivalent to the *arbitrary* assumption that any increase in the numbers of producers occupied in a given industry is invariably accompanied by an increase in the total amount of capital invested in the given industry. Secondly, there is an implicit arbitrary assumption that any extension of production also increases the supply of the given product on the same scale. Thanks to these two *arbitrary* assumptions the truism that 'competition lowers prices' receives an apparent basis (see our account of the way in which Smith reasons), but this does not make the assumption any the less arbitrary. The contradictory nature of the two principles on which all the conclusions of the classical school are based, namely the principle that every individual tends to pursue the greatest advantage and the assumption that competition tends to minimise prices, was evidently overlooked both by the members of the classical school themselves and by their numerous commentators (with the exception of Thornton, who enjoys no reputation as a theoretician of political economy; see W. T. Thornton, *On labour; its wrongful claims and rightful dues, its actual present and possible future*).[1] The tendency of competition to lower prices has been accepted as some sort of 'spontaneous' phenomenon completely independent of the economic calculation of competing individuals; at any rate we cannot find in the writings of economists of the classical school even the hint of an attempt to separate the effect of competition from the basic principle of the pursuit of the greatest advantage (or even an attempt to reconcile it with this situation, by accepting the effect of competition on prices as empirically given). The very possibility that such an important omission in the reasoning of the deductive school should be overlooked was undoubtedly a result of the imperfection of the 'dialectical' method which its members used. The honour of having constructed a completely scientific *theory of competition* belongs entirely to members of the

---

[1] The thought which runs as a guiding line through all Thornton's reasoning is that 'Dealers do not undersell each other merely for fun. Each is quite content that all the rest should sell dearly, provided he himself can sell as dearly ...' (Book III, Ch. 1, p. 61) The sole object of every merchant is to earn the greatest sum for all his goods, and therefore he will lower the price only if he can calculate that with this price reduction his sales will increase so that the total sum of his earnings will rise.

mathematical school of political economy, and mainly to the most talented of its members, the great 'forgotten' economist Augustine Cournot. Unfortunately, however, Cournot's immortal work had no effect on contemporaries and has been forgotten by new generations of economists.[1]

The next essay will be devoted to a critical account of Cournot's theory of competition. We shall attempt to prove by rigorous analysis that although it is generally accepted and has become a truism that unrestricted free competition tends to lower prices to the *essential production costs*, this is no more than an *arbitrary assumption*. This is at variance both with the facts of economic reality and with the basic hypothesis of economic theory that each tends to pursue his greatest advantage. We shall attempt, on the contrary, to demonstrate tangibly that, *as a general rule, unrestricted free competition invariably tends to raise actual production costs above the essential level*, i.e. above the *lowest* level *possible for a given state of production technique.*

Thus the value of products of the third category (i.e. goods infinitely reproducible by the application of labour and capital under conditions of zero rent), like the value of products of the first two categories considered above cannot, as a general rule, be determined independently of conditions of supply and demand (i.e. ultimately independently of the conditions of consumption).

The Third Essay, which will conclude our examination of the *general* elements of value, will be devoted to an analysis of the dependence of price on conditions of supply and demand.

[1] See L. Slonimsky's article 'Zabytye ekonomisty Kurno i Tiunen'' [The forgotten economists Cournot and Thünen], *Vostochnaya Evropa*, October 1878.

SECOND ESSAY

THE THEORY OF COMPETITION OF AUGUSTINE COURNOT

Dealers do not undersell each other merely for fun. Each is quite content that all the rest should sell dearly, provided he himself can sell as dearly . . .

W. T. Thornton

Cournot's theory and its fundamental error. An attempt to construct a rigorously scientific theory of price determination under unlimited free competition. The importance of unlimited free competition for the national economy as a whole; unlimited free competition and the chronic overproduction of goods; unlimited free competition and crises.

I. COURNOT'S THEORY OF COMPETITION

The abode of science is definitely not where it is sought and found by seekers after popular economic theories. Science does not subsist among collectors of published or factual rubbish, among coiners of high-sounding phrases, lovers of involved terms and definitions, resourceful critics and polemicists . . . but in a completely different and higher sphere, one which has been reached only occasionally by solitary and lucid intellects, whose reward for their achievement has been oblivion.

L. Slonimsky

Cournot writes:

'Every one has a vague idea of the effects of competition. Theory should have attempted to render this idea more precise, and yet, for lack of regarding the question from the proper point of view, and for want of recourse to symbols (of which the use in this connection becomes indispensable), economic writers have not in the least improved on popular notions in this respect. These notions have remained as ill-defined and ill-applied in their works, as in popular language' (Cournot, *Recherches*, 1838, p. 79 of English edition).

The starting point of Cournot's theory of competition is an analysis of the 'law of demand' (*loi de débit*), to which the fourth chapter of his book is devoted.

'Let us admit therefore that the sales or the annual demand D is, for each article, a particular function $F(p)$ of the price p of such article. To know the form of this function would be to know what we call *the law of demand* or *of sales*. It depends evidently on the kind of utility of the article, on the nature of the services it can render or the enjoyment it can procure, on the habits and customs of the people, on the average wealth, and on the scale on which wealth is distributed' (Cournot, 1838, p. 47 of English edition).

In view of this, Cournot does not himself attempt to give algebraic expression to this relationship and in general regards any such attempt as fruitless.[1] 'Since so many moral causes capable of neither enumeration nor measurement affect the law of demand, it is plain that we should no more expect this law to be expressible by an algebraic formulation than the law of mortality . . .' *ibid.*). He therefore confines himself to the most general analysis of the function $F(p)$.

---

[1] This is lightly undertaken by the newest members of the quasi-mathematical school; e.g. O. Effertz, *Arbeit und Boden*, Berlin, 1889, I, p. 138.

This function is (1) a *decreasing* function, i.e. as the price of a product rises its sale, as a general rule, declines; (2) a *continuous* function when the market is sufficiently large (in other words when the number of consumers is sufficiently large).

'We will assume that the function $F(p)$, which expresses the law of demand or of the market, is a *continuous* function, i.e. a function which does not pass suddenly from one value to another, but which takes in passing all intermediate values. It might be otherwise if the number of consumers were very limited: thus in a certain household the same quantity of firewood will possibly be used whether wood costs 10 francs or 15 francs the stere [1 stere = 1 m³], and the consumption may suddenly be diminished if the price of the stere rises above the latter figure. But the wider the market[1] extends, and the more the combinations of needs, of fortunes, or even of caprices, are varied among consumers, the closer the function $F(p)$ will come to varying with p in a continuous manner' (Cournot, 1838, pp. 49–50 of the English edition).

We know that the algebraic expression of the first characteristic of the function $F(p)$ is that the first derivative or differential coefficient $F'(p) = \mathrm{d}F(p)/\mathrm{d}p$ will be an essentially negative quantity.

Cournot proceeds from his general definition of $F(p)$ to an analysis of $F(p)p$, or in other words to an analysis of the relationship between gross revenue and the market price of the product.

'Since the function $F(p)$ is continuous, the function $pF(p)$, which expresses the total value of the quantity annually sold, must be continous also. This function would equal zero if p equals zero, since the consumption of any article remains finite even on the hypothesis that it is absolutely free; or, in other words, it is theoretically always possible to assign to the symbol p a value so small that the product $p \cdot F(p)$ will vary imperceptibly from zero. The function $pF(p)$ disappears also when p becomes infinite, or, in other words, theoretically a value can always be assigned to p so great that the demand for the article and the production of it would cease. Since the function $pF(p)$ at first increases, and then decreases as p increases, there is therefore a value of p which makes this function a maximum, and which is given by the equation,

$$F(p) + pF'(p) = 0, \tag{1}$$

[1] Cournot comments: 'It is well known that by *market* economists mean, not a certain place where purchases and sales are carried on, but the entire territory of which the parts are so united by the relations of unrestricted commerce that prices there take the same level throughout, with ease and rapidity' (Cournot, *Recherches*, 1838, pp. 51–2 of the English edition).

in which F', according to Lagrange's notion, denotes the differential coefficient of function F' (Cournot, 1838, pp. 52–3).

The expression for gross revenue $F(p)p$ may be written in the form $Df(D)$, where D is the quantity sold and $f(D)$ is the price expressed as a function of the quantity sold; we may therefore treat gross income as a function of the quantity sold D; if we express gross income by Y we have: $Y = Df(D) = \psi(D)$. Clearly the function $\psi(D)$ will have the same basic properties as $F(p)$: when $D = 0$, $\psi(D)$ will also be zero; as D increases, $\psi(D)$ will increase initially to reach a maximum at some value D_m, after which it will begin to decrease until it once again vanishes at some *finite* value of D.

In fact, as D varies from zero to D_0, the price p will vary between the level p_0, at which demand for the product ceases completely, and zero, and therefore $\psi(D)$ will vary as it does so in precisely the same way as $F(p)$ when p varies from zero to a quantity at which $F(p)$ vanishes, *but in reverse order.*

If we take the various quantities D as abscissae and the corresponding quantities $\psi(D)$ as ordinates, we obtain the 'demand curve' [or 'gross revenue curve'] OCD (Figure 1), with which we are already familiar from the preceding exposition (see the First Essay, on *The Theory of Value of David Ricardo*, Figure 1.2); this curve[1] was used for the analysis of monopoly prices [see First Essay, Section 4].

Having completed his analysis of the 'revenue curve', in the next chapter, Cournot proceeds to an analysis of monopoly prices and then

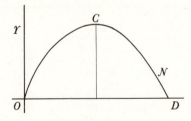

Figure 2.1

passes from this special case to market price determination in a market open to the free competition of entrepreneurs.

The best way to show the essential features of Cournot's theory of competition is to compile schedules of the kind used by von Thünen.

We shall begin by discussing price determination under monopoly conditions. Here, as previously, we shall take as our independent variable

[1] We follow Auspitz and Lieben in calling this curve a 'demand curve'; it would be more correct to call it a 'gross revenue curve'.

Q, the total supply of the commodity on the market; in this case, if we denote total gross revenue by Y, we have $Y = \psi(Q)$. As we have seen, $\psi(D)$ should have the following basic characteristics: when $Q = 0$, $\psi(Q) = 0$; at some finite value of the variable, $\psi(Q)$ should once again vanish; between these two limits $\psi(Q)$ should initially increase until it reaches the greatest possible value at some value of the variable, after which it begins to decrease until it once again vanishes; therefore, $\psi(Q)$ should have only one maximum and correspondingly no minimum. Let us assume $Y = \psi(Q) = aQ - bQ^2$; clearly the special form of the relationship between Y and Q we have adopted fully satisfies the foregoing requirements: when $Q = 0$, $aQ - bQ^2$ also vanishes; when $Q = a/2b$, the function $aQ - bQ^2$ is maximised; when $Q = a/b$, the function $aQ - bQ^2$ once again vanishes. Taking into consideration that $Y = \psi(Q) = f(Q)Q$, where $f(Q)$ stands for the price corresponding to the supply Q, we have:

$$p = f(Q) = \frac{\psi(Q)}{Q} = \frac{aQ - bQ^2}{Q} = a - bQ. \qquad (2)$$

Clearly as the variable increases the function $a - bQ$ will decrease, as it should in accordance with the basic characteristic of $f(Q)$.

In order to convert to numerical quantities, set $a = 1,000$, $b = 10$. We then obtain the following series of quantities:

$D = F(p)$ = sales actual supply = Q	$pD = \psi(D)$ = gross income = $1,000Q - 10Q^2$	$p = f(D)$ = the price of a unit of the product = $1,000 - 10Q$	$uD = \phi(D)$ = necessary production costs of D units = $100Q$	$pD - uD$ = net income from the sale of D units = $1,000Q - 10Q^2 - 100Q = 900Q - 10Q^2$
0	0	—	0	0
10	9,000	900	1,000	8,000
20	16,000	800	2,000	14,000
30	21,000	700	3,000	18,000
40	24,000	600	4,000	20,000
45	24,750	550	4,500	20,000
50	25,000	500	5,000	20,000
60	24,000	400	6,000	18,000
70	21,000	300	7,000	14,000
80	16,000	200	8,000	8,000
90	9,000	100	9,000	0
100	0	0	10,000	− 10,000 (loss)

1. Cournot's theory of competition

First assume that production costs are nil; in this case the most advantageous sales level for a monopolist entrepreneur will be sales of 50 units, since he receives the greatest total profit when sales are at this level: in fact, if he reduces his supply by one unit, his revenue will be 24,990, i.e. will be less than the revenue corresponding to a supply of 50 units; conversely, were he to increase his supply, even by one unit, his revenue would also fall to 24,990, and self interest would compel him to return to the former supply level.

Let us now assume that supply is in the hands of two separate entrepreneurs; assume for simplicity (as Cournot does) that supply is equally distributed between them. It is clear that in the case of two isolated entrepreneurs equilibrium can exist only when the existing total supply level will, at the same time, be the most advantageous *to each of them separately*.

Clearly this condition is not satisfied at a supply level of 50 units at which a monopolist entrepreneur arrives. In fact, the supply of each separate entrepreneur will be 25 units in this case and the revenue will be 12,500 units; should one of them increase his supply from 25 to 26 units, his revenue will change from 12,500 to 12,740,[1] i.e. will increase by 240 units. Admittedly, he will obtain this extra revenue only as long as the second entrepreneur's supply remains unaltered, but since, in accordance with Cournot, we make the invariable assumption supply = production, the second competitor, in his turn, is able to increase his supply *only by a corresponding expansion of production*; this always requires a considerable amount of time, during which the first entrepreneur will continue to enjoy excess income of 240 units. (Cournot uses the term *bénéfice momentané* for this extra profit.) If we make a similar calculation for a total supply of 51, 52, 53, . . ., 65 units we see that it is impossible for equilibrium to be established at any of these levels since it will invariably be advantageous *to the individual* entrepreneur to disturb the balance by expanding his own supply. When the total supply is 66 units the supply of each of the competing entrepreneurs is 33 units; the revenue is 11,220 units. Assume that one of them, still pursuing 'temporary profit' (*bénéfice momentané*) increases his own supply from 33 units to 34; in this case his revenue will be 11,220 units, i.e. will remain unaltered. We see therefore that when the total supply is 66 units it will no longer be advantageous to one of the competing entrepreneurs, between whom total supply is distributed, to expand his individual supply.

But if we assume that the total quantity produced is distributed not between two independent entrepreneurs, but *among a larger number*, e.g.

[1] Total supply here is increased from 50 to 51 units, and consequently the price will fall from 500 to 490. The revenue of the entrepreneur who expands his supply will therefore be $490 \times 26 = 12,750$.

103

among three, we see that when total supply is 66 units it will still be advantageous to each of them to disturb the equilibrium and expand his individual supply.

If total supply is 66 units, the supply of each competitor will be 22 units and the revenue of each will be 7,480. Assume, as previously, that one of them increases his supply from 22 to 23 units, in which case his income will alter from 7,480 to 7,590, i.e. will increase by 110 units. Therefore, on the assumption that total supply is distributed between three independent entrepreneurs, no equilibrium can be established when the total supply is 66 units (as existed with the assumption of two competitors). In this case equilibrium is established only when total supply is 75 units, as at this level it will no longer be advantageous to any of the three isolated entrepreneurs to expand his own supply in expectation of 'temporary advantage'[2] (i.e. in expectation of an increase in his individual revenue until such time as the other entrepreneurs react by a corresponding expansion in their own stocks). If we now introduce production costs in our calculations (taken to be 100 in our model calculation) we obtain exactly the same results: in this case also (as may be evinced from the tables, by applying the techniques used above) a monopolist would establish his supply at a lower level than that of two competing entrepreneurs;[1] two competitors would establish their supply at a lower level than that of three competitors and so on; but since the price corresponding to each larger supply is invariably lower, a monopoly price will always be greater than prices established by the competition of two isolated entrepreneurs; the level to which two competitors will lower prices will be higher than the level to which three competitors will lower it and so on.

This analysis shows that the equilibrium price level will be lower, the greater is the number of individuals competing in the market and that, in any case, however great the number of competitors, the equilibrium price will always be below the monopoly price set by an individual holding a monopoly in the market considered.

Since these conclusions are based on an arbitrarily selected relationship between supply and gross revenue (although one which satisfies all real

---

[1] Effectively, when total supply is 75 units, the supply of each of the three competitors will be 25 units and the revenue of each will be $25 \times 250 = 6,250$; should one of them increase his supply from 25 to 26 units, total supply will increase to 76 units and the price will be $1,000 - (10 \times 76) = 240$; consequently the revenue of the entrepreneur who expanded production will be $240 \times 26 = 6,240$, i.e. will be less than the income previously obtained before the balance was disturbed.

[2] It is evident from the table that a supply of 45 units will be the most advantageous supply level for a monopolist, since this will ensure the greatest net profit. It can be seen from the appropriate column of the table that the price corresponding to this supply level is 550.

requirements), it could be suggested that these conclusions are the *chance* result of this form of relationship.

In Chapter 7 of his book Cournot gives a purely abstract proof of the same hypotheses which rules out the possibility of any such reproach. In proceeding to this abstract analysis we shall quote the most important points of Cournot's theory in an extended form, since Cournot's highly compressed exposition does not lend itself to summary.

'Let us now imagine two proprietors and two springs of which the qualities are identical, and which, on account of their similar positions, supply the same market in competition. In this case the price is necessarily the same for each proprietor. If p is the price, $D = F(p)$ the total sales, D_1 the sales from the spring (1) and D_2 the sales from the spring (2), then $D_1 + D_2 = D$. If, to begin with, we neglect the cost of production, the respective incomes of the proprietors will be pD_1 and pD_2; and *each of them independently* will seek to make this income as large as possible.'

'We say each *independently*, and this restriction is very essential, as will soon appear; for if they should come to an agreement so as to obtain for each the greatest possible income, the results would be entirely different, and would not differ, so far as consumers are concerned, from those obtained in treating of a monopoly.'

'Instead of adopting $D = F(p)$ as before, in this case it will be convenient to adopt the inverse notation $p = f(D)$; and then the profits of proprietors (1) and (2) will be respectively expressed by

$$D_1 \cdot f(D_1 + D_2), \quad \text{and} \quad D_2 \cdot f(D_1 + D_2), \tag{3}$$

i.e. by functions into each of which enter two variables, D_1 and D_2.'

'Proprietor (1) can have no direct influence on the determination of D_2; all that he can do, when D_2 has been determined by proprietor (2), is to choose for D_1 the value which is best for him. This he will be able to accomplish by properly adjusting his price, except as proprietor (2), who, seeing himself forced to accept this price and this value of D_1, may adopt a new value for D_2, more favourable to his interests than the preceding one.'

'Analytically this is equivalent to saying that D_1 will be determined in terms of D_2 by the condition

$$\frac{\mathrm{d}[D_1 f(D_1 + D_2)]}{\mathrm{d} D_1} = 0 \tag{4}$$

105

and that D_2 will be determined in terms of D_1 by the analogous condition

$$\frac{\mathrm{d}[D_2 f(D_1 + D_2)]}{\mathrm{d}\, D_2} = 0 \tag{5}$$

whence it follows that the final values of D_1 and D_2, and consequently of D and of p, will be determined by the system of equations

$$f(D_1 + D_2) + D_1 f'(D_1 + D_2) = 0 \tag{6}$$

$$f(D_1 + D_2) + D_2 f'(D_1 + D_2) = 0. \tag{7}$$

'Let us suppose the curve $m_1 n_1$ (Figure 2.2) to be the plot of equation (6), and the curve $m_2 n_2$ that of equation (7), the variables D_1 and D_2

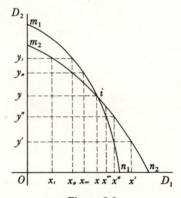

Figure 2.2

being represented by rectangular coordinates. If proprietor (1) should adopt for D_1 a value represented by ox_1, proprietor (2) would adopt for D_2 the value oy_1, which, for the supposed value of D_1, would give him the greatest profit. But then, for the same reason, producer (1) ought to adopt for D_1 the value ox_{11}, which gives the maximum profit when D_2 has the value oy_1. This would bring producer (2) to the value oy_{11} for D_2, and so forth; from which it is evident that an equilibrium can only be established where the coordinates ox and oy of the point of intersection i represent the values of D_1 and D_2. The same construction repeated on a point of the figure on the other side of the point i leads to symmetrical results.'

1. Cournot's theory of competition

'The state of equilibrium corresponding to the system of values ox and oy is therefore *stable*; i.e. if either of the producers, misled as to his true interest, leaves it temporarily, he will be brought back to it by a series of reactions, constantly declining in amplitude, and of which the dotted lines of the figure give a representation by their arrangement in steps.'

'The preceding construction assumes that $om_1 < om_2$ and $on_1 < on_2$; the results would be diametrically opposite if these inequalities should change sign, and if the curves m_1n_1 and m_2n_2 should assume the disposition represented by Figure 2.3.

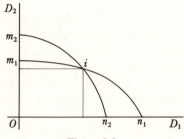

Figure 2.3

The coordinates of the point i, where the two curves intersect, would then cease to correspond to a state of stable equilibrium. But it is easy to prove that such a disposition of the curves is inadmissible. In fact, if $D_1 = 0$, equations (6) and (7) reduce, the first to

$$f(D_2) = 0 \qquad (8)$$

and the second to

$$f(D_2) + D_2 f'(D_2) = 0. \qquad (9)$$

The value of D_2 derived from the first would correspond to $p = 0$; the value of D_2 derived from the second corresponds to a value of p which would make the product pD_2 a maximum. Therefore the first root is necessarily greater than the second, or $om_1 > om_2$, and for the same reason $on_2 > on_1$.'

'From equations (6) and (7) we derive first $D_1 = D_2$ (which ought to be the case, as the springs are supposed to be similar and similarly situated) and then by addition:

$$2f(D) + Df'(D) = 0 \qquad (10)$$

107

an equation which can be transformed into

$$D + 2p \, \frac{\mathrm{d}D}{\mathrm{d}p} = 0 \tag{11}$$

whereas, if the two springs had belonged to the same property, or if the two proprietors *had come to an understanding*, the value of p would have been determined by the equation

$$D + p \, \frac{\mathrm{d}D}{\mathrm{d}p} = 0 \tag{12}$$

and would have rendered the total income Dp a *maximum*, and consequently would have assigned to each of the producers a greater income than what they can obtain with the value of p derived from equation (11).'

'Why is it then that, for want of an understanding, the producers do not stop, as in the case of a monopoly or of an association, at the value of p derived from equation (12), which would really give them the greatest income?'

'The reason is that, producer (1) having fixed his production at what it should be according to equation (12) and the condition $D_1 = D_2$, the other will be able to fix his own production at a higher or lower rate with a *temporary benefit*. To be sure, he will soon be punished for his mistake, because he will force the first producer to adopt a new scale of production which will react unfavourably on producer (2) himself. But these successive reactions, far from bringing both producers nearer to the original condition (of monopoly), will separate them further and further from it. In other words, this condition is not one of stable equilibrium; and, although the most favourable for both producers, it can only be maintained by means of a formal engagement; for in the moral sphere men cannot be supposed to be free from error and lack of forethought any more than in the physical world bodies can be considered perfectly rigid, or supports perfectly solid, etc.'

'The root of equation (11) is graphically determined by the intersection of the line $y = 2x$ with the curve $y = -F(x)/F'(x)$; while that of equation (12) is graphically shown by the intersection of the same curve with the line $y = x$. But, if it is possible to assign a real and positive value to the function $y = -F(x)/F'(x)$ for every real and positive value of x, then the abscissa x of the first point of intersection will be smaller than that of the second, as is sufficiently proved simply by the plot of Figure 2.4. It is easily proved also that the condition for this result is always realised by the very nature of the law of demand. In consequence the root of equation (11) is always smaller than that of equation (12); or (as every one believes without any analysis) the result of competition is to reduce prices.'

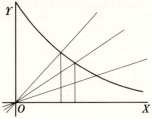

Figure 2.4

'If there were 3, 4, ..., n producers in competition, all their conditions being the same, equation (11) would be successively replaced by the following:

$$D + 3p\,\frac{dD}{dp} = 0; \quad D+4p\frac{dD}{dp} = 0; \quad \ldots; \quad D+np\frac{dD}{dp} = 0; \quad (13)$$

and the value of p which results would diminish indefinitely with the indefinite increase of the number n' (Cournot, 1838, pp. 79–84 of the English edition).

Before proceeding further consider whether the tendency of individual entrepreneurs to pursue 'temporary profit', causing price falls in a market with a plurality of sellers, is in fact, as Cournot assumes, a result of errors in economic calculation, or whether free competition would continue to be effective if all entrepreneurs were free of such errors.

It would be a correct economic calculus for each separate entrepreneur to abstain only if he could be certain that other entrepreneurs would similarly abstain. It is, however, impossible to derive such certainty from the fact that all other entrepreneurs are guided in their actions by correct economic calculus.

In fact, for each of the remaining entrepreneurs to abstain in his turn would be most in accord with correct economic calculus only if he could be certain that the others would abstain. If we denote by $p_1, p_2, p_3, \ldots$ the probability that the entrepreneurs (1), (2), (3), ... will abstain, and will be guided in their actions by correct economic calculation, we shall have a series of conditions:

$$\left.\begin{array}{l} p_1 = 1, \quad \text{if} \quad p_2 = 1; \quad p_3 = 1, \ldots, p_{-1} = p_2 p_3 p_4 \ldots = 1 \\ p_2 = 1, \quad \text{if} \quad p_1 = 1; \quad p_3 = 1, \ldots, p_{-2} = p_1 p_3 p_4 \ldots = 1 \end{array}\right\} \quad (14)$$

where $p_{-1}, p_{-2}, \ldots$, denote the probability that all producers apart from the first and second and so on will abstain. For $p_1 = 1, p_2 = 1, \ldots,$

109

it is not sufficient that these equations could, *in general,* exist; it is also necessary that they should have *already* existed (since the abstinence of the first, second and subsequent entrepreneurs is the result of a mental process, in which the facts expressed by our condition equations are the premises by which the conclusion is reached). Take some arbitrary point in time as the origin; let the time from which the equation $p_1 = 1$ comes into force (i.e. begins to correspond to what actually exists) be separated from the time taken as origin by an interval t_1; let the times at which the condition equations $p_2 = 1, p_3 = 1, \ldots,$ come into force be separated by the intervals $t_2, t_3, t_4, \ldots,$ in which case we should have $t_1 > t_2, t_1 > t_3, t_1 > t_4, \ldots,$ but if we deliberate in the same manner for the second equation $(p_2 = 1)$, we have $t_2 > t_1, t_2 > t_3 \ldots,$ but the assertions $t_1 > t_2$ and $t_2 > t_1$ are mutually exclusive and, consequently, the assumption that the statement $p_1 = 1$ actually holds becomes absurd. The same applies to any of the statements $p_2 = 1, p_3 = 1, \ldots$ (were the producers (1), (2), (3), $\ldots,$ to act not in isolation but in concert, then *from the time of their agreement* we would have $t_1 = t_2 = t_3 = t_4, \ldots$ reckoning from some arbitrarily selected time).

If we now turn from the simplest case, in which production costs were assumed to be zero, to a case in which production costs are greater than zero, the system of equations (6) and (7), (see p. 106), becomes

$$f(D) + D_1 f'(D) - \phi_1'(D') = 0 \Bigg\} \tag{15}$$
$$f(D) + D_2 f'(D) - \phi_2'(D_2) = 0 \Bigg\}$$

where $\phi_1(D_1), \phi_2(D_2), \ldots$ express the production costs of the first, second, and other entrepreneurs as a function of the quantity produced by them. When production costs are *proportional* to the quantity produced and are, additionally, *the same for all producers,* $\phi_1(D_1), \phi_2(D_2), \ldots$ may be presented in the form $uD_1, uD_2, \ldots,$ where u is the production costs of a unit of the product, and is the same for all the n entrepreneurs.

Therefore, when the given product is produced *in the absence of rent,* equation system (15) becomes

$$f(D) + D_1 f'(D) - u = 0 \Bigg\} \tag{16}$$
$$\cdots$$

If we sum the equations of system (14), we obtain

$$nf(D) + Df'(D) - \sum_{k=1}^{n} \phi_k'(D_k) = 0 \tag{17}$$

or

$$D + \frac{\mathrm{d}D}{\mathrm{d}p} [np - \sum_{k=1}^{n} \phi_k'(D_k)] = 0 \tag{18}$$

110

1. Cournot's theory of competition

When this equation is compared with the equation

$$D + \frac{dD}{dp}\,[p - \phi'(D)] = 0 \tag{19}$$

which defines price for the monopoly case, it may readily be shown, by an analysis similar to the foregoing analysis, that the level of p which may be determined from equation (18) is invariably smaller than p from equation (19). (See Cournot, 1838, Ch. 8.)

If we similarly sum the equation system (16), we obtain

$$nf(D) + Df'(D) - nu = 0 \tag{20}$$

or

$$D + \frac{dD}{dp}\,n(p - u) = 0. \tag{21}$$

The root of this equation will equal the abscissa corresponding to the point at which the curve

$$y = -\frac{F(x)}{F'(x)} \tag{22}$$

intersects the straight line

$$y = n(x - u). \tag{23}$$

The root of equation

$$D + \frac{dD}{dp}(p - u) = 0, \tag{24}$$

which defines the monopoly price of the product (when the absence of rent is stipulated), will equal the abscissa corresponding to the point where the same curve

$$y = -\frac{F(x)}{F'(x)} \tag{22}$$

intersects the straight line

$$y = x - u. \tag{25}$$

It is readily shown by a comparison similar to the one used by Cournot (section 44, Ch. 7; see Figure 2.3) that the root of equation (21) will invariably be less than the root of equation (24).

Cournot then proceeds to the most important point of the theory of competition: to an analysis of the formation of market prices under the influence of *unlimited* free competition.

111

'The effects of competition have reached their limit, when each of the partial productions D_k is *inappreciable*, not only with reference to the total production $D = F(p)$, but also with reference to the derivative $F'(p)$, so that the partial production D_k could be subtracted from D without any appreciable variation resulting in the price of the commodity. This hypothesis is the one which is realised, in social economy, for a multitude of products, and, among them, for the most important products. It introduces a great simplification into the calculations, and this chapter is meant to develop the consequences of it.

According to this hypothesis, in the equation

$$D_k + [p - \phi_k'(D_k)] \cdot \frac{\mathrm{d}D}{\mathrm{d}p} = 0, \tag{26}$$

the term D_k can be neglected without sensible error, which reduces the equation to

$$p - \phi_k'(D_k) = 0 \tag{27}$$

(Cournot, 1838, p. 90 of English edition).

We should obtain the same expression directly if we assumed that, in the expression for net income of the kth entrepreneur $D_k p - \phi_k(D_k)$, the level of p *was independent of the quantity* D_k. In fact, when p is independent of D_k the equation

$$\mathrm{d}\,[D_k p - \phi_k(D_k)] = 0 \tag{28}$$

will yield directly on differentiation (with respect to the variable D_k)

$$p - \phi_k'(D_k) = 0. \tag{27}$$

The equation system (15) therefore becomes

$$\left.\begin{array}{l} p - \phi_1'(D_1) = 0 \\[2mm] p - \phi_2'(D_2) = 0 \\ \vdots \\ p - \phi_n'(D_n) = 0. \end{array}\right\} \tag{15'}$$

If we add to these n equations the equation

$$D_1 + D_2 + \cdots + D_n = F(p) \tag{29}$$

we obtain a system of equations which suffices for definition of all the unknowns $p, D_1, D_2, \ldots, D_n$.

Cournot then considers two special cases: the case in which the function

112

$\phi_k'(D_k)$ is an increasing function and the case in which it is a decreasing function.

'In the hypothesis under consideration, all functions $\phi_k'(D_k)$ must be considered to increase with D_k. Otherwise the gross value of the product

$$pD_k = D_k \cdot \phi_k'(D_k) \qquad (30)$$

would be less than the costs of production, which are

$$\phi_k(D_k) = \int_0^{D_k} \phi_k'(D_k) \, dD_k. \qquad (31)$$

It is, moreover, plain under the hypothesis of unlimited competition, and where, at the same time, the function $\phi_k'(D_k)$ should be a decreasing one, that nothing would limit the production of the article. Thus, wherever there is a return on property, or a rent payable for a plant of which the operation involves expenses of such a kind that the function $\phi_k'(D_k)$ is a decreasing one, it proves that the effect of monopoly is not wholly extinct, or that competition is not so great but that the variation of the amount produced by each individual producer affects the total production of the article, and its price, to a perceptible extent' (Cournot, 1838, pp. 91–2 of English edition).

Between these two cases there is the case with which we are concerned at present, i.e. the case in which production costs are *proportional* to the amount produced, i.e. in which

$$\phi_k(D_k) = uD_k \qquad (32)$$

where u is a *constant* (or to be more precise is a quantity *independent of the variable D_k*).[1]

In this case $\phi_k'D_k$ becomes the constant u and ceases to be a function of D_k. Therefore, the equation system (28) becomes a series of identical equations:

$$p - u = 0 \qquad (33)$$

no longer containing the quantity D_k. In order to decide the level at which total supply D is established in this case, we must turn to the original expression of the income of the kth entrepreneur

$$D_k(p - u) \qquad (34)$$

---

[1] Because Cournot fails to consider this case at all, the whole of his subsequent conclusions relate only to those commodities where *rent* (in the Ricardian sense) unavoidably arises in their production. The same has to be said of all the conclusions of Auspitz and Lieben in their outstanding work *Untersuchungen über die Theorie des Preises*, Leipzig, 1889.

which may be written in the form

$$D_k[f(D_1 + D_2 + \cdots + D_k + \cdots + D_n) - u].\qquad(35)$$

Clearly when D_k is *immeasurably small* by comparison with the sum $D_1 + D_2 + \cdots + D_n = D$ the *second factor* of expression (35) may be taken to be a *quantity independent of the variable D_k* without any perceptible error in the conclusion, since the assumption that unrestricted free competition prevails amounts to the condition that D_k is so small relative to D that D_k may vary without any perceptible variation of D and $f(D) = p$ (see Cournot, 1838, Ch. 8). Therefore, *as long as the difference $(p - u)$ is greater than zero, it will be advantageous to each individual entrepreneur to expand his individual supply D_k without limit* and, consequently, *equilibrium cannot be established in production as long as the total supply (D) is smaller by a finite amount than D_0*, where D_0 is *the root of the equation*

$$f(D) - u = 0.\qquad(36)$$

As long as D is less than D_0, and consequently $(p - u) > 0$, each *individual* entrepreneur will retain the incentive to expand his partial production,[1] and when these *partial* expansions are added up, they will cause further expansion of the *total* production. Therefore when the total number of competing entrepreneurs increases without limit towards infinity, so that the partial production of each may be made as small as is desired in comparison with total production, the total volume of production will tend *indefinitely* to the *limiting quantity D_0*.

Consequently, *if we take the necessary costs per unit of product as* constant (in other words if we assume that *total production costs increase* proportionately *to the increase in the amount produced*), then *if unlimited free competition prevails, equilibrium will be established only when the total volume of production ($= supply$) is such that the difference between the price of the product and the necessary costs of its production becomes an infinitely small quantity (ultimately zero*). It is evident that this conclusion is fully compatible with the conclusion arrived at by Ricardo from the same propositions. The only difference is that in Cournot's theory this conclusion is rigorously based and elegantly combined with a general theory of price determination under free competition (the theory of temporary profit), whereas in the works of Ricardo and other classical economists the effect of unlimited free competition on prices was taken to be a *random factor unsuitable for further economic analysis*; as to price determination when the number of competitors is *limited* (finite), where it is more difficult to give a simple explanation, these economists did not even attempt to deal with such forms of the general principle of 'competition'.

---

[1] Since the partial income $D_k(p - u)$ will increase as D_k increases when $(p - u) > 0$.

1. Cournot's theory of competition

Before proceeding to the shortcomings of Cournot's analysis, we shall give graphic expression to Cournot's main formulas on the effect of unlimited free competition (in which we shall draw on the later writings of Auspitz and Lieben).

Let the abscissae of the curve ON (Figure 2.5) denote different amounts of partial supply D_k, and let the ordinates corresponding to them denote total gross revenue, on the assumption that the partial supply of the other entrepreneurs is unaltered.

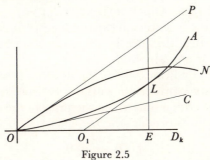

Figure 2.5

The smaller is partial supply D_k relative to total supply, the less curved will the line ON become until, ultimately, when D_k decreases indefinitely relative to D, the line ON will tend indefinitely to a straight line, so that on the assumption of unlimited free competition the ordinates of the straight line OP will express the gross revenue of the kth entrepreneur with an error smaller than an arbitrarily small quantity.

This is equivalent to Cournot's assumption that changes in partial supply D_k have no perceptible effect on total supply D and on $f(D)$, i.e. on the price of the product.

Now let the ordinates of the curve OA, whose equation is $y = \phi(D_k)$, denote the production costs of quantities expressed by the corresponding abscissae. In this case obviously the volume of partial production yielding the greatest total net income will equal the abscissa OE for which the tangent to the curve OA at the point L is parallel to OP.

In this case the tangent of the angle $P\hat{O}E$ is equal to the tangent of the angle $L\hat{O}_1E$; but the tangent of the angle $P\hat{O}E$ is equal to the price p, and the tangent of the angle $L\hat{O}_1E$ equals the production costs of the last unit of the product. We therefore see that partial supply D_k will expand until production costs of the last unit equal the price of the product. We find the same thing in the equation system (15) derived by Cournot.

Now let us assume that production costs increase strictly in proportion to the quantity produced; in this case the curve OA will become a straight line OC, and the tangent of the angle $C\hat{O}E$ will equal u, which is the necessary production costs of a unit of the product.

115

It can be seen from the figure that in this case, however much D_k may increase, the net revenue of an isolated kth entrepreneur, equal to the vertical distance between the straight lines OP and OC, will continuously increase.

Therefore, as long as the angle $P\hat{O}E$ is greater than the angle $C\hat{O}E$, each separate entrepreneur, acting according to quite correct economic calculus, will tend to expand his partial supply as much as possible (and consequently total supply D will continue to increase).

Only at the level D_0 for which we have $f(D_0) = p_0 = u$ will individual entrepreneurs lose the incentive to expand their own partial supply, since in this case the vertical distance between the straight lines OP and OC will become zero for any abscissa.

Therefore, under conditions where rent does not arise in the production of a given commodity, equilibrium will be established in production under unlimited free competition only when the price of the commodity falls to the necessary costs of its production, i.e. when

$$f(D) - u = 0. \tag{36}$$

This highly consistent conclusion is to be drawn from Cournot's whole theory of competition. We shall now see to what extent it is correct.

2. A CRITIQUE OF COURNOT'S THEORY OF COMPETITION

In order to obtain the temporary profit which is a stimulus to the expansion of the supply of competing entrepreneurs, it is essential that supply from other entrepreneurs should remain invariable, even if only for a short period of time. Equilibrium cannot be established at a price defined by the equation

$$d\,[F(p) \cdot D - F(p) \cdot u] = 0 \tag{37}$$

at which all the entrepreneurs receive the greatest total net profit, because at this price, and at the volume of supply corresponding to it, each separate producer may increase his net profit by increasing his supply, *provided that the supply of the other entrepreneurs (or of the other entrepreneur in the case of two competitors) remains unaltered* (Cournot, 1838, p. 83 of the English edition).

As Cournot shows, if the other entrepreneurs (or entrepreneur) reacted by altering their supply so that they instantly caught up with the first entrepreneur (as he expanded his supply in the pursuit of temporary profit), instead of increasing his income the first entrepreneur would immediately find himself in a worse position than before market conditions, defined by condition (37), were disturbed.

116

2. A critique of Cournot's theory of competition

Should we accept, in our research, the condition emphasised above? If, like Cournot, we assume that the quantity of a commodity *sold* in a given unit of time always equals the quantity *produced* in the same time, every expansion of supply must be matched by a corresponding expansion of production. Since this is *in general* a complicated matter, which necessitates a quite considerable time for its implementation even under the most favourable conditions (in an isolated industry), it may be accepted *as a general rule* that a certain finite time period, which can never be taken to be zero in our research, is needed for the implementation of every *expansion of supply*.

Completely different results would be obtained were we to accept that supply could expand *instantaneously* (even if only within certain limits). In that case *the time τ for which an entrepreneur who was the first to expand his supply* to more than the volume defined by the equation $D + p \, \mathrm{d}D/\mathrm{d}p = 0$ (see equation [12] above; Cournot, 1838, p. 82 of English edition) and by the condition $D_1 = D_2 = D_3, \ldots$ (see Cournot, *ibid*), *obtained a 'temporary profit' would be zero,*[1] since he would be *instantaneously* caught by the reaction of the other entrepreneurs (also striving to determine their supply to their greatest advantage), and he would find himself in a worse position than before the *status quo* was disturbed. In fact, if expansion of supply was *instantaneous* we should stipulate in our analysis that partial supplies $D_1, D_2, \ldots$ were equal *at each given minute* (by the same reasoning that led Cournot to stipulate $D_1 = D_2 = D_3, \ldots$ *after the establishment of equilibrium* (see Cournot, 1838, p. 82 of English edition)). In this case all of Cournot's formulas (*ibid.*) take the form

$$\mathrm{d}\,[D \cdot f(D)/n]/\mathrm{d}(D/n) = 0 \tag{38}$$

where D is the *total supply* and n is the *number of competitors*, so that $D_1 = D_2 = D_3 = \cdots = D_n = D/n$. If we transform these formulas we obtain n equations of the form

$$\frac{1}{n}\mathrm{d}\,[D \cdot f(D)] = 0 \tag{39}$$

[1] The *same consequences* will apply under the specific economic conditions not only when $\tau = 0$, but also for every positive value of τ, provided that τ is so small that the temporary profit which the entrepreneur can expect over the time period τ is insufficient to overcome the *inertia* which is an element of all human activities, and thus to cover the *risk* associated with every disturbance of the existing *status quo* in the market. If we denote the sum needed to overcome inertia and cover risk by ρ (this quantity will vary in relation to the individuality of the entrepreneur and to the nature of the enterprise), and the temporary profit by m per unit of time, *the inequality $m\tau < \rho$, in which both ρ and m are finite quantities, will be sufficient to maintain an existing equilibrium.* This comment is made in order to avoid the possible objection that all our subsequent deductions are incorrect because they are *based on an assumption which cannot be exactly fulfilled under real conditions.*

or, by multiplying each equation by n:

$$d\,[D \cdot f(D)] = 0 \qquad (40)$$

which, considering that $f(D) = p$ and $D = F(p)$, yields on differentiation

$$F(p) + p \cdot F'(p) = 0. \qquad (1)$$

It is therefore evident that when an *instantaneous* expansion of supply is possible for *any number of isolated* entrepreneurs competing in the market, the most advantageous general volume of supply will be *the same* as for a *monopolist* entrepreneur (or when the competitors have reached an agreement). *This deduction completely contradicts the whole of Cournot's theory of competition.* Therefore, Cournot's deductions hold only for his *arbitrary* assumption that *the amount of a commodity* sold *in each given unit of time corresponds exactly to the amount* produced *in the same unit of time.*[1] However are we entitled to accept this hypothesis? If we remain in the realm of abstract analysis (i.e. if we do not refer to the *contradiction with reality*) we may say that this assumption may be made only if it *does not contradict* our *basic hypothesis* that every individual tends to pursue the greatest advantage. Otherwise all our conclusions would be based simultaneously on mutually contradictory hypotheses and would be deprived of all convincing force. If, therefore, we are to accept Cournot's assumption with all its consequences, we have to consider whether it accords with the principle that individuals tend to pursue the greatest advantage.

Cournot asserts that if the supply of a commodity produced without costs is in the hands of n entrepreneurs, the level to which they will expand their production will be defined by the equation:

$$D + np\,\frac{\mathrm{d}D}{\mathrm{d}p} = 0 \qquad (13)$$

and he shows that the quantity determined from this equation will always be greater than the quantity determined from the equation

$$D + p\,\frac{\mathrm{d}D}{\mathrm{d}p} = 0. \qquad (12)$$

The question is whether, at such a level of production and, consequently, of market supply, the quantity sold in the same period will also equal the quantity D determined by equation (13). Let the supply of a product A be in the hands of n competing entrepreneurs. Let the *general volume of production* Q equal the quantity D_0 determined from equation (13).

---

[1] We shall see subsequently (Section 6) that the 'instantaneous' expansion of supply (instantaneous in a conventional sense, see the footnote on p. 117) is possible even then, whenever the actual degree of utilisation of the enterprises of a given industry is *less than their full capacity.*

2. A critique of Cournot's theory of competition

Let us denote the volume of production of each of the entrepreneurs by $q_1, q_2, \ldots, q_n$; we assume, as Cournot does, that $q_1 = q_2 = q_3 = \cdots = q_n$, in which case the *volume of production* of each individual producer will equal Q/n. Is it true, as Cournot asserts, that in this case *total supply* D will also equal Q, and the *supply* of each individual entrepreneur will equal Q/n? To solve this question we must prove that for a given volume of production such a volume of supply will correspond to the tendency of each entrepreneur to pursue the greatest advantage.

Supply will in fact equal production if it is at the level where each entrepreneur derives the greatest total advantage. If we assume, as does Cournot, that production costs are zero, the greatest total advantage will correspond to the greatest *gross* revenue for the quantity sold. The gross revenue of each producer will equal the product of the quantity sold by him $D_1, D_2 \ldots, D_n$ times the market price p. What is needed for this product to be greatest is that

$$\mathrm{d}(D_1 \cdot p) = 0; \quad \mathrm{d}(D_2 \cdot p) = 0; \ldots; \quad \mathrm{d}(D_n \cdot p) = 0. \tag{41}$$

What level of p will satisfy these equations? The total sale of a product A at a price p established in the market (common to all sellers by the assumption of uniqueness of the market price) is given by $D = F(p)$. Since none of the entrepreneurs has any advantage over the others, either in production or in sale (to exclude rent), the *probability of sale* of each unit of product will be the same for all entrepreneurs and will equal D/q. Since $q_1 = q_2 = q_3 = \cdots = q_n$, the number of units sold, $D_1, D_2, \ldots$ will also therefore be equal when $q_1, q_2, \ldots$ *are sufficiently large* (by virtue of Jacob Bernoulli's theorem);[1] in consequence of which we have:

$$D_1 = D_2 = \cdots = D_n = \frac{D}{n}. \tag{42}$$

If we insert this quantity in our equations (41), they all take the form

$$\mathrm{d}\left(\frac{D}{n} \cdot p\right) = 0; \tag{43}$$

---

[1] Bernoulli's theorem states: 'The probability P that the difference between the proportion of the expected number of occurrences of an event E and the number of trials and the probability p that this event will not exceed in absolute magnitude some arbitrarily small number when the number s of trials is large is close to unity (certainty) and tends to unity as s tends to infinity', from which it follows that 'the ratio of the expected number m of occurrences of an event E to the total number s of trials tends to the probability p of the event E as s increases to infinity' (see pp. 44–65 of *Teoriya veroyatnostei* [The theory of probability] by Professor Nekrasov, 1896). We know that Laplace provided a means of proving Bernoulli's theorem by which the *degree of approximation* could be assessed (using the formula $P = F(g) = \frac{2}{\sqrt{\pi}} \int_0^g e^{-x^2} \, \mathrm{d}x$); see Laplace, *Théorie analytique des probabilités* Paris, 1812, Ch. 8, p. 423; also Bunyakovsky, *Osnovy matematichescoi teorii veroyatnostei* [Principles of the Mathematical Theory of Probability].

which all become $d(Dp) = 0$ after taking the constant n outside the differential sign and simplifying. On differentiation this yields

$$D + p\frac{\mathrm{d}D}{\mathrm{d}p} = 0. \tag{12}$$

As shown by Cournot, the *quantity* D determined from this equation will always be *smaller* than the quantity D_0 determined from the equation

$$D + np\frac{\mathrm{d}D}{\mathrm{d}p} = 0 \tag{13}$$

and consequently smaller than the amount produced Q which is, by assumption, equal to D_0. Even if we considered, as a generalisation, the case of different production levels of individual producers, the results would be identical. In fact, when the market position of each producer is equally advantageous (when there is equal probability of sale) the total quantity $D = F(p)$ sold at the market price p would then be distributed *in proportion to the volume of production of each*, so that

$$D_1 : D_2 : D_3 : \ldots : D_n = q_1 : q_2 : q_3 : \ldots : q_n \tag{44}$$

from which

$$D_1 = \frac{Dq_1}{q_1 + q_2 + \cdots + q_n}; \quad D_2 = \frac{Dq_2}{q_1 + q_2 + \cdots + q_n} \tag{45}$$

and so on. Inserting these quantities in our equations, we have:

$$\mathrm{d}\left(\frac{Dq_1}{q_1 + q_2 + \cdots + q_n} \cdot p\right) = 0; \quad \mathrm{d}\left(\frac{Dq_2}{q_1 + q_2 + \cdots + q_n} \cdot p\right) = 0 \tag{46}$$

and so on, which, like the preceding equations (42) yield

$$D + p\frac{\mathrm{d}D}{\mathrm{d}p} = 0. \tag{12}$$

(Suppose Q is larger than D_0 determined from equation (13), i.e. larger than the volume to which, according to Cournot, n competing entrepreneurs will expand their production in the pursuit of temporary profit. The results would obviously remain the same, since *in the absence of production costs* the size of production is completely without effect on the volume of supply.)

2. A critique of Cournot's theory of competition

If we assumed that the quantity produced Q was in the hands of a single monopolist entrepreneur, the volume of supply yielding the maximum profit would continue to be determined by equation (12).

Clearly this conclusion is diametrically opposed to Cournot's conclusion. The foregoing analysis shows that even if n competing entrepreneurs were to expand the production of their product in pursuit of temporary benefit, the market price of the product could never fall below the monopoly price; the price fixed by a monopolist would also be most beneficial to each of the competing entrepreneurs. This conclusion is not dependent on the conventional assumption that all producers in the market have equal advantage. In fact, if we introduce in our equations different probability coefficients of sale, we have

$$d\left(\frac{D \cdot q_1 k_1}{q_1 + q_2 + \cdots + q_n} \cdot p\right) = 0; \quad d\left(\frac{D \cdot q_2 k_2}{q_1 + q_2 + \cdots + q_n} \cdot p\right) = 0, \quad (47)$$

and so on, which will also yield equation (12) because coefficients k_1, k_2, ... are independent of the variable for which the equation is differentiated.

If we now assume that the amount produced is *smaller* than the quantity D_m defined by equation (12), the price $p = F(Q)$, i.e. the price corresponding to a supply D equal to total production Q, will be established in the market both by a monopolist owner and by n competing sellers motivated by their greatest benefit. In fact, this price $p = F(Q)$ corresponds most closely to the price yielding the maximum advantage, and any price greater than $p = F(Q)$ corresponding to $D < Q$ will yield a smaller total advantage, both for a monopolist and for each of the competing sellers. Thus, whatever the quantity produced, *for a given quantity of production, the market price will be fixed at the same level, whether the total quantity produced is in the hands of one owner or of any number of entrepreneurs.*

Competition has an effect on the volume of production, but no effect at all on the volume of supply *for a given volume of production*.

In fact, if we now cease to regard the volume of production as *given*, and turn to an analysis of conditions determining it, we shall see that when the whole production is in the hands of one producer output is determined in a way quite different from the case of competing entrepreneurs. We have seen that, regardless of how the quantity produced is distributed, the volume of supply will be the same at each given moment (for which the volume of production is a constant). For outputs lower than D_m supply will equal the entire amount produced; for production levels greater than D_m supply will equal D_m.

Total net income (which is also gross income since production costs are

121

nil) accordingly will increase gradually as production expands from zero to D_m and will be greatest when production is D_m. If production was increased further, total revenue would remain unaltered. Therefore a *monopolist* who raised his output to D_m would remain at this amount, since further expansion of production could not increase his revenue (which equals the *total* revenue earned in the given branch of production). The situation will be different if the output of a given commodity is in the hands of *several independent* entrepreneurs. The share of each in total revenue will depend on the size of individual output: if the position of all entrepreneurs competing in the market is *equally favourable*, the share of each will be *strictly proportional* to the output of each; if their position is not equally favourable and *the probability of sale is not the same* for each of them, the share of each will be proportional to his output times the specific *coefficient of probability* of sale (see above). In any case, whatever the *initial* distribution of total revenue among individual entrepreneurs, if one of them, for example the kth entrepreneur, *expanded* his own output his revenue would increase in proportion to the increase in his *share of total output* (naturally assuming that his position in the market, i.e. the probability of sale, still remains unaltered). Provided the output of other entrepreneurs remains unaltered, *his share in total output* will naturally increase in *proportion* to the increase in his *own output*. Thus, if the output q_k of the kth entrepreneur was $1/n$ of total output, then *after expanding* his output to $2q_k$ it will be $2/n$ of total output, until other entrepreneurs, in turn, expand their own individual output. Consequently, until there is a reaction from the other entrepreneurs, his individual revenue will be doubled temporarily because his share in total revenue *has doubled*, whereas as we have seen *total* revenue remains *unaltered* when total output is increased beyond D_m. If we assume that the volume of production of the other entrepreneurs subsequently still remains unaltered, the individual revenue of the kth entrepreneur will tend to the limit $D_m f(D_m)$ when he increases his own output *indefinitely*. The *increase of revenue* corresponding to an expansion of output of the *same* magnitude would become *smaller and smaller*. In practice, however, every expansion of output by the first producer would invariably be followed, *even if not instantaneously*, by a reaction from other entrepreneurs (see the foregoing analysis by Cournot). This would take the form of an expansion, in their turn, of their own individual output; the proportion of total output represented by the output of the kth entrepreneur would return to the former level and, therefore, the incentive which initially prompted him to expand production would be reestablished *with its former force*.

Consequently, although at *each given moment for which production is a constant*, volume of supply and price will be determined in *exactly the same way* for a monopolist owner and for competing entrepreneurs, the actual *volume of output* will be *quite differently* determined in these two cases. The level of production set by a *monopolist* will equal the total supply yielding the greatest total revenue whereas *competing producers* in pursuit of temporary advantage will each increase their own output without limit and at the same time increase total output. This result evidently differs from Cournot's conclusion that the volume to which n entrepreneurs would expand total output would equal D, from equation

$$D + np \, \frac{\mathrm{d}D}{\mathrm{d}p} = 0 \qquad (13)$$

and would consequently be infinite only when $n = \infty$. On the other hand, under the assumption that supply and production are equal, production can never assume infinitely large dimensions, since when D is large *but finite*, p vanishes and, consequently, the incentive to expand production is lost, because when $p = 0$ the product pD also equals 0. In our hypothetical example of zero production costs, this expansion has no effect on the volume of supply and, consequently, on price: we have seen that the self interest of individual entrepreneurs will compel them to settle on a price p_m and the supply D_m corresponding to it, whatever the volume of production. This will not invariably be the case if we take production costs (which in reality are never zero) into consideration. This is the case we shall now consider.

3. THE CASE OF PRODUCTION COSTS GREATER THAN ZERO

Suppose that Q units of a product are produced in a time period, and the production cost of each unit is u. We denote by D the quantity sold in a time period. In this case gross revenue for the quantity sold will be $Df(D)$. We assume, for convenience, that the product concerned is perishable and cannot be stored, so that everything not sold shortly after production spoils and becomes unsuitable for consumption and for sale. In this case, whatever the quantity D, subject to the condition $D \leqslant Q$, the costs to be recovered by gross revenue will equal $u \cdot Q$. Therefore, the *net profit*[1] from D units sold will equal $Df(D) - Qu$. This net profit will be greatest when D satisfies the condition $\mathrm{d}[Df(D) - uQ] = 0$, which yields on differentiation

$$\mathrm{d}[D \cdot f(D)] = 0. \qquad (40)$$

[1] We follow Ricardo in *relating the average interest on capital* ('natural profit') to *necessary production costs*. Hence *what we understand here and subsequently by the net profit* of a given enterprise, or a given *industry, is the profit obtained* in the given enterprise or industry *over and above the 'natural profit' existing at a given moment in a given society* (in relation to the conditions under which the means of subsistence of workers are produced; in this respect see the First Essay, p. 58 *et seq.*). Therefore, *net profit is here the profit which would be taken* from a given enterprise *by an entrepreneur employing exclusively loan capital.*

This, consequently, is how a monopolist entrepreneur motivated by the aspiration for the greatest advantage would determine the quantity D (i.e. the amount sold).

Let us now consider how D will be determined when the production and supply of the product are in the hands of several n competing entrepreneurs. Let the total volume of production remain Q and let partial outputs be $q_1, q_2, \ldots, q_n$, so that $q_1 + q_2 + \cdots + q_n = Q$. By our assumption that the market situation is equally favourable to all entrepreneurs (an assumption made to exclude rent), when total sales are D, the sales of individual entrepreneurs will be defined correspondingly by $(q_1/Q)D$, $(q_2/Q)D, \ldots, (q_n/Q)D$ (a different definition of the share of each in total sales would imply that some entrepreneurs had a more advantageous market position than others). Accordingly the gross revenue of each will be equal to

$$\frac{q_1}{Q} Df(D), \frac{q_2}{Q} Df(D), \ldots, \frac{q_n}{Q} Df(D); \qquad (48)$$

and their profit

$$\frac{q_1}{Q} Df(D) - q_1 u, \frac{q_2}{Q} Df(D) - q_2 u, \ldots, \frac{q_n}{Q} Df(D) - q_n u \qquad (49)$$

(since necessary production costs per unit should be equal for all entrepreneurs in order to exclude rent). The level of total sales D most advantageous to each entrepreneur will be the quantity at which his individual net revenue is greatest. From conditions of the type

$$d\left[\frac{q_1}{Q} Df(D) - q_1 u\right] = 0 \qquad (50)$$

we obtain a series of identical equations

$$d[Df(D)] = 0 \qquad (51)$$

showing that, despite different individual volumes of production, the same volume of sales will be most advantageous to all individual entrepreneurs *for a given value of total production*. This volume of sales will actually be established in the market, since each person pursues the greatest advantage. If we compare the series of equations (51) obtained here with equation (40) we see that when the total volume of *production* is Q, the *sale* will be the same whether the whole output is in the hands of a monopolist entrepreneur or in the hands of any number of competing entrepreneurs (as we have not placed any restriction on n). So far we have assumed that the volume of production Q remains a constant when supply D is variously modified; but this holds only for each given moment; for longer periods of time the quantity Q itself should be taken to be a variable. Let us now consider at what level Q will be established when the entire output is in the hands of a monopolist and when it is in the hands of n competing entrepreneurs. In the interests of clarity we shall use a diagram. In Figure 2.6, let the abscissae of the curve ON denote the

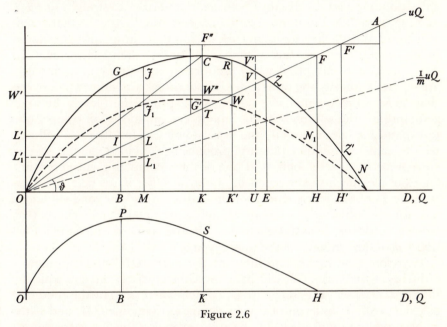

Figure 2.6

quantity sold in a time period, and the ordinates denote the corresponding revenue; this is a curve which is already familiar from previous figures. Let the tangent of the angle ϑ equal u, i.e. the necessary production costs of a unit of product. In this case the ordinates of the straight line OA will denote the production costs of quantities of product indicated by the corresponding abscissae; the vertical distance between the straight line OA and the curve ON indicates the net profit yielded in the industry considered for a volume of output equal to the corresponding abscissa *provided that the quantity produced and the quantity sold in the same time period are equal.* Clearly this condition will hold for all changes in the volume of production from zero to OK since, when the volume of production is less than OK, the most advantageous way of selling the quantity produced will be to sell the *whole* quantity produced in the time period. In fact, take any abscissa OM less than OK; the necessary production costs of the quantity corresponding to this abscissa will equal the line

125

segment ML; gross revenue from the sale of the *whole* quantity produced in the time period will equal MJ and the net profit will equal LJ; obviously the net profit for any volume of sale (per unit of time) smaller than OM, i.e. smaller than the volume of production in the same time period, will be less than LJ. In fact if we take a constant volume of production OM and vary the amount sold from OM to zero, the net profit corresponding to each amount sold (per time period) will equal the corresponding vertical distance between the horizontal straight line $L'L$ and the curve ON. But it may readily be seen from Figure 2.6 that whenever the quantity sold is less than OM, i.e. less than the quantity produced in the same time unit, this distance will be less than the segment LJ corresponding to net profit when production and supply in a time unit are equal. Naturally the same will also obtain for any other abscissa less than OK. Consequently, for changes of production levels between zero and OK the self interest of a monopolist producer will compel him to expand his sale by exactly the same amount. The situation will also be the same when the quantity produced is divided among several entrepreneurs. Let the output of one of the n competing entrepreneurs, for example the first entrepreneur, be $q_1 = Q/m$; if we take the gross revenue Y_1 of this entrepreneur for the ordinates and the total volume of sale for the abscissae, we shall obtain a partial revenue curve ON_1 (shown on the figure as a dashed line), the ordinates of which are a fraction $1/m$ of the ordinates of the total revenue curve ON.

Therefore, the highest ordinate of the curve ON_1 and the highest ordinate of the curve ON will have the same abscissa, and consequently the curve ON_1 will rise from O to C_1 (which is expressed by the condition $dY_1/dD > 0$). If total output per time period remains OM, and if the whole amount produced is sold, the gross revenue of the first entrepreneur will be expressed by the corresponding ordinate MJ_1 of the curve ON_1. His net income will be expressed by the segment J_1L_1, which is the vertical distance between the curve ON_1 and the straight line OA_1, the ordinates of which are a fraction $1/m$ of the ordinates of the straight line OA.

If we now reduce the volume of total supply in a time unit from OM to zero, the individual net income of the first entrepreneur for each given volume of sale less than OM will equal the corresponding vertical distance of the curve ON, from the straight line $L_1'L_1$ parallel to the horizontal axis. However, because of the property of the curve ON_1 that for all abscissae less than OK we should have $dY_1/dD > 0$, the vertical distance between this curve and the straight line $L_1'L_1$ will be less than L_1N_1 for all abscissae less than OM, i.e. will be less than the net income from sale of the whole quantity produced in the given time period. The same will evidently apply to any other volume of production less than OK (i.e. less

126

than the quantity which, when sold in unit time, will yield the greatest gross revenue). Consequently, the most advantageous sale for any number of entrepreneurs as well as for a monopolist, for all changes in production between zero and *OK*, will be the sale of the *whole* quantity produced in the time period. When the volume of output alters from zero to *OK*, total net income will be given by the vertical distance between the curve *ON* and the straight line *OA* regardless of whether monopoly or competition prevails.

If we now take the quantity produced in a time unit as the abscissae, and the highest net profit possible at a given volume of production as the ordinates, we obtain (see the lower part of Figure 2.6) the curve *OPS*, whose ordinates [for abscissae up to *OK*] equal the vertical distance between the straight line *OA* and the curve *ON* for the same abscissae. The abscissa *OM* corresponding to the greatest distance of curve *ON* from the straight line *OA* will correspond, in the new construction, to the greatest distance of the curve *OPS* from the horizontal axis of coordinates. We therefore see that when production varies from zero to *OK* net profit will initially increase until it reaches its maximum at a production level equal to *OB*, after which it begins to fall and ultimately reaches the level *SK* = *CT*. It is evident from the construction that this level is the difference between the greatest possible gross revenue in the given industry under the given market conditions and the necessary production costs of the quantity corresponding to this greatest gross income. We must now consider how net profit will alter when production is increased further beyond *OK*. It is readily appreciated from Figure 2.6 that when the volume of production is greater than *OK*, sale of the total quantity produced in the given time period will no longer be the most advantageous sale for a monopolist (i.e. the sale yielding the greatest net profit for the *given* volume of production).

In fact, let some quantity *OK′* > *OK* be produced during the period; if all this quantity is sold in the same period the monopolist will receive a net profit equal to *WR*. If we assume that the quantity produced is constant and if we vary the volume of sale from *OK′* to *OK*, we obtain, for net profit, a series of quantities corresponding to the vertical distance between the curve *ON* and the straight line *WW′* parallel to the horizontal axis. Since the ordinates of the curve *ON* will increase as the abscissa is progressively reduced from *OK′* to *OK* (since for abscissae greater than *OK* we invariably have $dY/dD < 0$) [where Y is total gross revenue], the vertical distance between the curve *ON* and the straight line *WW′* will increase as the abscissa decreases from *OK′* to *OK*. Conversely, when the abscissa is further reduced, this distance will once again begin to decrease (since we have $dY/dD > 0$ for abscissae smaller than *OK*). It is clear, therefore, that the most advantageous volume of sale for a volume of production OK' greater than OK will be the volume of sale which equals OK, since the greatest net profit (expressed by the segment CW'') corresponds to it. Consequently, this is the volume of sale which the monopolist entrepreneur will establish [if he happens to have produced a quantity OK].

Considering however the connection which exists between the ordinates of the curve ON and the revenue curve ON_1 it is not difficult to demonstrate by the same reasoning that this will also be the most advantageous volume of sale for any number of competing entrepreneurs, as is evident from the corresponding construction denoted by dashed lines (we have already given above the algebraic proof of this proposition).

Obviously the same will hold also for any other volume of production greater than OK. Therefore, when production is expanded beyond the level OK, the greatest total net income consistent with the given volume of production will be equal to the corresponding vertical distance between the horizontal straight line CF and the straight line of production costs OA. This will invariably be the case whether monopoly or free competition prevails. This distance will ultimately become zero at some production level OH.

If we now mark out on the horizontal axis in the lower part of Figure 2.6 a segment equal to OH and join the point H to the point S by a straight line, we shall obtain a line $OPSH$, whose ordinates will show the greatest possible net profit (at the corresponding volume of production) when production expands from O to the quantity OH at which the greatest possible net income becomes zero. This curve, as we have shown above, will be the same when all the sale is in the hands of a monopolist and when the total quantity produced is divided among an unlimited number of competitors. In reality, however, the volume of production itself (and not only the volume of sale within the limits of the quantity produced, as we have assumed above for methodological purposes) is determined by the economic calculation of the entrepreneurs engaged in a given industry. For a complete solution of the problem therefore it is not sufficient to show the level at which supply (and consequently price) will be established for each given volume of production, but it is also necessary to show the level at which production itself will be established under various conditions.

The curve $OPSH$ shows that the greatest total net profit will be yielded by the production level OB at which (see Figure 2.6) the vertical distance between the revenue curve ON and the straight line OA of necessary production costs will be greatest (for which the tangent to the curve ON at the point G should be parallel to the straight line OA). The gross revenue corresponding to this production level will equal BG (Figure 2.6); production costs will equal BI; and the net profit IG. For any further

3. The case of production costs greater than zero

increase in the production level the *total* net income will decline, as shown in the lower part of Figure 2.6. Therefore the self interest of the monopolist will prompt him to fix a volume of production equal to *OB*. The situation is different when production is in the hands of several competing entrepreneurs: although *total* net profit will be reduced when any one of them increases his own production, this *reduction of the total net profit* may be offset for an *individual* entrepreneur by an increase in *his proportion* of total profit. For this to occur it suffices that the first entrepreneur to expand his output be able to rely on the reaction from the other entrepreneurs (in the form of a corresponding expansion of their own output) not occurring instantaneously, but after some finite though very small interval of time. However, as we have already pointed out above, such a condition *invariably holds* whenever the question is one not of the expansion of supply (within the limits of production), but of *production*, since some degree of inertia (which frequently may even be very great) preventing instantaneous expansion is a feature of every industry.

Given this, as each entrepreneur by increasing his individual output *may expect* to increase proportionally his share of total revenue, *albeit temporarily*, all of Cournot's conclusions above on the effect of free competition apply fully to this case. However, instead of relating these conclusions, as does Cournot, both to production and to supply (which Cournot quite arbitrarily assumes invariably equals production), we ought to draw a rigorous distinction between these two questions; all conclusions stemming from the theory of 'temporary profit' ought to be related *exclusively* to the determination of the *production* level (since only in this case the prerequisites for the whole theory of 'temporary profit' will apply).

The following basic points may be established by applying Cournot's main conclusions to this case. First, several competing entrepreneurs will establish the total volume of output at a higher level than a monopolist. Second, when the number of competing entrepreneurs increases indefinitely (so that the individual output of each is infinitely small relative to the total output), they will tend to expand total output (in pursuit of temporary advantage) to the production level at which the greatest possible total net profit is zero. If we denote the equilibrium level of total production by Q^*, and the number of competing entrepreneurs among whom it is distributed by n, Q^* will in general be a function of n:

$$Q^* = \Omega(n) \tag{52}$$

and the relationship between Q^* and n will be such that

$$\left.\begin{array}{l} \Omega'(n) > 0, \\ \lim_{n \to \infty} \Omega(n) = Q_0 \end{array}\right\} \tag{53}$$

129

where Q_0 is understood as the root of the equation $R(Q) = 0$ and where $R(Q)$ is the total *net* profit as a function of total production, i.e. the equation of the curve *OPSH* obtained above in the lower part of Figure 2.6. The proof of this statement does not depend on the product being perishable and not storeable; it suffices that net profit (per time period) should be a *continuous* function of total production or, in more general terms, of the total *potential supply* (in the same time period). By potential supply we mean all those stocks available to the market during a given time period, i.e. the total output of the given period plus the quantity left over from the past periods.[1] In the case of *perishable* commodities the quantity remaining from previous periods is zero and, consequently, *potential supply equals the quantity produced.*

Let total potential supply during some time period (in other words total commodity stocks in the possession of the entrepreneur during this period) be S; let the greatest total net profit obtainable during this period at a given volume of potential supply be $R = R(S)$. Denote the value of S at which $R(S)$ is greatest by S_m; in this case S_m will be the limit of the expansion of potential supply by a monopolist entrepreneur. It is easy to see that when total potential supply S_m is divided among *several* entrepreneurs, it will be even more advantageous for each of them to increase his individual potential supply, and thus also raise total potential supply beyond S_m. In fact, denote by s the individual supply of each of n competing entrepreneurs among whom the total potential supply is divided; let $s = S/n$; in this case the individual net profit h of each individual entrepreneur under conditions excluding the occurrence of rent will be

$$h = \frac{s}{S_m} \cdot R \tag{54}$$

or, taking into consideration that $s = S/n$:

$$h = \frac{1}{n} R(S_m). \tag{55}$$

Now let one of the n entrepreneurs (for example the first), increase his individual stock ($=$ potential supply) by an amount δ, in which case his *new* net income h_1 throughout the period for which the potential supply of other entrepreneurs is constant (i.e. throughout the time they need to expand their enterprises) will be:

$$h_1 = \frac{s + \delta}{S_m + \delta} \cdot R(S_m + \delta) \tag{56}$$

[1] This sum will be the limit beyond which under no circumstance can actual supply be expanded; it is the *greatest possible supply* or, in other words, *potential supply,* the term we shall employ subsequently for brevity.

3. The case of production costs greater than zero

or, considering that $s = S/n$

$$h_1 = \frac{(S_m/n) + \delta}{S_m + \delta} \cdot R(S_m + \delta). \tag{57}$$

Since $R(S_m)$ equals *greatest* net profit, total net profit should be *reduced* when S_m is increased to $(S_m + \delta)$; let the increase of S_m by an amount δ correspond to a reduction in net profit by an amount Δ, so that $R(S_m + \delta) = R(S_m) - \Delta$. The quantities δ and Δ will always be quantities of the *same order* provided that $f(D) = p$, which figures in the expression for total net profit, is a *continuous* function, which holds for all mass consumption products (and in general for all products with a fairly wide range of consumers).[1] It may therefore be assumed as a general rule that the ratio Δ/δ is a *finite quantity*.

Since expressions (55) and (57) express *partial* net income as a function of *total potential supply*, we may write:

$$h = R_n(S_m); \tag{58}$$
$$h_1 = R_n(S_m + \delta).$$

If we subtract the former net income h from the new net income h_1 and divide by the increment δ, we obtain

$$\frac{h_1 - h}{\delta} = \frac{R_n(S_m + \delta) - R_n(S_m)}{\delta}. \tag{59}$$

If we now substitute for h and h_1 their magnitudes from equations (55) and (57), we obtain

$$\frac{R_n(S_m + \delta) - R_n(S_m)}{\delta} = \frac{(S_m/n) + \delta}{\delta(S_m + \delta)} R(S_m + \delta) - \frac{1}{\delta n} R(S_m) \tag{60}$$

and by replacing $R(S_m + \delta)$ by the expression $R(S_m) - \Delta$:

$$\frac{R_n(S_m + \delta) - R_n(S_m)}{(S_m + \delta) - S_m} = \frac{R(S_m) \ (n-1) - (S_m + n\delta)\Delta/S.}{n(S_m + \delta)} \tag{61}$$

If we now begin to reduce δ indefinitely, the left-hand side of equation (61) is converted to a *differential coefficient*, or in other words the first derivative $R_n'(S_m)$ with respect to the variable S. Therefore

$$\underset{\delta \to 0}{\text{Lim}} \frac{R(S_m + \delta) - R_n(S_m)}{(S_m + \delta) - S_m} = R_n'(S_m) = \frac{dR_n(S_m)}{dS_m}. \tag{62}$$

[1] Compare the remarks of Cournot on this question already cited in this Essay, Section 1, pp. 100–1.

When δ is reduced indefinitely, the right-hand side of equation (61) will tend to the limit

$$[R(S_m)\ (n-1) - R'(S_m)S_m]/nS_m,$$ (62a)

or[1]

$$\frac{R(S_m)\ (1-1/n)}{S_m} + R'(S_m)\frac{1}{n}.$$ (63)

Therefore:

$$R'_n(S_m) = \frac{(1-1/n)R(S_m)}{S_m} + \frac{1}{n}R'(S_m).$$ (64)

Clearly since the number n of competing entrepreneurs in the given industry *is greater than one*, when total potential supply is the quantity S_m beyond which it is no longer advantageous to a *monopolist* to expand his stocks (= potential supply), it will still be advantageous to each of the n competing entrepreneurs to expand his own partial stock $s = S_m/n$, and consequently also to increase the total stock S_m. In fact, since by assumption $R(S_m)$ is the *greatest* value of $R(S)$, then by the theory of maxima $R'(S_m) = 0$; inserting this quantity $R'(S_m)$ in equation (64), we obtain:

$$R'_n(S_m) = \frac{(1-1/n)R(S_m)}{S_m}.$$ (65)

The right-hand side of this equality is an *essentially positive* quantity, and therefore $R'_n(S_m) > 0$; consequently, *the partial profit $R_n(S)$ of each of the n entrepreneurs still continues to increase when the total stock increases above the quantity S_m*[2] (whereas the profit of a *monopolist* will already *be falling* when the total stock is increased beyond S_m). Equilibrium will be established only when the *total* potential supply reaches the quantity S_n defined by the condition:

$$R'_n(S_m) = 0$$ (66)

since only when total potential supply reaches this quantity will *none* of the n independent entrepreneurs continue to have an incentive to

---

[1] Since when δ decreases indefinitely the *ratio* $-\Delta/\delta$ tends to the *differential coefficient of* $R(S_m)$ *with respect to the variable S;* in fact: $-\Delta = R(S_m + \delta) - R(S_m)$, and consequently

$$-\frac{\Delta}{\delta} = \frac{R(S_m + \delta) - R(S_m)}{(S_m + \delta) - S_m} \quad \text{or} \quad \operatorname*{Lim}_{\delta \to 0} \frac{R(S_m + \delta) - R(S_m)}{(S_m + \delta) - S_m} = R'(S_m).$$

[2] This means that if we express the change in *partial* profit as a function of total potential supply in the form of a curve, this curve will be ascending at a point of potential supply S_m which yields the greatest *total* net profit (i.e. the tangent to the curve at this point will form an angle greater than zero with the horizontal axis).

expand his own partial potential supply (since every such expansion would be accompanied for that entrepreneur by an *immediate* reduction in his partial net profit). If in the equation $R_n'(S) = 0$ we replace $R_n(S)$ by its expression in terms of total profit $R = R(S)$ and the variable n, we obtain:

$$\frac{(1-1/n)R(S)}{S} + \frac{1}{n}R'(S) = 0 \qquad (67)$$

which may also be put in the form:

$$(n-1)R(S) + SR'(S) = 0. \qquad (68)$$

This equation is the most general expression of the equilibrium conditions in production (potential supply) for any number of competing entrepreneurs.

It is evident from equation (68) that the greater the number of competitors n the greater should be the value of S to satisfy this equation. Therefore, *the larger the number of independent entrepreneurs among whom total potential supply is divided the greater will be total potential supply at which equilibrium is established,* and consequently the lower *total* net profit earned throughout the industry (i.e. by all individual entrepreneurs combined). Finally, *when the number of competing entrepreneurs increases indefinitely, i.e. when $n \to \infty$, the equilibrium level of total potential supply will tend indefinitely to the limit S_0, where S_0 is total potential supply at which the* greatest possible *total net income is zero:*

$$R(S_0) = 0. \qquad (69)$$

In fact, when $n \to \infty$ the only value of S which can satisfy equation (68) is the value at which $R(S)$ becomes *infinitely small, since otherwise the first and second terms of the right-hand side of equation (68) remain incommensurate quantities* (since if $n \to \infty$ and $R(S)$ is a finite quantity, the first term will be infinitely great and the second will invariably be essentially finite), and therefore their sum can in no case be zero.

This conclusion *is of general significance,* for both storeable and perishable commodities, *since the only restriction placed on $R(S)$ is that $R(S)$ should be a continuous function,* which is invariably the case for mass production and sale. If we now substitute, for the symbol $R(S)$, the expression for total net profit previously given for the case of a *perishable* commodity, where potential supply always equals production alone, we obtain:

$$R(Q) = D \cdot f(D) - uQ = 0. \qquad (70)$$

If we add in the differential equation previously derived:

$$\frac{d[D \cdot f(D) - uQ]}{dD} = 0 \qquad (71)$$

we obtain an equation system which defines the unknown quantities D and Q. Since total production cost uQ is made up of the cost of the D units sold and the cost apportioned to them of the $(Q-D)$ perished units, the total cost can be represented in the general form:

$$D\left[u+\frac{(Q-D)u}{D}\right] \tag{72}$$

where u is necessary production costs of a unit of the product, and $(Q-D)u/D$ is additional unit cost *over and above its necessary production cost*. These costs will subsequently be referred to as *realisation costs or sales costs* [*izderzhki po realizatsii*] *and will be denoted by* v; unlike necessary costs, they vary with changes of the variables D and Q. We shall see subsequently that these costs v are a function of the ratio Q/D both in the present case and for storeable goods; we may, therefore, write:

$$v = \gamma(D, Q), \quad \text{or to put it another way} \quad v = \gamma(D/Q), \tag{73}$$

so that total cost is given by

$$uQ = D[u+\gamma(D, Q)]. \tag{74}$$

If we insert this new expression for total costs in our equations and replace $f(D)$ by the level of p from the market equation $p = f(D)$ we obtain:

$$p-u-\gamma(D, Q) = 0 \tag{75}$$

$$\mathrm{d}\{D[p-u-\gamma(D, Q)]\} = 0 \tag{76}$$

$$p = f(D). \tag{77}$$

The meaning of these equations can be expressed by the following *law* which, as we shall see subsequently, *is of general significance for all cases: the conditions for equilibrium in production and sale under unlimited free competition are* (1) *that total net profits obtained in a given industry should be* the greatest possible at the given volume of potential supply (in particular, with perishable goods, at the given volume of production); (2) *that this* greatest possible *net profit* should be zero. Both these conditions will be satisfied when actual supply D and potential supply Q reach the values defined by the set of equations (75) and (76). The market price established in this case will be determined from equation (77) and will be the *actual* equilibrium price *for the* given technical *conditions of production and storage of the product and for the* given psychophysiological *conditions of its use. Technical conditions of production* determine the constant u in the expression for necessary costs; *technical conditions of storage* determine the form of the function γ in the expression for realisation costs; the *psychophysiological*

3. The case of production costs greater than zero

conditions of use determine the form of the function f in the relationship between price and volume of sales.

Therefore we see that the condition that net profit should be zero, or in other words *that the price of the quantity sold should equal costs* of the quantity sold to be recovered (Ricardo's law) *is not* in itself *sufficient*. In fact, if we turn to Figure 2.6 we see that this condition (the only one required by Ricardo's law) will be satisfied when the volume of production is OE *provided that the quantity sold in a time period equals the quantity produced in the same period.* As shown by Figure 2.6, under this condition, the sum received for OE units produced will equal EZ, i.e. will exactly equal the production costs of the quantity produced (since point Z lies at the intersection of the revenue curve ON and the straight line OA representing production costs). Despite the fact that price equals production cost (the price of a unit of the product will equal the tangent of the angle ϑ, which also equals the production costs of a unit of the product), equilibrium cannot be established in this industry, since price and production cost will be equal only on condition that the *whole* quantity produced in a given time period is sold; whereas in practice (because of the basic premise that individuals tend to pursue their greatest advantage) *the whole quantity produced will not be sold, but only part of it,* namely the quantity OK, since *this is the volume of sale which, as we have seen, ensures to each separate entrepreneur the greatest net profit possible at a given volume of production.* However, it is evident from Figure 2.6 that the price corresponding to the supply level OK, equal to the tangent of the angle $C\hat{O}K$, will be greater than the tangent of the angle $Z\hat{O}K$ expressing the production costs which must be recouped in each unit sold.[1] Therefore, when the volume of production is OE equilibrium still cannot be established in this branch of industry, since new entrepreneurs will continue to enter it for as long as net profit exists and production will continue to expand as we have seen above. Equilibrium will be reached only when the volume of production reaches the limit OH at which, *however the quantity produced is sold*, this industry is incapable of yielding a net profit. With the most advantageous sales policy (when the volume of sale equals OK and price equals the tangent of the angle $C\hat{O}K$) ensured by the tendency of individual entrepreneurs to pursue the greatest advantage, net profit will be zero; with any other sales policy it will be negative (as appears from Figure 2.6, where the segment VV' represents the loss when the quantity sold is OU). Further production expansion will be impossible, since whatever the sales policy (i.e. whatever the ratio between the volume of sales to the volume of production in the same time period) quantities larger than OH cannot recover their

---

[1] Clearly these costs will be greater than necessary costs expressed by the tanget of the angle ϑ, since not only must their own necessary productive costs be recouped in the revenue, but also the production costs of units remaining unsold.

production costs at the price obtained. In fact, if the volume of production is greater than *OH*, for example *OH'*, then whatever the volume of sales and the corresponding price we shall always obtain a loss on sales. When the sale amounts to *OH'* (i.e. to the total quantity produced) this loss will be greatest and will equal *F'Z'* in Figure 2.6; when the sale is reduced the loss will be reduced initially and will reach its lowest point *CF"* when the quantity sold is *OK*; then it increases again. Therefore we see that the smallest loss possible will be greater than zero or, in other words, the greatest possible profit will be less than zero. It is evident from Figure 2.6 that the same will hold for any amount of production greater than *OH*. Consequently, when unlimited free competition prevails, as is shown in Figure 2.6, the volume of production will be fixed at the level *OH*; the volume of sale in the same period will be *OK*; price will be equal to the tangent of $C\hat{O}K$; gross revenue will be *KC*, and production costs to be recouped in the revenue will also be *KC*, i.e. will equal gross revenue; consequently, net profit will be zero. Compare these results of the effect of free competition with the situation which would prevail were a monopolist to control the industry considered. We see that a monopolist will fix his output at the level *OB* which, as shown by Figure 2.6, will yield him the greatest net profit. Following the previous argument, it is clear from Figure 2.6 that the most advantageous volume of sale for his volume of production will also be *OB*; total gross revenue will consequently be *BG*, the price of each unit equal to the tangent of $G\hat{O}B$; total costs to be recouped in the revenue will be *BI*; costs for each unit sold will be equal to the tangent of ϑ, and total net profit will be *IG*. Therefore we see that the market price under monopoly will be greater than the price established under unlimited free competition (since tan $G\hat{O}B$ > tan $C\hat{O}K$); production costs for each unit sold will be lower in the case of monopoly than when free competition prevails (since tan ϑ < tan $C\hat{O}K$). On closer analysis of this phenomenon we see that the increase of unit costs under competition arises because part of the expenditure incurred in the production and storage of unsold units also has to be recouped in each unit sold, in addition to its own necessary production costs. In our case these additional costs (i.e. the costs of each unit sold over and above its necessary production costs) are equal to necessary production costs of unsold units divided by the number of units sold, because of our assumption that the product is perishable and not storeable.

When we analyse storeable products we see that the limit to which sale could be expanded in a time period, i.e. the potential supply, would equal the volume of production in the same time period only in the *special* case where the most advantageous volume of sale in the period equalled the whole quantity produced. Otherwise some stock from the production of the preceding time period (or periods) would invariably remain on the

3. The case of production costs greater than zero

market at the beginning of each period, so that the limit of supply expansion per time period would be greater than the production by the total amount remaining at its beginning. If the quantity remaining at the beginning of a given time period is J units (from the production of previous periods), and if Q further units are produced during this period (according to the existing size of enterprises, which is invariable for the period), the limit which supply may reach in the time period will be $J + Q = S$. We refer to this quantity, S, as *potential supply* to distinguish it from *actual supply*, or sale, which we continue to denote by the letter D.

If we now assume that *potential supply* S in a time period is given, the volume of actual supply ensuring the greatest net profit possible per time period for a given potential supply is determined from the equation:

$$\mathrm{d}\left\{D\left[p - u - \frac{\gamma(S-D)}{D}\right]\right\}/\mathrm{d}D = 0 \qquad (78)$$

where u is necessary production costs of a unit of the product and $\gamma(S-D)$ is the cost of the unsold units $(Q-D)$ stored until the next period.[1] For methodological reasons we *still* continue to regard potential supply S *conventionally* as a given quantity; in reality the quantity S itself is determined by the tendency to pursue the greatest advantage. If all potential supply S is concentrated in the hands of a single monopolist, the most advantageous level of sales he would establish would be equal to the root of equation (78).

Clearly if potential supply S is not concentrated in one person's hands, but distributed between any number of competing entrepreneurs, the level of sale most advantageous *for each* competing entrepreneur *under conditions of zero rent* (i.e. on the assumption that production conditions, storage and sale of the product are the same for all competing entrepreneurs) would be the level ensuring the greatest *total* net profit for the given total potential supply which, consequently, was most advantageous for a monopoly owner of the whole potential supply. In fact, let the potential supply of any of n competing entrepreneurs, say the kth entrepreneur, be $S_k = S/m$, and let his sale be D_k; noting that market

[1] Additional costs will include the cost of storing the stock $(S-D)$ only for the time *beyond that objectively necessary*, i.e. for the time required by the natural discrepancy between the periods of production and consumption. We assume that storage costs arising from objective causes and therefore independent of economic calculation have already been included in necessary costs u.

Clearly *in a state of equilibrium* the sum of additional costs $\gamma(S-D)$ will equal the *cost of storing stock* $(S-D)$ *for a given time period.* In fact, in equilibrium D must necessarily equal Q (otherwise no equilibrium could exist) and $J = (S-D)$ *will be a constant*, since costs in *each* period should include *the storage cost of the stock J immobilised during the time period*, in addition to necessary costs of the D units sold (i.e. in addition to the sum uD).

position will be equally favourable to all entrepreneurs, D_k will equal D/m.[1] The gross revenue of the kth entrepreneur will equal $(D/m)f(D)$. Necessary costs will equal $S_k u = Su/m$. Additional costs will equal storage costs of $(S_k - D_k) = (S-D)/m$ units which, under zero rent conditions, will be m times smaller than the storage cost of a stock of $(S-D)$ units;[2] thus, if the storage cost of $(S-D)$ units is $\gamma(S-D)$, the additional costs of the kth entrepreneur will equal $[\gamma(S-D)]/m$, which for each unit sold gives

$$\frac{[\gamma(S-D)]/m}{D_k} = \frac{[\gamma(S-D)]/m}{D/m} = \frac{\gamma(S-D)}{D}. \tag{79}$$

The partial net profit of the kth entrepreneur will therefore be

$$\frac{D}{m}f(D) - \frac{D}{m}u - \frac{\gamma(S-D)}{D}\cdot\frac{D}{m} \tag{80}$$

or

$$\frac{1}{m}\cdot D\left[f(D) - u - \frac{\gamma(S-D)}{D}\right] \tag{81}$$

The derivative of this expression with respect to the variable D will be:

$$\frac{1}{m}\cdot d\left\{D\left[f(D) - u - \frac{\gamma(S-D)}{D}\right]\right\}. \tag{82}$$

Equating this quantity to zero, we obtain the equation

$$d\left\{D\left[p - u - \frac{\gamma(S-D)}{D}\right]\right\} = 0 \tag{83}$$

the root of which is identically equal to the root of equation (78) on p. 137.

[1] An equally favourable market position is expressed by the condition:

$$\frac{D_1}{s_1} = \frac{D_2}{s_2} = \cdots = \frac{D_k}{s_k} = \cdots = \frac{D_n}{s_n} = \frac{D_1 + D_2 + \cdots + D_n}{s_1 + s_2 + \cdots + s_n} = \frac{D}{S}.$$

From $D_k/s_k = D/S$ we have $D_k = D s_k/S$ and if we replace s_k by its value S/m we have:

$$D_k = \frac{D\cdot S/m}{S} = \frac{D}{m}.$$

[2] If the cost of storing the partial stock of $(Q-D)/m$ units was not m times smaller than the cost of storing the total stock of $(Q-D)$ units, this would signify that sale conditions were not the same for enterprises of different sizes; as a result of this some *differential* income (i.e. income accruing to enterprises favourably placed) would be incorporated unavoidably in total net revenue and, consequently, gross revenue in a state of equilibrium could no longer equal the necessary costs of the quantity sold. Under such conditions, as shown in the First Essay, the price of the product cannot be determined independently of the form of the function f in the expression $p = f(D)$, i.e. independently of demand conditions (see the Third Essay).

3. *The case of production costs greater than zero*

Of course, if differential equation (78) showed that the sales level D ensuring the greatest net profit for a given S was greater than S, D should be taken to *equal* S, since the quantity D is in general bound by the condition $O \leqslant D \leqslant S$. In any case, while total potential supply S is less than the root of the equation

$$\frac{\mathrm{d}[Sf(S) - uS]}{d} = 0 \qquad (84)$$

the most advantageous sale level will always equal *total potential supply*, i.e.:

$$D = S. \qquad (85)$$

A monopolist motivated by maximisation of profit would fix his potential supply equal to the root of equation (84), since this volume of potential supply would ensure him the greatest absolute net profit when sales equal potential supply. If S was increased further the greatest possible net profit (not absolutely, but at the given level of S) in general would decrease (see below for greater detail).

At some quantity greater than the root S_m of equation (84), the most advantageous volume of supply for the given S ceases to equal the whole potential supply; from that point the costs to be recouped in gross revenue will invariably include, in addition to the necessary production costs of the quantity sold, further additional costs due to storing speculative stocks, which are objectively superfluous. When S is increased further these additional costs also continue to rise until, ultimately, total costs swallow up the entire gross revenue at some quantity S_0, so that net profit $R_0 = R(S_0) = 0$. Clearly further increase in potential supply cannot be advantageous to any of the n competing entrepreneurs (however many there are). Also it is not difficult to demonstrate, by techniques analogous to those used when analysing instances of perishable products, that when unlimited free competition prevails equilibrium cannot be established *at a quantity less than* S_0. But at this volume of potential supply the best actual supply will, *as a general rule*, invariably be less than potential supply; consequently, total costs to be recouped in gross revenue unavoidably *exceed the necessary production costs* of this quantity. In order to clarify the mutual relationship of various cost elements let us return to the construction which we used to analyse the previous case (i.e. the case of commodities which cannot be stored). In Figure 2.7 the gross revenue curve and the straight line representing the necessary costs will naturally be the same as previously (Figure 2.6). We now assume that potential supply is a constant equal to the abscissa OH, and that actual supply is a variable. As we gradually reduce actual supply from the total available

139

stock to zero, the sum of costs to be recouped in the gross revenue will be successively expressed by the corresponding ordinates of a line *FF'*.

We shall refer to this curve briefly as the *total costs curve*. This curve may vary according to the properties of a given commodity and to general storage conditions (in certain circumstances it may become a *straight line*), but *it can never coincide with the line OA representing necessary production costs*. It could coincide with the straight line *OA* only *if there were no additional expenditure connected with the storage of goods*. Since this is not so, and cannot be so for any commodity, all the ordinates of the curve *FF'*, apart from ordinate *FH* corresponding to sales *OH* equal to the entire quantity produced, will always be greater than corresponding ordinates of the

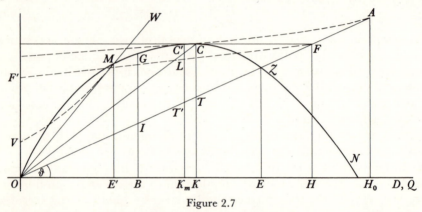

Figure 2.7

straight line *OA*. The difference between necessary production costs and total costs to be recouped in gross revenue (a difference expressed on the graph by the vertical distance between the curve *FF'* and the straight line *OA*) we call 'costs incurred in sale' (or realisation costs) of the quantity sold. *Therefore the curve FF' could also be regarded as a curve of 'costs incurred in sale'*: however it should be remembered that costs incurred in sale do not correspond to the *entire ordinates, but to segments* of the ordinates of the curve *FF'* above the points where they intersect the straight line representing necessary costs. We shall not consider special forms of the line *FF'* now. It is sufficient to establish here the most general relationship between sales for a given volume of stocks and 'total costs' of the quantity sold. We have already seen that the curve *FF'* cannot have points in common with *OA* other than point *F* (at which production and supply per time period are equal); we should add that, whatever the properties of a given commodity, *the curve FF' cannot become a descending curve*. Hence if $Z = Z(D)$ is the equation of this curve, $Z'(D)$ cannot be less than zero; because when the unsold (carried over) commodities perish entirely the curve *FF'* becomes a horizontal straight line. There-

3. The case of production costs greater than zero

fore, if the cost of storing the goods until the next period was greater than the loss suffered if they perished completely (and the cost of the amount perished was transferred to the units sold), the entrepreneur would not store unsold goods, since it would be more *advantageous* for him to leave these goods to perish. *Therefore, the value* $Z'(D) = 0$ *is the lowest value which the first derivative of this function in general can assume.* For commodities *suitable for storage* $\mathrm{d}Z(D)/\mathrm{d}D$ would be in general *greater than zero* and, consequently, the curve *FF'* should take the form depicted in Figure 2.7, with larger ordinates corresponding to larger abscissae.

Finally, the curve *FF'* should satisfy the requirement that *the angle formed with the horizontal axis by a straight line drawn from any point of the curve FF' through O should be greater, the farther this point of the curve lies from the point F.* The curve *FF'* should satisfy this condition whatever the nature of the commodity concerned and whatever its specific conditions of storage. In fact, *provided that storage costs* of a unit of a given product per time period *are not zero* (as in reality), the costs *to be recouped per unit sold* in general *will be greater, the larger the ratio between unsold and sold units.* Each smaller abscissa of the curve *FF'* should be therefore necessarily matched by a greater tangent of the angle (and consequently a greater angle, since the angles relate in the same way as the tangents) formed with the horizontal axis by a straight line drawn from the corresponding point on the curve through O; the tangent of this angle shows graphically the costs to be recouped in the price of each unit sold. Clearly this requirement is also fully satisfied by the form of the line representing costs incurred in sale adopted previously for perishable commodities (a horizontal straight line). Consequently, *total costs* (i.e. essential costs plus costs incurred in sale) of a commodity of any kind (perishable or unperishable) *charged to each unit sold are, for a given production level, a continuous[1] decreasing function of the level of sale in a given time period.* Ricardo lost sight of this when constructing his theory of production costs. We have found above that, for a perishable commodity, equilibrium would be established in the example we analysed (see Figures 2.6 and 2.7) at a potential supply equal to *OH*, since at this level of potential supply the *greatest possible* total net profit (corresponding to a sale equal to *OK*) would be zero.

In the case of a storeable commodity, instead of the straight line *FC* we obtain some other line *FF'*, and the most advantageous sales level when the production level is *OH* would be the quantity OK_m for which the vertical distance between the curves *ON* and *FF'* was greatest. From Figure 2.7 we can see clearly that OK_m should be less than *OK*; it is also clear that at this sales level the industry considered would still yield a net profit (equal to the segment *LC'*). Consequently, when unlimited free

[1] Within the limits of *possible* changes of the variable, i.e. changes from *zero to the total quantity produced.*

141

competition prevails, equilibrium could still not be established at a volume of potential supply corresponding to the abscissa *OH*, since at this volume of total supply it would still be advantageous to *each* of an infinitely large number of independent entrepreneurs to enlarge his own partial potential supply (in the pursuit of 'temporary profit'). By reasoning as before (see pp. 135–6 above) we reach the conclusion that equilibrium will be established in a given industry only when output (to be more precise potential supply) is equal to OH_0, at which point the curve showing the behaviour of *total*[1] costs as sales decrease from total potential supply = OH_0 to zero *is tangential to the curve ON*. The most advantageous sales level for this magnitude of potential supply will equal the abscissa of the point C' of tangency[2] of both curves. Since at this sales level net profit will be zero (for all other volumes of supply it will be a negative quantity, as is evident from Figure 2.7) all incentive for the further expansion of potential supply by individual entrepreneurs (in the pursuit of temporary advantage) is eliminated. The equilibrium conditions are algebraically expressed by the set of equations:

$$pD - uS - vD = 0 \tag{86}$$

$$\frac{\mathrm{d}(pD - uS - vD)}{\mathrm{d}D} = 0 \tag{87}$$

where D is total actual supply, S is total potential supply, u is the necessary production cost per unit of product, p is the unit price and v is the additional cost of *each* of the D units sold, over necessary production costs (at a potential supply equal to S). We add to this market conditions (which are ultimately demand conditions):

$$p = f(D) \tag{77}$$

and storage conditions expressed by the equation:

$$V = \gamma(S - D) \tag{88}$$

where V is total storage cost for the stock $(S - D)$ throughout the time exceeding the period objectively required for the sale of this stock. This equation can be put in the form:

$$\frac{V}{D} = \frac{\gamma(S - D)}{D} \tag{89}$$

or:

$$v = \frac{\gamma(S - D)}{D}. \tag{90}$$

---

[1] I.e. equal to necessary costs + costs incurred in sale.

[2] We have placed the point of tangency in Figure 2.7 at C', since under conditions closest to reality (see below) *when potential supply increases the total costs curve will be shifted upwards, while remaining parallel to its former position.*

3. The case of production costs greater than zero

The system of equations (86), (87), (77) and (90) is adequate for determining all the unknowns: S, D, p, v, from the viewpoint of theoretical *economy*.

If we eliminate unknowns p and v from equations (86) and (87) by substitution, we obtain two basic equations defining the levels of actual and potential supply in terms of the same known quantities in a state of equilibrium:

$$Df(D) - uS - D\frac{\gamma(S-D)}{D} = 0 \qquad (91)$$

$$\frac{d[Df(D) - uS - D\gamma(S-D)/D]}{dD} = 0. \qquad (92)$$

If further we consider that potential supply is

$$S = J + Q \qquad (93)$$

we may present our basic equations as

$$Df(D) - uS - D\frac{\gamma(J+Q-D)}{D} = 0 \qquad (94)$$

$$\frac{d[Df(D) - uS - D\gamma(J+Q-D)/D]}{dD} = 0 \qquad (95)$$

and since in equilibrium

$$Q = D \qquad (96)$$

these equations become:

$$Df(D) - uD - D\gamma\left(\frac{J}{D}\right) = 0 \qquad (97)$$

$$\frac{d[Df(D) - uD - D\gamma(J/D)]}{dD} = 0. \qquad (98)$$

The system of equations (86), (87), (77), (90), (93) and (96) is sufficient for determining all quantities dependent on economic calculation: Q, J, S, D, p and v in terms of economically known quantities.

As we have shown, the price corresponding to this equation system is graphically represented by the tangent of the angle formed with the horizontal axis by a straight line from the origin to the point of tangency of the gross revenue curve ON and the total costs curve FF'.

In this state of equilibrium (Figure 2.7) gross revenue is equal to $K_m C'$;

total costs to be recouped in this revenue will also equal $K_m C'$, so that net profit will be zero. Total costs will continue to be divided into two parts: essential production costs $K_m T'$ of the quantity sold and *sales costs*, equal to $T'C'$. It is clear from Figure 2.7 that with the new form of the line representing costs incurred in sale, total sales costs recouped in gross revenue will be greater than in the previous case when we assumed that the commodity was perishable (when the curve of costs incurred in sale was a horizontal straight line). In fact, segment $C'T'$ will invariably be greater than segment CT because of the basic properties of curve ON. Clearly although this difference might vary when the form of curve FF' changes (with a change in storage conditions), it cannot vanish unless the curve FF coincides with the straight line OA representing necessary costs (except, of course, at point F), but this would contradict the actual situation as we have seen.

Consequently, whatever the properties of a given commodity (in particular, its storeability), as a general rule equilibrium will be established in a given industry *at a price higher than necessary production costs*.

Price may equal necessary production costs only exceptionally when the *necessary* production costs of a given product are so large that *they exceed the price corresponding to the maximum gross revenue*, i.e. *the price (equal to the tangent of the angle $C\hat{O}K$) which would be set by a monopolist* if he could obtain the product free. For instance if essential production costs are equal to the tangent of the angle $W\hat{O}K$ a horizontal straight line drawn through the point M where the cost line OW intersects the revenue curve extends to the left *outside* the revenue curve, so that for any supply less than OE' (more than which cannot be produced in this case) the entrepreneurs will suffer a loss *if the commodity is not storeable*. Therefore supply will be exactly equal to the quantity produced, and as a result the price will be established at the level of necessary production costs. However, even if necessary production costs were so large, the price would be fixed at the level of these costs *only if the commodity was completely unsuitable for storage*.[1] For storeable commodities which satisfy permanent needs (i.e. the majority), for which the total cost curve is close to the line of necessary production costs, the 'total costs' curve would always be *inside* the revenue curve, as indicated by a dashed line MV, even with the large necessary production costs we have assumed. Consequently, *the equilibrium price would nevertheless be established at a level higher than the necessary production costs of the product*. However, even those cases where extremely high

---

[1] In reality, *even for goods which are not storable the price could be established at a level higher than the necessary production costs* even in this case of high necessary production costs greater than tan $C\hat{O}K$. Here we provisionally assume the contrary only because, for methodological considerations, we are *still* assuming that the accumulation of non-productive stocks is the *only* means of limiting supply. This in fact is not so: see next section.

necessary production costs cause the price to be established at the level of these costs cannot serve as confirmation of Ricardo's *law*. In this case the equality of price and necessary production costs would be merely a *transient* phenomenon corresponding to a low state of industrial technology and would disappear with further improvement in production methods. Therefore Ricardo's law is inapplicable even to commodities in whose price rent is not embodied in any form. Equality between the market price and the costs which the entrepreneurs should recover from this price may be established *not only by reduction of the market price to the necessary production costs* (as was assumed by Ricardo), *but also by a simultaneous increase in the costs* falling on the quantity sold, *above the level of the necessary* production costs of this quantity, by the addition of the costs incurred in sale. The contribution of each of the aspects referred to in the price equation and the level at which the price will be established will depend in each specific instance on the shape of the total production costs curve and of the *revenue curve*. From Figure 2.7 it appears that *we may arbitrarily alter the equilibrium price, raising it to a greater or lesser degree above the level of necessary production costs, by leaving the production costs curve unchanged*, and by altering the form of the demand curve alone. Consequently, the price of products in the third category, like the price of products in the first two categories (monopoly products and those which yield rent) may not be determined independently of the form of $f(D)$; and it changes with it, as supply and demand conditions change,[1] even if *necessary production costs* remain *completely unaltered*.

APPENDIX TO SECTION 3

The System of Equations for Competitive Equilibrium*

In reality it is by *trial and error* that entrepreneurs arrive at the price which ensures them highest total profit for a given volume of available stocks. By varying the price and comparing the net profit corresponding to different price levels they are able to find with a sufficient degree of approximation the price level consistent with their tendency to pursue the greatest advantage. The same operation is repeated for every change in the conditions of production and sale of products.

It is extremely important to note here that at all fluctuations preceding the establishment of an equilibrium price[2] (*prix d'équilibre, Gleichgewichtspreis*), the price will invariably fluctuate *downwards*, i.e. from a higher to a lower level and not *vice versa*: the converse may occur only as a result of *errors in economic calculation by entrepreneurs*. In fact, let the equilibrium price be p_m, and let the

---

[1] These are, ultimately, the conditions of use of the product; see the Third Essay.
[2] I.e. the price *closest* to the economic calculation of *each* entrepreneur.

* *Ed. note.* See Equations (86), (87), (77), (90), (93) and (96) above.

sale in t units of time at this price be D_m. Now let us assume that before the price is established at p_m it passes successively in t units of time through a series of values $p_1 > p_2 > p_3 > \cdots > p_m$. In this case the total quantity sold in t units of time will also equal D_m; it cannot be less than D_m because in that case the utility of the last unit bought would be greater for the consumer than the utility of the sum of money for which a unit of the product is offered in the market[1] and, consequently, it would be to the consumer's advantage to expand his purchase since by continuing to trade he would be increasing his utility. Consequently, the total volume of sale will be the same whether the price p_m is established immediately or whether it passes through a number of successive values: $p_1 > p_2 > p_3 > \cdots > p_m$, but clearly the *sum received for D_m units will be less in the former case than in the latter.* When the price p_m is established immediately, gross revenue will be $p_m D_m$; when the price passes through a number of successive values from p_1 to p_m, gross revenue will be

$$\frac{1}{k_1} p_1 D_m + \frac{1}{k_2} p_2 D_m + \cdots + \frac{1}{k_m} p_m D_m \tag{99}$$

where

$$\frac{1}{k_1} D_m + \frac{1}{k_2} D_m + \cdots + \frac{1}{k_m} D_m = D_m. \tag{100}$$

Completely the opposite would obtain if the price were to pass through a series of values $p_1 < p_2 < p_3 < \cdots < p_m$ before being established at the level p_m. An excellent graphic analysis of the question of 'multiple prices' (*prix multiples*) may be found in Dupuit's works, *De la mesure de l'utilité des travaux publics* (1844) and *De l'influence des péages sur l'utilité des voies de communication* (1849). The same question is treated in algebraic form by Launhardt (*Mathematische Begründung . . .*, Sections 9 and 10). For our present purposes it is important to note simply that *in their search for the most advantageous price* (which is still not known to them from previous experience) entrepreneurs, guided in their actions by correct economic calculation, invariably begin with higher prices and move to lower prices until they reach a point at which further price reduction begins to reduce their total net profit.

---

[1] In fact, the *utility of the last unit to be brought* or the 'marginal utility' of a product is, as we shall see below, a function of the total quantity bought. As this quantity increases, marginal utility decreases and, conversely, as it decreases marginal utility increases. Therefore, when $D < D_m$ the utility of the last unit bought will be greater than when the total sale is D_m; if we denote the marginal utility of the quantity D by U and the marginal utility of the quantity D_m by U_m we have $U > U_m$; but U_m should in any case *equal* the utility of a sum of money p_m for the consumer (otherwise consumers would not acquire D_m units of the product at a price p_m, since in this case they would exchange greater for lesser utility), and therefore U should be *greater* than the utility of this sum to the consumer.

4. *Unlimited free competition and the national economy*

The price actually established in the market will correspond *exactly* to the price defined by the equation system derived by us above (pp. 142–3) only if the *conditional* assumptions on which our theoretical conclusions are based are *fully* satisfied in reality. These assumptions are: (1) that the conditions under which rent (in the Ricardian sense) occurs are completely absent in the production and sale of the given commodity; (2) that the number of entrepreneurs competing in the same market may be assumed to be greater than any finite quantity, so that the supply and production of each of them is an infinitely small quantity relative to the total supply and production; (3) that all the entrepreneurs are guided in their actions by *correct* economic calculation.

Ultimately these *three* assumptions may be reduced to the first *two*, since the third assumption is implicit in the second. In fact, provided that the number of entrepreneurs operating separately and independently from each other is greater than any finite quantity, their errors, as random variables (which are moreover confined within very narrow limits since every entrepreneur strives his uttermost to avoid them) should by virtue of the *law of large numbers* be mutually compensating. Therefore *total* supply and *total* production will tend asymptotically to the quantity which would be determined if entrepreneurs were *completely free of errors* of economic calculation.

4. THE SIGNIFICANCE OF UNLIMITED FREE COMPETITION FROM THE VIEWPOINT OF THE NATIONAL ECONOMY

We now return to our comparison of the phenomena arising when monopoly and unlimited free competition prevail in a given industry. We have seen that in general monopoly price is higher than the price established under free competition in the market. The production costs which the monopolist has to recoup in this price do not exceed the necessary production costs, since a monopolist is always able to produce just so much as he calculates may be sold, and does not incur any additional sale costs (we assume that those costs incurred in sale arising from the difference in the periods of production and consumption are already included in the necessary production costs). Therefore, the whole difference between the necessary production costs and the sale price remains to the free disposal of the capitalist as net income: he may consume or invest this income in further production *but, in any case, this sum will not disappear without trace for the national economy as a whole*. The situation is different when free competition prevails. Admittedly, the price of the product is lower, so that consumers gain from not paying *so much* above the necessary production costs; even so, as we have shown, they still pay more than the necessary production costs.

What happens to this surplus? It is no longer at the free disposal of the sellers: *it is entirely spent on non-productive expenditure* on storage of the commodity (in the broad sense, i.e. including insurance charges) *for longer than the time required* by the conditions of use and production; or on covering the cost of amounts of a non-storeable commodity which are not sold immediately and perish. Consequently, if the monopolist uses the same production techniques as competing entrepreneurs, the results of monopoly and free competition for the national economy *as a whole* may be expressed as follows: *When monopoly prevails, the national economy as a whole loses nothing: what is taken from the consumers over and above the necessary production costs is at the disposal of the monopolist as a particularly high monopoly profit: conversely, when free competition prevails, the entire sum paid by consumers over and above the necessary production costs is lost without trace to the national economy, by its expenditure on non-productive costs (i.e. costs the expenditure of which does not increase the sum total of benefit or satisfaction).* Therefore the thesis that free competition ensures the greatest productivity of existing means of production, which has become practically axiomatic in classical political economy (see the Appendix to Section 4), is simply based on the incorrect assumption that free competition is capable of reducing the price of products to the *necessary* production costs under all conditions of production and use, and that it falls as these costs fall. (Here we do not deal at all with the *ethical* question of how equitable is the transfer from the consumers to the monopolist.)

At first it might seem strange that *free* entrepreneurs (i.e. motivated in their actions solely by their own considerations of the greatest advantage) should build up stocks which are completely unnecessary (since not destined to be sold at the time), and which bring them nothing but harm (since by their additional expenditure on storage they raise the costs which have to be recouped in the price of the units of the commodity which are sold). In fact, if for example every one of n competitors sells a units of a commodity in a time period, when production and consumption periods coincide, why should each have stock greater than a units in that period? After all, this dead stock only raises the total costs of the enterprise, and it would appear to be most rational to eliminate the excess entirely by reducing the stock per time period to the quantity actually sold in that period. In fact, it would be advantageous to each competitor to destroy the dead stock, but *only on condition that other competitors did the same.*

Stocks of commodities in the struggle for sales play the same role as intensified armament of the Powers in *peace time.* Expenditure on such armament appears completely pointless since it does not yield any *apparent* result; its significance is purely negative and may be understood only if we consider one Power beginning to disarm when the others remain in their former position. Not only would the position of this Power deteriorate *in the event* of a disturbance to international peace, but the very fact of its disarmament would be an *incentive to a disturbance of the peace*. The other Powers for whom a favourable outcome of a struggle (and the benefits associated with it) with this state (or with a given combination of states including the state which has disarmed) would have been in doubt (owing to the balance of power) could now count on victory should a struggle commence. Precisely the same thing would occur in the market if one or more of the competitors were to liquidate their 'dead' stocks: the remaining competitors would immediately feel in a better position and therefore it would seem advantageous for them to disturb the existing equilibrium (by lowering the price existing in the market). The new equilibrium which would be established after mutual reactions would be less favourable to the competitors who had destroyed their 'surplus' stocks, since every increase of sale occurring as a result of reduction in the former market price *would accrue only to the competitors who had maintained their surplus stocks*. Therefore, the competitors who had destroyed their 'surplus' stocks would find themselves, ultimately, in a worse position than before.

APPENDIX TO SECTION 4

When we speak of the importance of the system of unlimited free competition to the national economy as a whole we invariably have in mind a *theoretical* rather than a practical assessment of this system. In other words we have in mind only those consequences of unlimited free competition that *necessarily* stem from this form of economic organisation.

Both dialectical economists and economists who have used the precise techniques of mathematical analysis agree on the significance of unlimited free competition for the national economy. Thus, for example, Walras states:

> 'Production in a market ruled by free competition is an operation by which services can be combined and converted into products of such a nature and in such quantities as will give the greatest possible satisfaction of wants within the limits of the double condition, that each service and each product have only one price in the market, namely the price at which the quantity supplied equals the quantity demanded, and that the selling price of the products be equal to the cost of the services employed in making them' (Walras, p. 255 of the 1954 English edition; see pp. 256–7 for the significance of this statement for economic policy).

Auspitz and Lieben (*Untersuchungen*, 1889 *passim*) arrive at the same conclusions on the significance of unlimited free competition for ensuring the greatest 'general benefit' (*Gemeinnutzen*).

The only exception is Launhardt, who arrived at completely opposite conclusions concerning free competition. 'The result of the struggle over price depends entirely on the ability and perseverance of the various owners. The contention that the unimpeded operation of free competition, *laissez faire*, leads always to a solution favourable to the general wellbeing is, therefore, completely erroneous. . . .' 'Here only the proof was to be given, that the unimpeded action of free competition, *laissez faire*, satisfies neither the requirements of justice nor of general welfare' (Launhardt, 1885, pp. 43–4).

However, Launhardt's theory of competition suffers from the following major defects:

(1) it cannot be of *general* significance, since the main premises were arrived at on the basis of an analysis of *particular* (arbitrary) examples.

(2) it cannot have *any* immediate significance (without appropriate correction), since the particular form of the utility curve adopted by Launhardt $(y = f(x) = ax - a_1x^2)$ does not correspond to reality (see our Third Essay), while the conclusions obtained from the analysis refer to economic policy, which is concerned with actually existing phenomena.

(3) even if, after making the necessary corrections in Launhardt's analysis, the final conclusions remained unaltered, it would not be possible to accept that they demolished the opposite theory of the supporters of unlimited competition, since what Launhardt understands by 'unlimited free competition' in his research is something quite different from what all other economists understand by this term. This is already evident from the fact that Launhardt investigates the effect of free competition (in relation to total benefit) in instances of *isolated* exchange, i.e. exchange in which the parties are monopoly owners of two different commodities (see Sections 7, 8, 9 and 10; it is only from Section 11 onwards that he begins to examine instances of exchange between *many* owners, but his analysis of the effect of unlimited competition ends in Section 10). Clearly as a consequence of this his conclusions are quite different from those of other economists who have analysed the effect of genuine free competition, like Walras.

In addition, the actual *quantity of the commodity* in the possession of each of the two parties involved in the exchange is assumed to be a *given* quantity in Launhardt's analysis (and not a variable influenced by the economic calculation of the producers of these commodities), and it is assumed that both owners have received their commodity as a gift, *without expenditure* on their part (the analysis of production costs does not begin until Part 2 of *Die Gutererzeugung*, Section 19 and following). Therefore, what Launhardt understands by free competition is not at all what is usually understood, but merely 'freedom of exchange transactions', i.e. a situation in which the price of a commodity is determined by the free play of the opposite interests of seller and buyer irrespective of whether each of the parties involved in the exchange determines his price as a monopoly owner of this commodity or under the pressure of competition from other sellers or buyers of the same product.

5. SOME CONSEQUENCES OF THE UNEQUALLY FAVOURABLE SITUATION OF INDIVIDUAL ENTREPRENEURS

The main aim of this Second Essay is to show that the necessary production costs cannot be an *independent* regulator of the value of products in

5. The unequally favourable situation of individual entrepreneurs

Ricardo's third category (i.e. to products in the price of which *there is no rent*; we have already proved this proposition for commodities of the first two categories in the First Essay). Therefore we have naturally assumed systematically in the whole of the preceding analysis that all entrepreneurs competing in the market of a given commodity do so under equally favourable conditions for the production, storage and sale of that commodity. However, some of the conclusions we arrived at in proving this proposition are also important *in their own right*, as well as in their bearing on the *main* object of this essay. One of our conclusions is that *non-productive* costs incurred in sale, raising the equilibrium price above necessary costs, arise unavoidably under the influence of competition between entrepreneurs (under certain conditions). It is undoubtedly extremely important to establish whether this conclusion is *necessarily* related to the methodological assumption that all competitors are equally favourably situated, or whether, given a certain relationship between the use value of the product (its importance to consumers) and its necessary production costs (in other words the level of productivity of labour in the given industry), this category of costs is *a necessary result of free competition, irrespective of the assumption that competitors are equally favourably situated.* The establishment of price under conditions in which various categories of *differential income* may arise is a question relating to the *theory of rent*, which should form the independent subject of one of the later essays; since this problem lies essentially outside the framework of this essay, we shall deal with it only in so far as it is absolutely essential for answering the question formulated above. To begin with, since *we are not concerned* here *with a detailed analysis* of the form of the *additional costs* incurred in sale, *but only with the fundamental question of the relationship between this category of costs and the assumption that competing entrepreneurs are equally favourably situated,* we shall give to the general expression for costs incurred in sale $\gamma(Q-D)$ a special form which will *in fact incorporate almost all instances* of the formation of *non-productive costs.* Namely, if we replace the expression $v = \gamma(Q-D)$ by the special form $v = (Q-D)c$, where the coefficient c is some *finite* quantity *independent of the variables Q and D,* we shall cover by this form *all cases* where the cost of storage of the stock (for a *given* time) increases *in proportion* to the amount stored (which is in fact the case *in the overwhelming majority* of instances). For non-storeable commodities the coefficient c takes the value u, i.e. is equal to the necessary production costs of a unit of the product. Therefore, the formula $v = [(Q-D)c]/D$, in which c may assume any value provided that it is a *finite quantity independent of the variables Q* and D, *applies not only to storeable commodities, but also to commodities unsuitable for storage* (in which case $c = u$). By taking $\gamma(Q-D) = (Q-D)c$, we considerably simplify the analysis of equilibrium price. In this case the

151

total costs curve for a potential supply of OE (see Figure 2.8) becomes a *straight line* running from Z in such a way that the tangent of the angle formed by this line with the straight line OZ representing the necessary costs equals the coefficient c. Consequently the angle β formed by the straight line ZL with the horizontal axis is equal to the difference $(\vartheta - \alpha)$. By virtue of the general properties of the 'total costs line' this angle β should be greater than zero, but smaller than the angle ϑ. Therefore, the

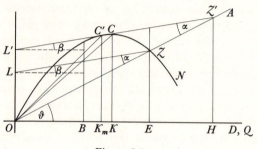

Figure 2.8

abscissa for which the vertical distance between the straight line LZ and the curve ON is greatest should be greater than the abscissa OB, but smaller than the abscissa OK; where the abscissa OB corresponds to the greatest vertical distance of the curve ON from the straight line OA, and the abscissa OK to the greatest vertical distance of the curve ON from the horizontal axis. Consequently *the best volume of sale for the owner of the stock OE will be the sale equal to the abscissa OK_m for which the vertical distance between the curve ON and the straight line LZ is greatest.* The price corresponding to this sale is equal to the tangent of $C'\hat{O}K$. If we now raise the total stock beyond OE, the straight line representing total costs will be successively shifted *upwards parallel to itself*, until at some output OH it becomes tangential to the curve ON. The line $L'Z'$ becomes tangential to the curve ON at the point C'. As long as *necessary production costs u and coefficient c*, i.e., the *conditions of storage, remain unchanged, the total costs line should form the same angle β with the horizontal axis* whatever its movements when the total stock is increased, since the angle β is still defined as $\beta = (\vartheta - \alpha)$. We now consider the case where the total stock Q is not concentrated in the hands of one owner, but is distributed between n separate entrepreneurs, so that each holds stocks of $q_1, q_2, q_3, \ldots, q_n$ units; and *the conditions of production and storage* of the products *are unequal for the separate entrepreneurs.* Let the *necessary costs be* respectively $u_1, u_2, u_3, \ldots, u_n$, and storage costs be $c_1, c_2, c_3, \ldots, c_n$; the net profit of each, $R_1, R_2, \ldots, R_n$ will correspondingly equal:

152

5. The unequally favourable situation of individual entrepreneurs

$$
\left.
\begin{aligned}
R_1 &= D_1 f(D) - D_1 u_1 - \frac{D_1(q_1 - D_1)c_1}{D_1} \\[2ex]
R_2 &= D_2 f(D) - D_2 u_2 - \frac{D_2(q_2 - D_2)c_2}{D_2} \\[1ex]
&\vdots \\[1ex]
R_n &= D_n f(D) - D_n u_n - \frac{D_n(q_n - D_n)c_n}{D_n}
\end{aligned}
\right\} \tag{101}
$$

and, if $q_1 = Q/m_1$; $q_2 = Q/m_2$; ...; $q_n = Q/m_n$, and consequently, as we still assume that *the probability of sale is the same for all,* $D_1 = D/m_1$; $D_2 = D/m_2$; ...; $D_n = D/m_n$ we obtain

$$
\left.
\begin{aligned}
R_1 &= \frac{1}{m_1}\left[D \cdot f(D) - D u_1 - \frac{D(Q - D)c_1}{D} \right] \\[2ex]
R_2 &= \frac{1}{m_2}\left[D \cdot f(D) - D u_2 - \frac{D(Q - D)c_2}{D} \right] \\[1ex]
&\vdots \\[1ex]
R_n &= \frac{1}{m_n}\left[D \cdot f(D) - D u_n - \frac{D(Q - D)c_n}{D} \right]
\end{aligned}
\right\} \tag{102}
$$

and $R_1, R_2, \ldots, R_n$ become greatest at the volume of D defined by the conditions:

$$
\left.
\begin{aligned}
d\left\{ \frac{1}{m_1}\left[D \cdot f(D) - D u_1 - \frac{D(Q - D)c_1}{D} \right] \right\} &= 0 \\[2ex]
d\left\{ \frac{1}{m_2}\left[D \cdot f(D) - D u_2 - \frac{D(Q - D)c_2}{D} \right] \right\} &= 0
\end{aligned}
\right\} \tag{103}
$$

and so on.

The roots of equations (103) will be denoted as $D_I, D_{II}, \ldots, D_N$, and the corresponding price levels will be denoted as $p_I, p_{II}, \ldots, p_N$.

Suppose $D_I > D_{II} > D_{III} > \cdots > D_N$, so that $p_I < p_{II} < p_{III} < \cdots < p_N$. Whatever price p greater than p_N is established in the market some entrepreneurs will be compelled by their self interest to call a price below p. Since two prices cannot exist for the same commodity in the same market, the other entrepreneurs (whose interest would be to establish a price greater than p) will have to accept this price. Therefore, equilibrium *will be established* in the market *only at the price* p_N, since only

153

at this price *there will be no advantage for any entrepreneur in lowering the price further.*

The meaning of the equation for N from which the equilibrium price p_N is determined is expressed by the following law. *When the production and storage conditions of the products* (i.e., *coefficients u and c*) *are not the same* for individual competing entrepreneurs, *the total volume of sale and the price will be established at the same level which would be decided by a monopoly owner of production Q placed under the same conditions of production and storage of the commodity as the competitor to whom it seems advantageous to lower the price of the product further than is done by the other entrepreneurs.* Therefore, when the situation of individual entrepreneurs *is not equally favourable,* for *additional non-productive costs* to occur in the given industry *it is sufficient that the necessary production costs of a unit of the given commodity* should be lower for the entrepreneur to whom it seems advantageous to lower the market price below the price which maximises total gross revenue under the given conditions of demand (i.e. consumption). Consequently, for non-productive additional costs to occur, in the example above it is sufficient that the necessary production costs of a unit of the product should be less for the nth entrepreneur than the price p_{max} determined from the equation:

$$\frac{d[F(p) \cdot p]}{dp} = 0. \tag{104}$$

Provided u_n is less than the root of this equation, the total costs to be covered by gross revenue *should inevitably include the non-productive additional costs* resulting from the inequality between potential and actual supply.

If the necessary costs of the nth entrepreneur are $u_n < p_{max}$, while the necessary costs of all the other entrepreneurs are greater than or equal to p_{max}, non-productive additional costs will be incorporated only in the costs of *the nth enterprise.* However, if condition $u < p_{max}$ holds for the other entrepreneurs, the additional costs must necessarily be included in the costs of *each entrepreneur.* Therefore, *for additional costs to be a usual phenomenon it is sufficient that the average costs necessary* in a given state of technology *should be less than p_{max}.* In other words, they should be less than the price at which the greatest sum is taken from consumers, given the importance of the need the given product satisfies. *The more important is the need* the product satisfies (and, consequently, the more difficult it is for consumers to make do without this product completely or in part when it becomes dearer), and *the more advanced is the technique* of its manufacture (in other words, the higher is the productivity of labour in this industry), *the greater,* naturally, is the *probability* that *non-productive costs* for the storage of speculative stocks (i.e. stocks exceeding the reserve objectively needed for the regular supply of the market) will be a *usual* phenomenon in the given industry. In the present state of technology the condition that average necessary production costs should be less than p_{max} undoubtedly holds *in all the most important and extensive branches of industry*, i.e. in the production of the overwhelming majority of *prime necessities* intended for mass consumption. Considering a *specific case*, we have to decide whether a monopoly *producer* who obtained the whole of the given product *free of charge* would set a price *higher* than the level prevailing under *unlimited free competition*; if the answer, based on the available trading statistics, is *affirmative*, this proves that the *necessary production costs are already below the price* p_{max} in the given state of technology.

We have concluded above that the equilibrium price established in the market for a given potential supply Q, distributed between entrepreneurs who are not *equally favourably* situated, will equal the price which would be set by a *monopoly owner* of the entire stock operating under the same conditions of production and storage of the nth *entrepreneur* for whom it was most advantageous to lower the market price. Therefore it is very important to consider how *changes in the conditions of production and storage* of a product, at a given constant volume of potential supply, affect the price set by a monopolist (motivated by the desire for the greatest advantage).

From Figure 2.8 we can see that the smaller is the angle β between the total costs line and the horizontal axis, the farther to the right on the curve ON (reckoning from the point O) will be the point at which the vertical distance between this curve and the total costs line is greatest (since at that point the tangent to the curve ON should be parallel to the straight line representing total costs). Consequently, the lower will be the price at which a monopoly owner of the stock would obtain the greatest net profit (which equals the tangent of the angle formed with the horizontal axis by a straight line drawn to the origin from this point, at which the vertical distance between the curve ON and the total costs line is greatest). However, since $\beta = (\vartheta - \alpha)$, this angle will be greater, the greater is the angle ϑ, whose tangent equals u, and the smaller is the angle α, whose tangent equals the coefficient c.* Therefore, the *price which secures a monopoly owner of a given stock the greatest net profit will be higher, the higher are the*

---

* *Ed. note.* It appears that the coefficient c should be equal not to tan α, but to tan α', where tan $\alpha' = (\tan \vartheta - \tan \beta)$. In fact the correct sequence of steps for the construction of the figure should be the following: take an angle α', such that tan $\alpha' = c$ (i.e. unit storage costs which are known); find the angle β for which the relation is satisfied tan $\beta = (\tan \vartheta - \tan \alpha')$; we then have $\alpha = \vartheta - \beta$, where α is the same as in Figure 2.8 and satisfies the condition postulated by Dmitriev $\beta = \vartheta - \alpha$. Therefore in general tan $\alpha \neq c$, and the meaning of α in the figure and the way it is arrived at should be modified. Dmitriev's subsequent argument also has to be slightly modified, but since α varies directly with α', the substance of Dmitriev's argument still holds.

155

necessary production costs u and the lower are storage costs c. Evidently from the equality $\beta = (\vartheta - \alpha)$, if u and c are raised by the same amount, the price which secures a monopolist the greatest profit will remain unaltered.

An interesting practical conclusion follows from this: since in practice the *main elements* of storage costs are *insurance premia* (to cover possible loss or deterioration of the product) and *interest on the capital* invested in speculative stocks, *storage costs are approximately proportional to the original value of the product stored* (i.e. to the necessary costs of its production in the narrow sense). Therefore, the lower are necessary production costs of the product for a given entrepreneur, the lower, *caeteris paribus*, his storage costs for this product per time period. *This reduces the significance of a difference in the situation of individual entrepreneurs in relation to production and sale.*[1] Finally, the unequally favourable situation of individual entrepreneurs *in relation to sale*, given our previous assumption that $\gamma(Q - D) = (Q - D)c$, *cannot have any effect on price determination* for a given potential supply (as may readily be established by altering the expressions for the net profit of individual entrepreneurs according to the assumption that the probability of sale of a unit of the commodity is not the same for each of them).

We cannot give a complete analysis of the laws governing price determination when individual units of a product are produced and sold under unequal conditions until (in one of the later essays) we have given a *full* account of the theory of rent (since Ricardo's theory analysed in the First Essay does not deal with the question in its entirety). At present we can analyse the determination of 'equilibrium price' merely for cases involving only the simplest form of rent, whose laws were studied by Ricardo.

Ricardo restricted his study to the rent arising from inequality in the necessary production costs of individual units (or batches) of the same commodity *by imposing the condition that at each given moment the quantity produced equals the quantity sold* (with a difference not exceeding the 'necessary' stocks which have to be kept because of the natural difference in the periods of consumption and production; as we have already noted above, the storage costs of such stocks should be charged to the *necessary* production costs).

Therefore, the rent *examined by Ricardo*[2] can in fact occur *in a capitalist system only if industrial capital* (in the narrow sense, i.e. capital devoted exclusively to the *production* of a product) and *trade capital* are completely separated. In this case, the price at which a product will be transferred

---

[1] Remember that we are at present exclusively concerned with price determination for a *given* potential supply; the complete solution of the problem of *equilibrium price* when the situation of individual entrepreneurs is not equally favourable is the object of a full theory of rent.

[2] As we have already pointed out in the First Essay, Ricardo's theory of rent is not confined to the case of land rent and rent from mines: he uses these two special cases only as examples to clarify the *general laws of rent*.

from the capitalist producers (who do not hold any speculative stocks) to the capitalist merchants, who are the middle men between the producer of the commodity and its consumer, will in fact be regulated by the law of price established by Ricardo for products yielding rent; in this case the price will equal the necessary costs of the last unit of the product to be produced. However, in this case the price at which the product will be transferred to its *direct consumers* will not be equal to the necessary costs of the last unit to be produced (or, if the necessary stocks are in the hands of capitalist merchants, these necessary costs + the cost of storing the necessary stocks).

As we have done earlier, in Figure 2.9 we measure the quantities produced along the abscissae and the production cost of these quantities by the corresponding ordinates. Then, if the product considered is such that necessary production costs per unit increase as the total quantity produced increases, we shall obtain (see Figure 2.9) an ascending curve

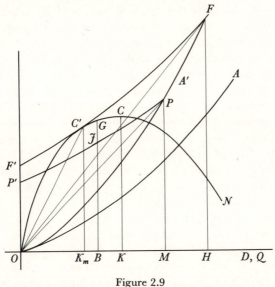

Figure 2.9

OA, the *Kostenkurve* of Auspitz and Lieben, which we know from the First Essay. By applying the methods of the previous Essay we obtain from this original curve a derived curve OA', the *Angebotskurve* of Auspitz and Lieben, whose ordinates express the amounts (in the same unit in which production costs are expressed) which merchant capitalists should pay to induce capitalist producers to supply (in the wholesale market) the quantities of produce expressed by the corresponding abscissae. Suppose the total quantity produced is equal to OM; the total sum paid by the

157

merchant capitalists for OM units is equal to MP, and unit cost of the product for the merchant capitalists is equal to tan $P\hat{O}M$.

Since all the *merchant* capitalists obtain the product at the same price, the price at which they will find it most advantageous to dispose of their stocks will be determined by principles we have already analysed above. In this case the price at which the product is sold to consumers is equal to the tangent of the angle $G\hat{O}M$ formed with the horizontal axis by a straight line drawn from the origin through the point G, corresponding to the greatest vertical distance between the curve ON and the 'total costs curve' PP' (whose ordinates express costs which should be recouped in the price of quantity sold for an available stock equal to OM and a sale equal to the corresponding abscissa OB). Since the greatest vertical distance of curve ON and PP' (equal to the segment GJ) is greater than zero for the total volume of stocks OM we have assumed, the self interest of entrepreneurs will compel them to continue to expand stocks beyond OM, in pursuit of 'temporary benefit'. With a proof analogous to those above we can easily show that equilibrium will be established in the sphere of production and sale only when the *quantity produced* (equal to the quantity bought by the merchant capitalists, since we have assumed that producers do not themselves build up speculative trading stocks) is fixed at some quantity OH at which the 'total costs curve' FF' is *tangential* to the 'revenue curve' ON, and the *volume of sale* is established at a quantity OK_m equal to the abscissa of the point of tangency C'. The price at which the *merchant* capitalists will sell their stocks is equal to the tangent of the angle formed with the horizontal axis by a straight line drawn from the origin through the point C' of tangency of the curves ON and FF'. It is evident from the construction that the total sum payable by consumers at this 'equilibrium price' for quantity OK_m is equal to the segment $C'K_m$; the amount needed from this total sum to cover expenditure *actually* incurred by the producers of OK_m units of the product is equal to the segment K_m; the sum needed to cover the rent of capitalist producers will be equal to IL; and finally the remainder of gross revenue equal to segment LC' will cover 'costs incurred in sale', i.e. non-productive expenditures resulting from the struggle of entrepreneurs competing for sales.

From Figure 2.10 it is readily seen that the 'equilibrium price' of products in the second category can equal the '*necessary production costs*' *of the last unit to be produced* only if necessary production costs of the last unit of the total quantity produced OK, equal to the quantity yielding the greatest possible gross revenue under given market conditions, is greater than the price at which this quantity OK can be sold.[1] In this

---

[1] This conclusion stems from the basic properties of the 'total costs curve'.

case the 'production cost' curve and the derived 'supply curve' assume a position similar to that of OA and OA' in Figure 2.10.

Even in this case, however, the market price only *may equal* necessary production costs *but definitely need not do so invariably*; whether it does depends on the particular form of the 'total costs curve', depending in turn on the particular properties of the product, the interest rate, technical conditions of storage and other factors. If the 'total costs' curve for a stock equal to OE passes *outside the curve* ON (i.e. does not intersect it), as is

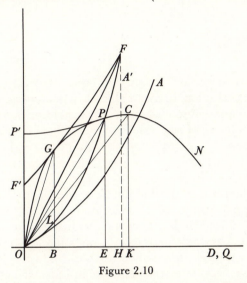

Figure 2.10

shown by the line PP', the market price of the commodity will exactly equal the necessary costs of the last unit to be produced, i.e. tan $P\hat{O}E$. If storage conditions (in the broad sense) of the product are more favourable, so that the total costs curve for a stock OE *intersects* the curve ON, the total volume of stocks will be expanded beyond OE, and the volume of sale will be established at some level OB less than the new volume of total stocks OH. Consequently, costs incurred in sale will no longer be zero and price will no longer equal necessary costs of the last unit to be produced. In this case necessary costs of the last unit produced will be equal to tan $F\hat{O}H$, as is clear from Figure 2.10; and the price at which the commodity will be sold to consumers will be equal to tan $G\hat{O}B$; the total amount of 'costs incurred in sale' paid by consumers will be expressed by the segment GL.

Therefore, *for non-productive costs to arise in sale when rent in the Ricardian sense exists, it is sufficient that the necessary costs of the last unit out of a total output equal to the supply yielding the greatest gross revenue should be less than the price at which this quantity yielding the greatest gross revenue may be sold.* If $\phi(x)$

159

is the equation of the 'production cost curve', and $Y(X)$ is the equation of the 'demand curve' (gross revenue), for the possibility that non-productive costs arise in sale it will be sufficient that *for the quantity X satisfying the condition*:

$$\frac{\mathrm{d}Y(X)}{\mathrm{d}X} = 0 \qquad (105)$$

we should have:

$$\frac{\mathrm{d}\phi(X)}{\mathrm{d}X} < \frac{Y(X)}{X}. \qquad (106)$$

In our analysis 'necessary production costs' may naturally be understood in the broadest sense, to mean all cost in general falling on a unit of product between the commencement of production and its transfer to direct consumers, *provided only that these costs are not a function of sale*, i.e. provided they depend *exclusively* on the quantity produced. Therefore, our conclusion applies both to the case where there is a difference in production conditions in the strict sense, and where the difference is in the distance of the place of production from the place of sale.[1]

Therefore, the price may equal the necessary production costs of the last unit (the unit produced under the worst conditions), just as price may in general equal necessary production costs, only at a low level of technique, and this equality should inevitably cease with industrial progress. However, even at the very lowest level of technique we may nevertheless always raise the price of a product above necessary production costs when unlimited free competition prevails by approximately modifying the conditions of demand. In fact, as we have just shown, the price *may equal* the necessary costs of the last unit to be produced only until the 'supply curve' OA' intersects the 'revenue curve' ON to the left of the point where the vertical distance between the curve ON and the horizontal axis is greatest; but, by arbitrarily modifying the form of the curve ON (by correspondingly modifying the *demand* conditions) we may always make it intersect the curve OA' *to the right* of the point where the vertical distance between ON and horizontal axis is greatest, *whatever the form of OA and its derivative OA'* (and whatever the storage conditions of the product).

We shall return to examine more complicated instances of the equilibrium price determination of products with rent as part of their price in

---

[1] The analytical method and its ultimate conclusions will naturally remain completely the same whether these additional costs incurred in sale, resulting from unequal situations in the market, are borne by the capitalist producer, or carried over by a corresponding reduction in the wholesale price to the merchant capitalist.

one of the later essays, after analysing the cases of rent which Ricardo and later economists failed to examine, where inequality of conditions concerns costs which are a *function of the volume of sale as well as the volume of production.*

6. COMPLICATIONS RAISED BY THE ASSUMPTION THAT POTENTIAL AND ACTUAL PRODUCTION OF ENTERPRISES ARE INDEPENDENT VARIABLES

We have assumed so far that the potential production of each enterprise exactly equals its actual production at each given time; in other words, that the quantity actually produced per period always equals the greatest quantity which can in general be produced by a given enterprise in the same period. However, this assumption would be justified only if it had been proved that the full utilisation of an enterprise's capacity is *always most advantageous* to the entrepreneur. This hypothesis cannot be proved since it is contradicted by both theoretical considerations and direct observation of reality. Let the greatest possible production of an enterprise equal H units per time unit. Initially we assume that the enterprise is in the hands of a monopolist; what quantity will he actually produce when motivated by the pursuit of the greatest advantage? To simplify the question, let us assume that in a given industry there is complete separation of trading and productive functions, so that the producer does not have any trade capital and works not to stock but exclusively to order (since speculation in stocks requires trade capital as well as industrial capital, and, in addition, a knowledge of the state of the world market, which is something not normally possessed to a sufficient degree by entrepreneurs exclusively specialised in the productive function).

This assumption will simplify our analysis. At a price p, let the sale of our entrepreneur equal D, and gross revenue pD. Since $D = F(p)$, then also $pD = \psi(D)$. Let the volume of sale be D and the gross revenue Y; in that case $Y = \psi(D)$. We construct a curve ON corresponding to this equation; this is the 'revenue curve' with which we are already familiar. Suppose the segment OH (Figure 2.11) correspond to H units, i.e. to the greatest quantity which the given enterprise can produce. In that case, if unit production costs when the enterprise is in *full operation* equal $\tan \vartheta$, the costs of OH units will equal HP. But since the gross proceeds for OH units equal only $HW < HP$, full capacity utilisation will entail a loss correspondingly equal to the segment WP.

Suppose our entrepreneur, while leaving the *potential* output of his enterprise unaltered, begins to contract *actual* output from OH to zero. It can be seen clearly that the *total production costs* for the total quantity produced *will not decrease in proportion* to this quantity, *but more slowly*, so that if this happens *the costs chargeable to each unit* produced *will increase* continuously. Therefore production costs of quantities smaller than *OH* will be expressed not by the corresponding ordinates of the straight line *OP* (as would have been the case if the size of the entire enterprise, i.e. its production capacity, had been reduced correspondingly to the reduction in the quantity produced), but by the ordinates of the line *P'P* corresponding to some equation $\Theta(Q)$. This curve should satisfy the main condition that the tangent of the angle formed with the horizontal axis by a straight line drawn from any point on this curve should be greater than the tangent of the angles formed with the horizontal axis by straight lines from all the points lying *to the right* of the given point. The second condition which the curve *PP'* should satisfy is that a greater ordinate should correspond to each greater abscissa (which is algebraically expressed by the condition $d\Theta(Q)/dQ > 0$).

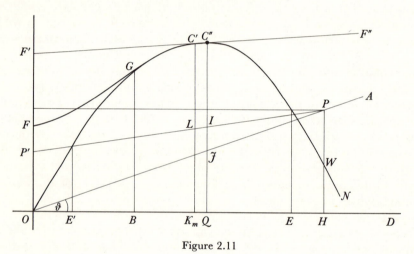

Figure 2.11

This requirement stems from the fact that *in each enterprise* (whatever the ratio of constant capital to circulating capital in it) there are *invariably* certain *costs which fall as its actual production falls* (for an unchanged potential production). Therefore, the *line PP'*, unlike the 'total costs' curve previously analysed, *can never become a horizontal straight line*.

Thus when production per time unit is reduced from *OH* to zero, net profit will initially increase; for a volume of output equal to *OE* net income will be zero; for all quantities between *OH* and *OE* it will be negative, although absolutely smaller than the loss *PW* corresponding to full capacity utilisation. For quantities smaller than *OE* but greater than *OE'*, profit will be greater than zero, and it will be greatest for some quantity OK_m corresponding to the greatest vertical distance between the curves ON and PP'[1] (represented graphically by the fact that the tangents to the curves ON and PP' at the points C' and L are parallel). This volume of production OK_m should be selected by a monopolist entrepreneur acting in the pursuit of his greatest advantage. Clearly this volume OK_m is far less than the *potential* output of the enterprise (by the segment K_mH). Now suppose the industry considered is operating under free competition. Let the number of competitors be n; the potential output of *each* enterprise will be $a_1, a_2, a_3, \ldots, a_n$ units. Let the *total* potential production of n competing enterprises remain H units. What will be the level of actual output established through each separate competitor seeking the greatest individual advantage?

Using the methods above it is easy to show that in this case the volume of actual output will also equal OK_m, i.e. will be the same as if monopoly prevailed in the industry concerned. In fact we have seen that with any increase of actual output beyond OK_m the *total* net profit is *reduced*; therefore an increase of output beyond OK_m may be advantageous to an *individual* producer only if his proportion of the total net profit is thereby *increased* to such an extent that his partial profit is raised despite the reduction in the total. This kind of phenomenon occurred when we assumed, purely for methodological reasons, that actual output was invariably equal to the potential production of enterprises, and consequently that *an expansion of production was impossible without a* corresponding *expansion of enterprises*, which, as we have noted, *invariably requires a considerable time to elapse*. However, this kind of phenomenon will no longer be possible with the different assumptions which we have now made.

In fact, when enterprises *operate below capacity* (as follows from the condition $OK_m < OH$) *production can expand within the capacity limits of enterprises* so rapidly that the first entrepreneur to expand his output (in the hope of immediate profit) will *immediately* be caught up by the reaction from other entrepreneurs (also seeking to achieve the most advantageous volume of production for themselves), who will correspondingly expand their own partial outputs. Consequently the time *during which he will enjoy the 'temporary profit' will vanish* or, at least, will so nearly vanish that the *total* 'temporary profit' which he can expect will be insufficient to prompt him to disturb the existing equilibrium. (A disturbance always entails a risk, so that total immediate profit should always exceed some finite quantity, and should at least equal the insurance premium to cover the risk entailed in the pursuit of market advantage.) When each of the competitors is capable of immediate expansion of output and when their situation in the market is equally favourable the total sale will be distributed between them *at each given*

[1] Within limits defined by the requirement that the difference of the ordinates of the curves ON and PP' should be $\geqslant 0$.

moment in proportion to the productive capacity (= potential output) of their enterprises. If the total sale is denoted by D, we have for partial sales:

$$\frac{Da_1}{H}, \frac{Da_2}{H}, \frac{Da_3}{H}, \ldots, \frac{Da_n}{H}. \tag{107}$$

Due to the uniqueness of market price, we obtain for partial gross revenues:

$$\frac{Dpa_1}{H}, \frac{Dpa_2}{H}, \frac{Dpa_3}{H}, \ldots, \frac{Dpa_n}{H} \tag{108}$$

and for partial net profits we have:

$$\frac{Dpa_1}{H} - \frac{Da_1u}{H}; \quad \frac{Dpa_2}{H} - \frac{Da_2u}{H}; \quad \ldots; \quad \frac{Dpa_nu}{H} - \frac{Da_nu}{H} \tag{109}$$

where u is understood as the actual production costs of each unit sold (i.e. the costs corresponding to the *given* level of operation of the enterprise). But clearly since the *technical* situation of the enterprises is the same (i.e. their *necessary production costs* are identical), *these costs will be the same for all the competing entrepreneurs, since they depend on the ratio between potential and actual production of the enterprise, and this ratio* (under conditions excluding the occurrence of rent) *will be* consistently *the same* (at all values of the variable D) *for all the entrepreneurs.*

If we compare the expressions we derived:

$$\frac{a_1}{H}(Dp - Du); \quad \frac{a_2}{H}(Dp - Du); \quad \ldots; \quad \frac{a_n}{H}(Dp - Du) \tag{110}$$

with the expression for the net income of a monopolist:

$$Dp - Du \tag{111}$$

we see the magnitude of the variable D maximising expression (111) will be equal[1] to the magnitude maximising expression (110).

Consequently, when the potential production of enterprises remains unaltered, the volume of actual output will be determined in exactly the same way regardless of whether the whole industry is in the hands of a monopolist or unrestricted free competition prevails (unrestricted since no limitations are imposed on n). But we have already shown above that it may be advantageous to a monopolist to fix his actual output at a much lower level than the potential production of his enterprise. We now see that this will also hold for any number of competing entrepreneurs. The

---

[1] Since $\mathrm{d}[a_1(Dp - Du)/H] = \mathrm{d}[a_1(Dp - Du)/H] = \cdots = \mathrm{d}(Dp - Du)$.

level at which the volume of actual output will in fact be established for a *given* volume of production capacity of the industry is question of fact and is dependent on the form of the 'revenue curve' ON and the 'total production costs curve' PP'. When the *necessary*[1] production costs are very large the 'total production costs curve' may follow the course indicated in Figure 2.11 by the line FG. With the curve in this position the most advantageous volume of actual output will be OB, corresponding to *full* operation of the enterprise. However, this will be merely a temporary phenonon corresponding to a low level of industrial technique.

Consequently, for each given period for which the size of enterprises may be taken to be constant (since the size of enterprises may alter only after a considerable time has elapsed), the volume of operation will be continuously determined in such a way that the difference $(D \cdot p - D \cdot u)$ will be greatest.

If in this difference we express p as a function of D we have

$$DF(D) - Du. \tag{112}$$

The quantity u is in its turn a function of D, so that the entire expression becomes

$$Df(D) - D \cdot \Theta(D). \tag{113}$$

This expression does not contain the quantity H, but only because we have hitherto assumed it to be a constant and therefore discarded it in the expression $u = \Theta(D,H)$.

However, for longer time intervals the productive capacity H of an enterprise is itself a variable and conforms with the entrepreneurs' tendency to pursue the greatest advantage. We now apply precisely the same reasoning as before when considering 'potential supply'. When monopoly prevails, the equilibrium level of H ultimately will be determined so as to yield the greatest net profit when the enterprise is fully utilised (i.e. when $D = H$); whereas when unlimited free competition prevails H will increase (because of entrepreneurs striving to pursue 'temporary benefit') until the curve showing the behaviour of total costs when the volume of actual output is reduced from the productive capacity of the enterprise to zero becomes tangential to the 'revenue curve', as shown in Figure 2.11 by line $F'C''F''$. At *any smaller* productive capacity of the enterprise the 'total costs curve' should inevitably intersect the 'revenue curve' and, consequently, the industry considered will still yield a *total net profit greater than zero* at the most advantageous actual output volume (= actual supply). This net profit will equal the greatest distance between the 'total costs curve' and the 'revenue curve'. However, under such conditions each individual entrepreneur will still

---

[1] I.e. the costs incurred by the operation of enterprises at full capacity.

have the incentive to expand the productive capacity of *his own* enterprise to increase *his own share in total profits* temporarily, until there is a reaction from other competitors. *When the number of competitors is sufficiently large* the expansion of one enterprise by a finite number of times cannot have any perceptible effect on *total profit*, and therefore for an entrepreneur who succeeds in expanding the production capacity of his enterprise earlier than the others *the increase in his share of total profit will amount to an increase in his individual profit*. Consequently equilibrium may be established only when the production capacity of the industry is such that the 'total costs' curve assumes the position $F'C''F''$ in Figure 2.11.

The volume of actual output when this happens will equal the abscissa OQ corresponding to the point of tangency of the curves ON and $F'C''F''$, since at this volume of actual output entrepreneurs will receive the greatest possible profit for the given (joint) size of the enterprises. Equilibrium is algebraically expressed by the set of conditions:

$$Df(D) - D \cdot \Theta(D, H) = 0 \tag{114}$$

$$\frac{\mathrm{d}[Df(D) - D\Theta(D, H)]}{\mathrm{d}D} = 0 \tag{115}$$

which is completely analogous to those derived above for the case where the *variables* were actual supply D and the potential supply S (Section 3). The difference is that additional expenses filling the gap between necessary production costs OJ and gross revenue QC''' will not come from costs incurred in the storage of non-productive stocks, but from *the operation of enterprises below capacity*.

From the viewpoint of the national economy this result of free competition is in no way better than the accumulation of non-productive stocks and is one further proof of how incorrect is the assertion of the Classical school that free competition ensures the greatest productivity of the resources of a country (see the Appendix to Section 4).

To simplify the analysis we assumed above that producers of a given product had no trading capital and therefore were unable to produce for stock (working only for a previously ensured sale). If we now assume that producers also combine trading functions in the same corporate body, they will find themselves in a dilemma in each given instance in determining the most advantageous relationship between size of enterprise and volume of sale: should they contract actual output to the volume of sale, and thus be satisfied with the operation of the enterprise below capacity, or should they operate the enterprise fully, reaching the limits of supply (to the most advantageous quantity) by building up stocks (which naturally accumulate whenever the sales per period become less than the output of the same period). Each producer-merchant, seeking the greatest advantage, will select the method of limiting supply ensuring him the greatest net profit. Finally, there will possibly be cases where it will be more advantageous, up to a certain limit, for him to contract production itself and thereafter leave it contracted, and continue the further restriction of supply to the most advantageous volume by slowing down the sale of the quantity actually produced, thus building up non-productive stocks or *vice versa*. *In these latter cases non-productive expenditure* filling the gap between the equilibrium price of the product and necessary production costs *will be formed, simultaneously, of storage expenditure* in the broad sense *and of additional costs due to the operation of the enterprise below capacity*. How the situation will develop in each case is a question of fact and a solution of the problem will not be difficult once given the 'revenue curve' and the 'total costs curve'. In this case the methodology will be the same as above, except that the number of variables incorporated in the net profit expression to be maximised will be greater.

A detailed examination of the various cases concerned will not be made here, since a *general* analysis of these cases does not reach any significant conclusions.

APPENDIX TO SECTION 6

It is evident from this analysis, *inter alia*, that non-productive costs arising from the struggle of competing entrepreneurs for sales, when unlimited free competition prevails, would also continue to exist when all the middle men, through whose hands a commodity passes before reaching the consumers, disappear (hence the pointlessness of consumer societies as a *general* measure). *In fact, even when the commodity is directly transferred from producers to consumers it will still remain possible for non-productive costs to occur* (under the influence of competition between producers) *arising from operation of the enterprises below capacity*. Therefore, even in such a hypothetical state of affairs (to which the proponents of consumers' associations aspire as to an ideal) *the consumers will nevertheless continue to pay in the price of a commodity a sum greater than its necessary production costs*. The occurrence of non-productive costs will become impossible only when consumer and producer *merge in the same person* (even if a corporate body), i.e., in other words, *when an exchange economy is once again converted into a natural economy*. While an exchange economy (which we are only just beginning to analyse) continues to exist and unlimited free competition prevails, the consumer will invariably pay in the price of the product a series of non-productive costs, which are a net loss to the national economy as a whole, in addition to necessary production costs.

7. THE ECONOMIC CONSEQUENCES OF TECHNICAL PROGRESS

Up to now we have assumed necessary production costs to be constant. Let us now assume that the necessary production costs per unit of product vary from the level $u_m = \tan C\hat{O}K$ (see Figure 2.12) to some level $u_0 = \tan \vartheta_0$, where ϑ_0 is an arbitrarily small quantity but greater than zero. If we also assume for the sake of simplicity that the commodity is not storable, in equilibrium the additional costs of the quantity sold will vary from zero to some finite quantity, less than that expressed by the segment CK by some arbitrarily small amount. At each given time these additional costs will be equal to the distance of the point C from the point where the straight line CK intersects the line of necessary production costs. The smaller is the tangent of the angle formed by this line with the horizontal axis, the closer the point at which it intersects CK will move to the point K and, consequently, the greater will be the sum of additional [i.e. sales] costs falling on the quantity sold.[1]

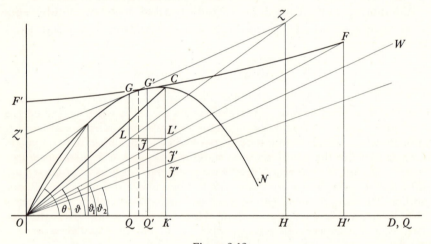

Figure 2.12

The *sum* of the additional expenditure is proportional not only to the *quantity* of dead stocks but also to their *value*; hence when necessary production costs tend to the limit zero, for the additional expenditure to tend to the limit RK, which equals some finite quantity, the quantity of dead stocks should tend to become *infinitely large*.

Therefore, if we denote the quantity of reserve stocks by S and the necessary production costs of a unit of the product by u, we shall have $S = S(u)$, and $S(u)$ will be a *continuously decreasing function* of u within the

---

[1] Clearly when the necessary production costs per unit of product are *exactly zero*, the sales costs falling on the quantity sold will also be zero, whatever the ratio of the volume of sale to the volume of available stocks of the commodity.

limits of variation of u from some finite quantity at which costs incurred in sale first arise to a quantity arbitrarily close to zero. Clearly $S(u)$ will satisfy the same basic property as we derived above for this relation not only for non-storable commodities but, in general, for any commodity.

Suppose the original level of necessary production costs of a unit of the product equals $\tan \theta$ (see Figure 2.12); at this level of necessary production costs equilibrium will be established, in accordance with the general principles previously established, at some total production level OH for which the 'total costs curve' ZZ' (i.e. a curve showing the behaviour of costs on the quantity sold when sales alter from the total quantity produced OH to zero) will be tangential to the curve ON. The equilibrium volume of sale will be equal to OQ, which is the abscissa corresponding to the tangency point G of the curve ON and the curve ZZ'.

In this case additional sales costs will equal the quantity LG. Construct a horizontal straight line from L to the intersection with CK (the ordinate corresponding to the greatest vertical distance of the curve ON from the horizontal axis) and construct a straight line through the point of intersection L' from O; this straight line will form a new angle ϑ with the horizontal axis which will be less than the angle θ by some finite quantity.

Assume that, as a result of technical progress, necessary production costs have fallen from the level equal to $\tan \theta$ to the level equal to $\tan \vartheta$. *At this new level of necessary production costs equilibrium will be established at some* new volume of total production OH' for which the 'total costs curve' FF' will be tangential to ON. The tangency point G' of this new 'total costs curve' for the new level of necessary production costs and of total production, will lie somewhere between the point C of greatest vertical distance of the curve ON from the horizontal axis and the point T, where the vertical distance of the curve ON from the straight line OF is greatest. This tangency point G' of the 'total costs curve' cannot lie *to the right* of C, because of the general properties of this curve regardless of its particular form, as we have already shown. Also, it cannot lie *to the left* of point G; in fact, suppose the equation of the curve ON is $Y = \psi(X)$, that of the curve FF' is $Y = \zeta(X)$, and that of the straight line OF is $Y = \varphi(X)$; in that case, by virtue of the basic properties of the curve FF' we shall have $d\zeta(X)/dX < d\varphi(X)/dX$; therefore, for the abscissa for which $d\zeta(X)/dX = d\psi(X)/dX$ we invariably have $d\psi(X)/dX < d\varphi(X)/dX$, and since the derivative $d\psi(X)/dX$ is a decreasing function of X, it is clear that if the condition $d\zeta(X)/dX = d\psi(X)/dX$ holds for some X_a, the equality $d\varphi(X)/dX = d\psi(X)/dX$ will hold for some value of the variable $X_b < X_a$.

If the tangency point occurred at the point C, the sum of the additional

169

sales costs would be $= CL'$ (as is shown in the figure). If the tangency point occurs to the left of C, the vertical distance of the straight line OF from the curve OD, expressing additional sales costs, will *invariably be greater* than GL, but by virtue of the property of the curve ON the segment CL' should invariably be greater than the segment GL. Consequently, wherever the new tangency point occurs (defining the volume of sale at the new level of necessary production costs $= \tan \vartheta$), the additional sales costs of the quantity sold will invariably be greater than the additional sales costs of the quantity sold earlier at the higher level of necessary costs $= \tan \theta$. When necessary production costs alter from $u = \tan Z\hat{O}H$ to $u_1 = F\hat{O}H'$ whatever the particular form of the curves ZZ' and FF' additional sales costs should inevitably increase *at least by an amount equal to* $CL' - GL$. Suppose that, when necessary production costs are u_1, the total costs curve is tangential to the curve ON at some point G'; draw a horizontal straight line from the point J to the intersection with KC and a new straight line OW from O through the point of intersection J'. We indicate the tangent of the angle $W\hat{O}H$ as u_2; if we assume necessary production costs to equal u_2 and argue as before, when necessary production costs decrease from the level u_1 to the new level u_2 additional sales costs will again increase *at least by the amount* $(CJ' - G'J)$; if we continued to reduce necessary costs by *equal amounts*, so that $(u - u_1) = (u_1 - u_2) = (u_2 - u_3)$ and so on, the least quantities by which additional sales expenditure should increase would be found to be greater than those obtained above; thus, if we took $u_2 = \tan \vartheta_1$, where ϑ_1 satisfies the condition $(\theta - \vartheta) = (\vartheta - \vartheta_1)$ [and $u_3 = \tan \vartheta_2$], the least quantity by which the additional sales costs would increase when necessary costs altered from u_2 to u_3 would be an amount $(CJ'' - G'J)$ greater than $(CJ' - G'J)$, and so on.*

Consequently, when necessary production costs are successively reduced by finite quantities the total sales costs of the quantity sold will increase simultaneously by finite amounts until, as necessary costs tend infinitely to zero total sales costs will tend to the greatest possible gross revenue for the product considered in the market. Also, since additional sales costs cannot increase without a corresponding rise in reserve stocks, when necessary production costs are successively reduced there should be an increase in the non-productive reserve stocks accumulated by competing entrepreneurs in the struggle for sale, in addition to an expansion of sales. This increase in non-productive reserve stocks should take place even faster than the increase in additional sales costs, since

---

* *Ed. note.* The identification of the various angles mentioned and their relations in Figure 2.12 appear obscure and possibly unrigorous (see editorial note, p. 155). However the following argument – that in the competitive model technical progress is bound to raise unproductive expenses for excess stocks or unused capacity – is not affected.

7. *The economic consequences of technical progress*

these costs are *an increasing function not only of the quantity of the stocks but also of their value* to the producers and this *value should* naturally decline continuously as necessary production costs are reduced.

Therefore an *expansion of output following a reduction of necessary production costs will,* in general, *extend not only to an expansion of supply but also to an increase in excess commodity inventories.* This circumstance should completely alter our view of the progress of industry under continuously rising labour productivity (which reduces the necessary production costs of commodities). On the basis of his theory of value, Ricardo and his followers maintain that every reduction in production costs gives rise to an expansion of output until *the price once again comes into equilibrium with necessary production costs at a supply equal to the new volume of production,* after which the expansion of output ceases and equilibrium is reestablished in the industry.

Consequently, if we wish to express the progress of industry graphically, and if we take time on the abscissae (since technical progress is, generally speaking, a function of time), and the volume of production on the ordinates (the quantity produced per unit of time), we shall obtain a broken line of the kind depicted in Figure 2.13. The horizontal segments correspond to periods when there is no change in labour productivity; the points A, B, C correspond to moments when some improvements appear in a given industry; the ascending segments correspond to periods of expansion of enterprises resulting from the cheapening of production. If such expansion could take place instantaneously, these segments would become vertical, as in the dashed line, but since in reality an instantaneous expansion of output is unthinkable, the angles α, α', α'', ... will invariably be greater than a right angle. The smaller are the periods of stagnation, i.e. periods during which the established equilibrium is not disturbed by cost-reducing improvements in an industry, or in other industries connected with it, the more will this broken line tend to an ascending curve of the kind depicted in the same figure by a dotted line.[1]

Our broken line will assume a different form if we base its construction on the conclusions reached from our criticism of Ricardo's theory. We saw that, in general, after each reduction in necessary production costs, equilibrium will be established at some greater volume both of supply *and of reserve commodity stocks.* For example, suppose the initial volume of supply is Q and the volume of the commodity stock J, and the equilibrium volume of sale after the cheapening of production is established at a quantity $Q' > Q$ while the volume of the commodity stock is now at a

[1] Whether this broken curve is concave or convex will depend on whether we assume that labour productivity increases ever more rapidly (which is closer to the actual state of affairs, at least within certain limits) or ever less rapidly, but this question is not important for our purposes. [This seems to suggest that Figure 2.13 is on a semi-logarithmic scale. *Ed.*].

171

new level $J' > J$. In order to sell Q' units per period, output should also be raised to Q' units per period. Suppose it has already been raised to this limit; by how much is production to be further expanded for commodity stocks to increase by the quantity $(J' - J) = C$? If production per period is raised to $Q'+B$ when sales per period equal Q' the stock increase will accumulate in C/B time units. Clearly should production continue to equal $Q'+B$ after this period, the stock would continue to increase beyond the level J' at which the price of the product equals total average cost of sales. Therefore at the end of C/B time units production should be reduced once again to Q' units per period. Otherwise, producers would be unable to recoup production costs in the price. Clearly the need to *reduce* output after some period will remain whatever the magnitude of the increment B. Of course, this reduction need not be instantaneous, but may be gradual, so that the level of production will take successive values $(Q'+B) > (Q'+B_1) > (Q'+B_2) > \cdots > Q'$ during the reduction from $(Q'+B)$ to Q'. In this case, of course, more units of time than C/B will be needed to build up the stock to the level J'.

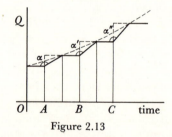

Figure 2.13

For the sake of simplicity we have assumed that the stock increment C begins to be built up after production reaches the new volume of sale Q'. In fact, *every* production expansion will be distributed (in accordance with the laws analysed above) between a sales expansion and a stocks increase. But this, naturally, cannot alter the situation: in building up a stock equal to some *constant* quantity, *output must contract, instantaneously or gradually, after the expansion*; were this not so the stock could not become a constant at any moment but would always remain an increasing function of time.

Considering this, we should give our curve (Figure 2.13) a form different from that adopted by Ricardo: instead of an ascending broken curve we obtain an undulating line, rises alternating with falls, as depicted in Figure 2.14. *A continuous rise in labour productivity* (and consequently a reduction of necessary costs) in any branch of industry *will be accompanied not by simple expansion of that branch*, as Ricardo assumed, *but by the successive alternation of periods of expansion and contraction*, although, as is evident from Figure 2.14 (and as we have demonstrated analytically), output will remain at a higher level after each contraction than before the preceding expansion, so that *on the whole* our broken line is ascending.

This conclusion is extremely important for the construction of a correct theory of industrial crises. A later essay will be devoted to an elaboration of this theory; here we shall give only a few comments. If the output of products and their sale (understanding by sale the transfer of the product to *consumers* and not to retailers) is in the hands of the same individuals (or corporate bodies), the need for successive expansions and contractions of output, under the influence of technical progress, would not entail the inevitable industrial upheaval we see in reality in the alternation of periods of industrial expansion and stagnation. In fact, were stocks to accumulate in the hands of *their producers*, their growth at each moment would be a true indication of how close they are to the limit beyond which further increases of stocks would become disadvantageous (since net profit would become negative). Therefore producers would invariably be able to identify precisely the point at which further production expansion should be halted and production be gradually reduced, so that, by the

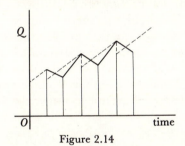

Figure 2.14

time production finally falls to the *new* sales level, total accumulated stocks would not exceed the quantity economically advantageous (see the preceding analysis). The situation will be quite different if, as actually occurs, activities of production and sale of commodities are in the hands of separate specialised classes. In this case, industry knows nothing about the actual sale of commodities to consumers. Producers work for the demand of wholesale merchants and follow it blindly, but naturally an expansion of *this* demand does not, and cannot, give producers any indication on the state of demand by the actual consumers of the product. An increased demand for a commodity by wholesale and even small merchants is in no sense a definite indication of an increase in their sales; *they may buy more* not only to expand their sales, but also *in order to increase their dead stocks* if such an increase conforms with their pursuit of the greatest advantage. However, a producer specialising purely in the activity of production has no means of distinguishing between a demand increase by

173

merchants standing between him and consumers due to an actual expansion of consumption and an increase directed merely to increase dead commodity stocks in the hands of merchant retailers. At the same time the producer, not knowing this, cannot know whether it is a permanent increase (where the extra quantity demanded is due to a sales increase), or a temporary increase inevitably followed by more or less rapid contraction, after accumulation of stocks is no longer advantageous to merchants. Therefore, with the separation of trading and industrial functions (in the strict sense), production is bound to follow blindly the demand of merchants without knowing to what extent reliance may be placed on the permanence of this demand.

Considering this analysis of the effect of cheapening of production on the progress of industry, clearly when trade and production activities are divorced *gradual* contraction of output will no longer occur. In fact, production will expand as long as demand by merchants keeps expanding, and merchants will expand demand until a further expansion of stocks is disadvantageous to them; then they will *immediately* restrict demand to the volume of sales, i.e. reduce it by the whole amount previously devoted to increasing stocks. For it to be otherwise, merchants would have to suffer a loss from the sudden contraction of output (in which case they would gradually begin to restrict their demand in good time), but this would be possible only if production and sale were *in the same hands*, which is not the case. When these activities are divorced, merchants have no concern for the interests of producers: their demand ceases as soon as its further expansion is no longer advantageous to them, and they are completely indifferent to the consequences of this sudden contraction for the producers.

Therefore, as industrial technique advances, demand by merchants will follow the dashed curve in Figure 2.14. In this case, what will be the curve depicting the corresponding production movement? For this we have to consider the consequences for industrialists of a sudden contraction of output corresponding to the vertical parts of our broken line. Every sudden contraction of production, however comparatively small the constant capital (in the Ricardian sense) engaged in it, invariably entails great losses, arising because it is impossible to withdraw immediately from production and realise the capital engaged in it in the form of machines, tools etc.

In fact, when there is a *general* contraction of production it is impossible to find purchasers for machines, tools etc. suitable for the production concerned, since, at that time, they are of no use to anyone because of continuous technological progress, a purchaser hoping to sell them later, at a more favourable time, cannot pay much more for them than their scrap value. Producers will be left therefore with one of two possibilities: either reducing output by working below full capacity, while maintaining the enterprise at the same size, i.e. the same constant capital; or continuing to work at full output, maintaining the former volume of sale by a corresponding price reduction. In either case they will work at a loss: in the first because of the excessive increase in production costs, and in the second because of the excessive price falls.

As a general rule, the second course is, in fact, more advantageous for them or, to be more precise, less unprofitable. It is better to sell cheaper (even if at a loss) than to suddenly restrict output to a new, lower volume of sale (since such a sudden restriction would be even more disadvantageous; this may readily be proved analytically as we shall demonstrate in the second part of this work; moreover, all the information needed for this purpose is already contained in the earlier analysis of the curves of demand, supply and production costs). This is the beginning of what is usually known as over-production: more of the commodity is produced in each unit of time than can be sold at a price covering the costs incurred.

The price keeps dropping at an accelerating rate, since it falls further the more the market is filled with unsold goods and the more producers have to lower prices to sell the newly produced quantity.

The appearance in the market of cheaper goods (sold by the producers at a loss) further devalues stocks already in the hands of traders. Stocks previously fully in accordance with correct economic calculations will now become excessive, i.e. become unsaleable without loss; the further this proceeds, the greater will be this loss.

Wishing to avoid even greater loss, merchants decide to sell their stocks at any price, merely to get something for them. The effect of this mass sale of trading stocks is that the price begins to fall with fearful rapidity. There is the additional factor of loss of confidence which inevitably accompanies any industrial upheaval; credit contracts at the same time. Bankruptcy follows bankruptcy; every liquidation throws on to the market masses of goods sold for trifling sums, depressing the price even further. Enterprises close one after the other, production falls rapidly, and hardly any new commodities reach the market. Former stocks, very heavily devalued, gradually pass from the principal markets into ever smaller channels of commodity circulation; thus the markets are gradually cleared, the panic abates, and the price stops falling. The crisis comes to an end. Many of the weaker enterprises will have perished. A few of the more viable, having withstood the shock of the crisis, now remain, but even they will have suffered large losses. They now need to compensate themselves for what has happened, but prices remain low. A mass of commodity stocks remains in the retail trade network (it would be incorrect to regard that intensified sale of stocks while prices fall during crises as an intensification of consumption: the goods sold merely pass from the hands of large merchants to those of smaller merchants, who take advantage of the general fall in prices to build up their own stocks against a future, more favourable time). To win through, the remaining enterprises must adapt themselves to adverse conditions. The only means of making enterprises profitable is to reduce necessary production costs. Hence the attempts to introduce improved productive methods. This would have been impossible during the worst phase of the crisis because there was no credit. Moreover, there would have been no point in such improvements because of the impossibility of foreseeing the limits to price falls and therefore the impossibility of deciding whether a given improvement would be advantageous, or whether savings in costs so effected would be entirely swallowed up by the decline in market value of the product and, therefore, whether expenditure on improvement would merely accelerate catastrophe, by using up the last available resources of the enterprise (since such improvements could not possibly be carried out on credit during crises). When the crisis ends, on the contrary, although prices remain low there are no longer grounds to fear a further fall; indeed, the more the resale of stocks clears the market, the greater is the hope of a price rise, since *output* is greatly reduced after a crisis; also, loan capital is cheap. The bulk of *fixed* incomes will have continued to accrue in the hands of rentiers of various kinds even during the crisis (see Tugan-Baranovsky's theory of credit); when confidence is restored, uses for these accumulations will be actively sought. Therefore, conditions become most conducive to the introduction of all kinds of production improvements. In fact, the history of industry shows that most major improvements are introduced at these times. Consequently, production cheapens, prices strengthen increasingly (until industry has expanded excessively once again), and a period of industrial expansion begins.

But this expansion already embodies the nucleus of a new crisis; the fall in production costs which causes industrial expansion is, at the same time, the fatal cause of new overproduction (when the production and trade activities are separated). All the phenomena examined above are repeated in the same sequence.

The situation is different when the production and trade activities are combined in the same entrepreneurs. As we have already noted above, in this case producers will be aware at any time of whether they are producing to expand sales (where 'sales' are strictly defined as the transfer of the product to *consumers*), backed by an expanding consumption of the product, or whether they are working to raise stocks.

In the latter case they are able invariably to contract their output gradually so that by the time output falls to the volume of sales in the same period (and, consequently, by the time equilibrium is established in the

176

productive sphere), the quantity of stocks accumulated in their hands does not exceed the quantity at which the price of the product exactly covers the total unit costs. Consequently in this case the only subsidiary result of an increase in labour productivity (if we regard the price fall as the main result) will be an increase in non-productive stocks, which will be accumulated without any apparent industrial upheavals (in contrast to cases where production and trade activities are separated); a chronic increasing general 'overproduction' will become apparent instead of the successive alternation of periods of industrial upsurge and ruin. We can see that this *'overproduction' is in no sense a result of errors of economic judgement*, i.e. it is not a consequence of the inability of production to adapt to excessively variable demand (which is moreover unknown at each given moment), but is a direct result of the struggle of competing entrepreneurs, *each of whom is motivated in his own actions by quite correct economic judgement*. To explain overproduction in an entire industry (which is in the hands of a vast number of entrepreneurs), and even more so in all branches of industry, in terms of *errors of economic calculation* (stemming from excessively complicated conditions in the modern market) is entirely to ignore or fail to understand the 'law of large numbers', on which the whole theory of statistical research is based.

The larger is the number of independent entrepreneurs who meet in the market, the more will errors in their economic judgement be mutually compensating[1] and the less will they be capable of affecting the volume of *total* sales, or the *total* commodity stocks.

We have also seen that when non-productive stocks are accumulated in the hands of producers, they always have the choice of producing more than the saleable quantity (i.e. advantageous to sell) in the same period and thereby building up non-productive stocks in their own hands, or contracting their output to the volume of sales, by operating their enterprises below full capacity. In the latter case, the result of an increase in labour productivity will not be *commodity stagnation* but stagnation in production; instead of loading the market with commodities which cannot be sold, producers will begin to operate their plants at less than full capacity, for fewer days in the week, will begin to shorten the working day and so on. In other words, the pattern of chronic stagnation, chronic *excess of enterprises*, will appear in the sphere of production.

Consequently, the more middle men between producer and consumer are eliminated, the greater will be the change in the effect of technical progress on the advance of industry; periodic industrial upheavals will

---

[1] Since all the conclusions of probability theory concerning random variables and their *means* are fully applicable to the individual errors of entrepreneurs (treated as random variables).

be increasingly evened out, and their place will be taken by the *chronic stagnation* of trade and industry.[1]

These conclusions, arrived at purely by deduction, are fully confirmed by reality; this is a further proof that the basic premises of Ricardo and other members of the deductive school are so close to reality, despite the various limitations to which they are subjected under the conditions of real life, that rigorously logical conclusions drawn from them are found to be fully in accordance with the facts of life and may therefore serve for the correct interpretation of observed phenomena. The change noted during the last quarter of the nineteenth century in the nature of industrial stagnation both in England and America and in other countries with a developed industry coincides strikingly with the gradual elimination of the merchant middle man inevitably standing between producer and consumer.

In this section we have not aimed to give a complete theory of industrial crises even in general outline; we have merely attempted to indicate the basis which a correct theory of free competition, taken in conjunction with the theory of production costs as the ultimate regulator of value, may provide for an explanation of (periodic and chronic) *general overproduction of commodities*. In order to give a *finished* theory to industrial crises, it is first necessary to provide a firm foundation for the theory of monetary circulation, which considerably complicates the schematic outline of a crisis given above and has, hitherto, been one of the least elaborate areas of theoretical political economy. This task will be the subject of a future part of our work.

---

[1] The spread of what are known as 'forward markets' (*Terminhandel*) leads to the same result as the elimination of middlemen in trade: forward contracts make non-productive 'reserve stocks' unnecessary since they make it possible to sell goods which have still not been produced but merely can be produced (in conformity with the productive capacity of the enterprise).

THIRD ESSAY

THE THEORY OF MARGINAL UTILITY

'Values differ but they are not capricious'

F. Galiani

Development of the foundations of marginal utility theory in the writings of Galiani (1750), Senior, Rossi, Dupuit and others. The later phase: Gossen (1854) and the Austrian school. Marginal utility theory in its 'developed form': the writings of Walras, Jevons, Launhardt, Auspitz and Lieben and other members of the mathematical school. The psycho-physiological foundations of marginal utility theory: the Fechner-Weber law; the theories of Buffon, Laplace and Bernoulli; the views of the most recent physiological psychology: Wundt and others.

So far we have regarded the form of the 'demand [gross revenue] curve' as empirically given. However, to end the analysis here would be a methodological error, since the form of the demand curve is itself dependent on an *economic* factor: the economic calculus of the consumers of the product. We cannot regard our analysis as complete until, as a result, we have obtained facts which lie outside the realm of the science of *economics* and are the subject of other disciplines (including psychology, physiology, biology, physics and mechanics).[1] What determines the form of the 'revenue curve', and what is the explanation for the daily observed fact (expressed in the form we adopted for the revenue curve) that the functional relationship between the volume of sale and market price is such that an expansion of sale is invariably observed whenever price is reduced and, conversely, that restriction of sale always causes a rise in price?

Tugan-Baranovsky states, 'Only the theory of marginal utility provides us with a fully scientific explanation of the fact which has long been known that the price of commodities is dependent on the quantity in which they are offered in the market', and continues, 'it is only from the viewpoint of this theory that we may refer to the *law* of supply and demand as a *scientific* law rather than a crude empirical generalisation'.[2] It is impossible not to be in full agreement with these words of Tugan-Baranovsky, but at the same time it should not be thought that the honour of having solved this problem belongs entirely to the Austrian economic school headed by Menger, with whose name the 'theory of marginal utility' is usually associated. An impartial analysis must lead to the conclusion that *the Austrian school* as such (Menger, Böhm-Bawerk, von Wieser and others) *added very little* (unless much significance is given to the introduction of new terms) *to what had been done* before them *for the solution of the problem.* Quite apart from such nineteenth-century writers as Senior,

---

[1] 'Investigation of the causes of value should not cease until we arrive at facts which lie outside the realm of the science of economics. In analysis of the subjective causes of value such facts will be physiological and psychological laws, since political economy cannot take upon itself the tasks of psychology and physiology. In relation to the objective causes of value the limit will be facts inherent in the natural environment (e.g. the fact that gold is rarer than iron) and social facts dependent on the general nature of the social order, the social institutions etc. Political economy is not a natural science and does not incorporate the whole sphere of sociology. *The sphere of investigation of each science should be limited so that the investigation may be brought to a conclusion.* But the task of a scientific theory of value may be regarded as completed only when the investigation has been carried to such a conclusion'. (Tugan-Baranovsky, Teoriya predêl'noi poleznosti, [The theory of marginal utility], *Yuridicheskii Vestnik*, 1890, p. 215). A similar view is also expressed by C. Menger in his work: *Untersuchungen über die Methode der Socialwissenschaften und der politischen Oekonomie insbesondere*, Leipzig, 1883.

[2] Tugan-Baranovsky, 'The Theory of Marginal Utility', p. 212.

Rossi, Dupuit and some others, in whose works the main elements of marginal utility theory are quite clearly shown (we do not include Gossen since the 'founders of the school' of marginal utility themselves acknowledge him as their forerunner), we find *all the information* needed for the construction of a *finished* theory of marginal utility in the work of such an 'old' economist as Galiani[1] (the first 'positivist' in political economy, who hitherto has not been properly appreciated in the literature). We do not wish to assert that *everything* concerning the theory of marginal utility had been said in 1871, which is the year normally accepted as the inception of the marginal utility school, and that nothing remained to be added. On the contrary, much remained to be done to convert the theory of marginal utility into a fully scientific theory, but this was to be the work not of the Austrian scholars mentioned above, but of the group of economists who used in their works the only method which could profitably be employed in this case (by virtue of the *complexity* of the question), namely the mathematical method, the method of precise knowledge. These included Walras (who may justifiably be regarded as the creator of marginal utility theory), Launhardt, Auspitz and Lieben, Jevons (although he may be regarded as only partly a member of the *mathematical* school in political economy, despite the fact that he is often referred to even as the 'head' of this school). We shall give below a detailed analysis of marginal utility theory in its developed form (briefly indicating the main stages through which this theory has passed in its development), but for the present we shall turn to the first attempt to solve the question of the functional relationship between the volume of sale and the price of a product.

Under this heading we should firstly include all the so-called 'theories of supply and demand'. It would be pointless to waste time on a detailed examination of the obscure and confused arguments of the proponents of these theories.

This is a subject in which everything is confused, everything is indefinite, beginning with the very concepts of supply and demand. Each individual defines them in his own way, and we frequently find these terms used in different senses even by the same author (in different places). An example of this is provided by J. S. Mill, who frequently departs in his studies from the original definition which he gave of the concept of demand and its quantitative expression (this has been justifiably pointed out by Cairnes).[2] Most often authors completely avoid any *precise* definitions, and content themselves with general, meaningless phrases.

[1] F. Galiani, *Della Moneta* (1750), in P. Custodi (Ed.), *Scrittori classici italiani di economia politica*, Parte moderna, Vol. 3, Milan, 1803.
[2] J. E. Cairnes, *Some leading principles of political economy newly expounded*, London, 1874, pp. 23–8.

The actual *form of the relationship* between price, on the one hand, and supply and demand, on the other, remains no less indefinite; most authors define it in terms which at first glance appear very specific: price is dependent on the *ratio* between supply and demand, and alters in direct proportion to demand and in inverse proportion to supply. However, this definiteness is only seeming, since hardly any of the economists whom we are considering mean a ratio in the *mathematical* sense by *the ratio between supply and demand*. The few exceptions are some of the early Italian economists such as, for example, Valeriani, Genovesi and Verri, of whom the last-named adopts an unusual definition of supply and demand, understanding by demand the number of purchasers, and by supply the number of sellers, so that the whole formula is expressed by him in the form: 'the price of things varies directly with the number of buyers and inversely with the number of sellers',[1] but what other meaning should be attached to this 'ratio' remains completely unclarified.

The matter is slightly improved by the correction made by John Stuart Mill, who replaced the concept of the 'ratio' of supply and demand by the concept of the 'equation' of supply and demand (see Mill, *Principles of Political Economy* (1848), Book III, Ch. 2 & 4, pp. 446–8 of 1909 edition). Although Mill's formula is undoubtedly more realistic, it still remains only the most successful formulation of the problem, and in no sense its solution.

Mill's 'theory' states no more than that the price actually established in the market will be the price at which demand equals supply. However, to state this is to state the self-evident fact that the total quantity *sold* in the market at a given moment cannot be either greater or less than the total quantity *bought* at the same moment (and *vice versa*). Why this equality of supply and demand is established at different levels of total sale of the product at different prices is a question which remains completely unanswered in Mill's theory.

Cairnes's very verbose theory fails to contribute anything further to an *understanding* of the formation of market prices. The concept of 'reciprocal demand'[2] which he introduces is of great methodological convenience, but, like Mill's correction, its apparent refinement of the theory of supply and demand does not touch the essence of the problem. The theories of supply and demand which are closest to the correct approach are those which went beyond quantitative expression of supply and demand and attempted to clarify the matter by the introduction of the concept of the rate of demand (and supply). This was the approach followed by Storch (*Cours d'économie politique*, 1815, Vol. 1, pp. 91–3) in

---

[1] P. de Verri, *Meditazioni sulla Economia Politica*, (1771), P. M. Custodi (Ed.), *Scrittori classici italiani di economia politica*, Parte moderna, Vol. 15, Milan, 1814, § 14, p. 47.

[2] See Cairnes, 1874, pp. 23–6.

the present century and by Steuart[1] in the last century. However, these theories cannot be regarded as 'pure' theories of supply and demand, but border on theories in which value is based on the use value of products, i.e. ultimately on human needs.[2]

However, they were unable to solve the question, since they could not resolve the notorious 'contradiction' between exchange value and use value.

Therefore, all theories of supply and demand, from the first attempts to such scientific 'last words' as, for example, the work of Pichenot (*The law of supply and demand*), which is a kind of summary of all that has been said on this question by the various proponents of this theory, suffer from the same common defect that while giving a detailed *description* of the phenomenon (sometimes even slightly too detailed), they completely fail to do what they set out to do, namely to *explain* the phenomenon which they set out to analyse. In this respect, Pichenot's work is typical of this trend: having *enumerated* with amazing detail all the factors capable of affecting price level, he concludes 'The foregoing factors of price . . . enter into real life in the most various combinations, creating the apparent diversity of prices and their fluctuations' (*The law* . . ., p. 85). However, he completely fails to consider the laws governing the interaction of these factors one with another, and the nature of the functional relationship between them (or their resultant) and price.

The words of Rossi, who formulated the main defects of the theory of supply and demand as long ago as the 1830s, are fully applicable to all these theories. He states:

'Some economists have said that the law determining prices is nothing other than the ratio of supply to demand: the price of any good stands in a direct relationship to demand and in an inverse relationship to supply. . . . Although this hypothesis is not apparently open to refutation (one only has to attend an auction . . .), it is nevertheless

---

[1] Zalessky (1893, p. 95) was therefore unjust to conclude that Storch was the *first* to point out the difference between the volume and rate of supply and demand. Steuart (1767) had published 48 years before Storch (1815). Admittedly, Storch expressed his views with greater clarity and definiteness.

[2] For example, *Storch* assumed that 'The value of objects is their relative utility, attributed to them by those who use them to satisfy their needs' (*Cours*, 1815, p. 49). *Steuart's* theory of value may be regarded as a production costs theory only on the basis of a misunderstanding, since he saw production costs (in which he did not include profit) as *merely the lower limit* below which sale price could not fall; he related any excess in the sale price above necessary costs exclusively to the conditions of supply and demand (the concept of a common mean level was alien to him), which were therefore the *ultimate* regulator of price in his theory. Failure to realise this may arise from Steuart's inconsistent use of terms, since he treats the 'real expense of making the goods' and 'intrinsic value' as synonyms (see J. Steuart, *An inquiry into the Principles of political oeconomy*, 1767, Book 2, pp. 141–404 of 1966 ed.).

erroneous because it fails on a fundamental point, because its formula does not reach the heart of the matter; in other words, it is a formulation of the problem rather than its solution. We seek a law of price, and they tell us that it is directly related to demand and inversely related to supply. This is all very well, but what then determines supply and demand? What makes supply and demand what they are and not something different? What is the law of supply and demand? It is evident that these economists have halted at the threshold of the problem.'[1]

The more clearly one of these authors attempts to formulate the theory of demand, the more obvious does it become that the *data are inadequate*, and that this inadequacy prevents all these theories from advancing beyond an apparent solution of the problem, which is a solution in words alone. It is for this reason that most supporters of the theory of supply and demand attempt to enshroud their deliberations in a fog of general phrases behind which there is no content.

For them supply and demand are not facts amenable to scientific analysis, but 'conjuring terms' (to use the expression of Cairnes[2]), 'by pronouncing which difficulties may be exorcised, and obstacles of all sorts removed from our path'.

Now that the solution of the problem is in front of us it is clear that the reason for the failure of all these theories is not to be found in errors of logic in the reasoning, but in the fact that the *data* themselves were inadequate for solving the problem. For a correct solution of the problem it was necessary to carry the research beyond the limits of the market in the strict sense and to seek the causes of price changes when sale expands and contracts in the sphere of *consumption* and the psychological and psychophysiological laws by which it is governed.

Here, however, the investigator immediately came up against an obstacle which for long seemed insurmountable. We are referring to the

[1] Rossi, *Cours d'économie politique*, Vol. III, Lesson 3 p. 46 of the second edition, Paris, 1843. Elsewhere Rossi states: 'It is perfectly true that, at the moment of exchange, one thing is worth the other. But is this anything other than the same question in different terms?

To say that the exchange value derives from the ratio between supply and demand, that it varies directly with demand and inversely with supply, is again to say something perfectly true, but this expression tries also to explain how external events take place. It is an expression sufficient for ordinary needs. . . . The expression explains sufficiently what actually happens in the markets' (*Cours d'économie politique*, Vol. I, Lesson 4, p. 49).

[2] Cairnes, 1874, p. 17. It is interesting to compare this quotation from Cairnes with the words of Rossi, who expresses almost the same idea in practically the same terms: 'There is no economist who does not assert that supply and demand are the two regulating elements of the market: therefore there is no gap in their system. Then we ask in turn: What is supply and demand? What is expressed by these two somewhat magic words by which one pretends to answer all questions and solve all problems?' (Rossi, *Cours*, Vol. I, Lesson 4, pp. 65–6 of the 1843 edition).

'contradiction' between exchange value and use value, which was continually advanced as an argument against the acceptance of use value, or utility, as a regulator of the proportions in which goods are exchanged. This contradiction was long ago noted by Le Trosne, in his polemic against Condillac who had stated 'Value is in the evaluation that we make of things, and this evaluation is relative to our need' thus indicating our needs as the basis of value (Condillac, *Le commerce et le gouvernement*, 1776, p. 15); Le Trosne stated that if value were in fact to be determined by our subjective evaluation of goods, then 'the most necessary things would have the greatest value' (Le Trosne, *De l'intérêt social*, 1777, p. 892). The same is also noted by Adam Smith: 'The things which have the greatest value in use, have frequently little or no value in exchange; and, on the contrary, those which have greatest value in exchange, have frequently little or no value in use' (Smith, Book I, Ch. 4, p. 42 of the 1814 edition). This assertion is also repeated by Ricardo[1] quoting from Smith. Some of the instances in which such a contradiction is apparently to be noted are undoubtedly merely a consequence of an incorrect and arbitrary interpretation of the terms 'utility' and 'use value'.[2] This has already been noted by Rossi, who stated:

[Smith] 'said that diamonds have an exchange value out of proportion with their use value. No, gentlemen, the value of diamonds is perfectly proportional to its utility, taking this word in the sense that economists must give to it. Utility is the property of satisfying a need, whether this is real or imaginary, permanent or temporary, physical or intellectual. . . . Scarcity is here an indirect means of satisfaction; it satisfies that need of our nature consisting in the desire to have what others have not got. It is a need that may be condemned by the moralist, and that reason must contain within just limits, but it is a need for the satisfaction of which men are willing to make great sacrifices' (Rossi, *Cours*, Vol. I, Lesson 4, pp. 73 and 74 of 1843 edition).

However, these exceptions aside, there still remains a mass of instances in which exchange value and use value do not coincide. We know that Proudhon developed this contradiction between use value and exchange value in the greatest detail in his essay *Système des contradictions économiques* (1846). He states: 'Use value and exchange value are in an eternal con-

---

[1] Ricardo, *Principles*, Ch. 1, 'On Value'.
[2] The first economist to give a completely correct definition of the concept of utility is undoubtedly Galiani: 'I call utility the aptitude of an object to procure us happiness. . . . All that produces a real pleasure is useful'. (Galiani, *Della moneta*, Ch. 2, Book 1, pp. 59 and 61 of 1803 edition).

flict' (p. 75); in his view it is impossible to find an explanation for this contradiction: 'The contradiction inherent in the notion of value has no visible cause, nor possible explanation' (p. 71). Proudhon, however, was late in his assertion; leaving aside Rossi and Senior, who wrote earlier than Proudhon, we can already find an explanation of this apparent contradiction in Galiani, in whose opinion the proportion in which products are exchanged is exclusively dependent on the subjective valuation placed on the product by the individual.[1] What determines the importance of a thing to the individual? Firstly, the *primary utility* (*utilità primaria*) of the thing, i.e. the importance which the thing will have for the individual if the need which it serves has not been satisfied at all (e.g. the significance of bread and gold for a starving beggar).

The *primary* utility of things is therefore dependent on the importance of the needs which they serve. However, *specific* utility, i.e. utility in a given specific instance, is dependent not only on prime utility or, in other words, *on the importance of the need* which the thing satisfies, but also on the *extent to which this need has been satisfied* or, in other words, on the relationship between need and satisfaction.[2] Galiani does not have a special term to denote this specific utility, this specific subjective value which determines the exchange proportion in each given case (corresponding to what is now known as marginal utility, final degree of the utility, *Grenznutzen*). However, he has no need of such a term, since in his use of words the term 'value' means only the subjective valuation placed on things by the parties to the exchange. Therefore we may summarise Galiani's theory[3]

---

[1] Therefore it could be said that the evaluation, that is value, is a notion of the proportion between having one thing or another in the judgement of a man' (Galiani, 1750, p. 58 of 1803 edition).

[2] Galiani uses the term 'scarcity' (*rarità*) for the relationship between need and satisfaction defined as follows: 'I call scarcity the proportion between the quantity of a thing and the use made of it' (1750, p. 72 of 1803 edition).

[3] Because of the lack of terms at Galiani's disposal for various economic concepts, *some phrases* in his essay may give rise to an incorrect interpretation of his theory. In order to make a correct appraisal of Galiani's theory of value we must carefully compare all the separate places in his essay where he deals with the question of utility and scarcity (the examples which he gives contribute greatly to clarification): see Ch. 2, pp. 58–89; examples: pp. 67–9; Ch. 4, pp. 75–6, 1803 edition. There is a noteworthy statement by Galiani to the effect that although prices are dependent on the variable needs of man, they are nevertheless not random: 'Values differ but they are not capricious' (p. 83; see also earlier from the words '*Assai si è detto . . .*' p. 82). It therefore follows that Galiani understood that the fact that prices were dependent on a subjective evaluation did not prevent them from being *conditioned*, and consequently did not make it impossible to discover the *laws* governing prices. It is interesting to compare this with Ingram's statements on Cournot's writings (Ingram, *History of Political Economy*, p. 234). It turns out that Galiani had a more correct view of the 'positive' sciences than Ingram, a member of the 'positive' school of political economy. It is also important to note Galiani's division of products into *two classes* (*due classi*): into articles the quantity of which may be increased by the application of labour, and into those the quantity of which is dependent on their natural abundance ('When we discuss the quantity of a thing, I maintain that there are two classes

as follows: the exchange value is determined by the subjective value of a thing to the individual; this is determined in its turn by two factors:

(1) the importance of the need which the thing is capable of satisfying and (2) the extent to which the need is satisfied.

The 'contradiction' noted by Proudhon is completely eliminated in this theory: although the need which a good satisfies may be very great, the importance of the good to the consumer will be very minor if that need has been practically completely satisfied. This gives rise to the apparently strange fact that articles which satisfy the most pressing needs may *when conditions change* (when the need is fully satisfied) possess very low use value for the individual (which is correspondingly reflected in the exchange proportion). This is noted by Galiani himself:

'If then somebody wonders how is it that all the most useful things have a low value, while the less useful ones have great or exhorbitant value, he will have to realise that this world is so well constructed with marvellous providence for our own good, that utility in general does not correspond to scarcity: indeed the greater the primary utility of a thing, the greater its abundance is, hence its value cannot be great' (Galiani, 1750, p. 69 of 1803 edition).

It is therefore in Galiani that we find the first clear idea concerning *relative use value*. He states:

'I understand that others say that a pound of bread is more useful than a pound of gold. My answer is: this is a disgraceful play of words, deriving from the lack of realisation that *more useful and less useful are relative notions*, and that they are measured according to the different conditions of individuals. If we are talking of a man who has no bread and no gold, certainly bread is more useful; facts confirm this because nobody will be found to give up bread to die of starvation in order to take the gold. Those who dig mines never forget to eat and to sleep. But to a satiated person what is more useless than bread? It is good for him then to satisfy other desires. Therefore these metals are companions of luxury, that is of the situation where primary needs have already been satisfied' (Galiani, 1750, p. 68 of 1803 edition, emphasis added).

The use value of the same product is not some invariable quantity, exclusively dependent on the importance of the need which it serves. The value of a thing to man may vary from some infinitely large amount to

---

of objects: for some the quantity depends on the degree of abundance in which nature produces them, for others it depends only on the work and labour employed in them', 1750, p. 73 of 1803 edition).

nothing as the need for this thing is satisfied. But since in Galiani's opinion the exchange value is determined exclusively by the relative importance to the individual consumer of the things exchanged, it becomes quite evident that the value of each thing (relative to others) falls as its supply increases. The problem of the relationship between market price and 'supply and demand' had, therefore, already been solved in principle by Galiani, in precisely the same way as by the marginal utility school. Very little that is new can be found in the writings of the Austrian school when we compare them with Galiani's theory (apart from a more highly developed terminology which gives rise to an *outwardly* more elegant theory). Even in the theory of 'production goods' (*Productivgüter*), which occupies so much space in the writings of this school, we find the same views expressed by Galiani (concerning the value of labour). Galiani assumed that production goods acquired their value from the first-order goods which they served to produce. The only new element here is what is known as von Wieser's law,[1] which provides a solution for the case in which the same production good is used in the production of *several* first-order goods. The most recent theoreticians of marginal utility are also in complete agreement with Galiani on the significance of labour as a production good of higher order (*Gut höherer Ordnung*; compare Galiani, 1750 Ch. II, pp. 75–8; Böhm-Bawerk *Wert, Kost. und Grenznutzen*, p. 333; Wieser, *Ueber den Ursprung*, pp. 105–07; *Der Natürliche Werth*, Vienna, 1889, p. 168).[2]

The theory propounded by Galiani remained unnoticed and the contradiction between exchange value and use value was once again raised in the writings of Smith, Ricardo and other members of the classical school. The theory of the functional relationship between the *use* value of a good and the quantity of it at the disposal of the consumer (which is the essence of marginal utility theory) was further developed in the 1830s in the writings of Senior and Rossi.

Senior stated that

'Not only are these limits to the pleasure which commodities of any given class can afford, but the pleasure diminishes in a rapidly increas-

---

[1] See F. von Wieser, *Ueber den Ursprung und die Hauptgesetze des Wirthschaftlichen Werthes*, Vienna, 1884. 'No part of the productive stock shall in any industry be used for the production of a less important product while it could be used for the production of a more important one elsewhere' (pp. 148–9).

Böhm-Bawerk gives the following formulation of the same law: 'The value of a unit of means of production depends on the marginal utility and value of that product having the least marginal utility of all those products which could have been used to produce the unit of means of production in an economical way' (E. von Böhm-Bawerk, 'Grundzüge der Theorie des wirthschaftlichen Güterwerths', *Jahrbücher für Nationalökonomie und Statisik*, 1886, p. 169).

[2] All that is original is von Wieser's theory of the *different* evaluation placed on labour in our time and under a primitive social order.

ing ratio long before those limits are reached. Two articles of the same kind will seldom afford twice the pleasure of one, and still less will ten give five times the pleasure of two. In proportion, therefore, as any article is abundant, the number of those who are provided with it, and do not wish, or wish but little, to increase their provision, is likely to be great; and, so far as they are concerned, the additional supply loses all, or nearly all, its utility. And in proportion to its scarcity the number of those who are in want of it, and the degree to which they want it, are likely to be increased; and its utility, or, in other words, the pleasure which the provision of a given quantity of it will afford, increases proportionally' (Senior, *An outline of political economy*, pp. 11–12 of 1938 edition).

He further commented: 'We have already stated that the utility of a commodity, in our extended sense of the term utility, or, in other words, the demand for it as an object of purchase or hire, is principally dependent on the obstacles which limit its supply' (p. 17 of 1938 edition).

The theory of marginal utility is here formulated with such clarity as to leave nothing further to be desired. What remained to be clarified in more detail was the *mechanism* of the equalisation of marginal utility in exchange (even for instances of *isolated exchange*, since more complicated cases are amenable only to *mathematical* analysis;[1] such an analysis is to be found in Rossi's *Cours*, a work which we have already frequently had occasion to quote).

Like the present-day theoreticians of marginal utility, Rossi sees utility as the basis of exchange (market) value, and like these theoreticians he recognises that the utility of an article is not an invariable constant for the same product, but a function of quantity: 'Those who seek in utility the cause of exchange value are careful to explain that the scarcer a useful object becomes, the more its utility increases' (*Cours*, Vol. I, Lesson 5, p. 83 of the 1843 edition).

Turning to the effect of use value on exchange value, Rossi makes the assumption of isolated exchange:

'We have put into contact two men in a given situation, one having two loaves of bread, the other two bottles of water; one dominated by an irresistible need for water, the other dominated by an irresistible need for bread, and both equally convinced that they will die today unless they can satisfy their pressing need, and equally convinced that

---

[1] It is interesting to note Roscher's view which exemplifies the methodological views of the historical school in general, that 'the more complicated are the facts and phenomena to which the mathematical method is applied, the more its advantages evaporate' (W. Roscher, *System der Volkswirthshaft*, I; *Die Grundlagen der Nationalökonomie*, Stuttgart, 1900, Introduction, Ch. III, Section 22).

tomorrow this need will disappear. We have asked what is the exchange value of this bread and water, and we have recognised that bread represented the value of water, and water the value of bread, because in our hypothesis on one side there is an infinite need to have bread, to the extent that we can apply the word "infinite" to man, and the conviction that the second bottle of water is useless; on the other side, there is an infinite need for that bottle of water and the conviction that the other loaf is useless. Is it not clear that when these two parties take each other by the throat – if you allow me to use this expression – one must hand over the bottle of water, the other the loaf? The two compelling forces are the same, and exchange must take place.'

'Now, change something in one of these positions. Suppose that the need for water is not so urgent anymore, or multiply the number of loaves, or weaken the conviction of the uselessness of these objects for tomorrow; briefly, introduce mentally some change in the situations, and you will find that the results will not be the same. Economists will tell you that the conditions of supply and demand have changed, but fundamentally what has changed? The basic element of value, that is need, whether this has changed because utility is lower, or the means of obtaining the goods have increased, or the quantity of goods has changed and they are not as scarce or abundant as before' (*Cours*, Vol. I, Lesson 5, pp. 92–3 of 1843 edition).

It is hardly necessary to add that neither Rossi nor Senior admits the possibility that production costs should *directly* affect the establishment of *market prices*: in their view the *only* way to bring market prices into line with production costs is to alter the supply of the product in the market. Senior stated this with particular force: 'if all the commodities used by man were supplied by nature without any intervention whatever of human labour, but were supplied in precisely the same quantities as they now are, there is no reason to suppose that they would either cease to be valuable, or would exchange in any other than their present proportions'.[1]

It is impossible not to be in complete agreement with these words by Senior. A reduction of production costs cannot *in itself* cause the market price of a product to fall: until output of the product increases, the *only* result of a reduction of production costs will be excessive profits for the entrepreneurs engaged in this industry. But, as we have seen, even when output is increased, this need not always be followed by an increase in sale, and consequently by a reduction in market price. Market price will

[1] Senior, *Outline*, p. 24 of 1938 edition. Malthus expressed the same thought in the statement '... no change can take place in the market prices of commodities without some previous change in the relation of the demand to supply' (*Principles of political economy*, Ch. 2, Section 3, p. 71 of the 1836 edition).

fall when and *only when* the *supply* of the product is raised, since only an increase in sale (leading to a more complete saturation of the demand for the given product than before) can alter the *valuation which purchasers place upon the product* (on which alone the market price of the product is dependent). Were the sellers to take it into their heads, *without increasing supply*, to lower the price below that which the purchasers were prepared to pay at a given volume of sale, the only result of this would be the development between them and the consumers of a class of middle men into whose hands the whole of the 'difference' would fall.

Cournot states, 'The price . . . is fixed by the law of demand, whether or not there is competition' (i.e. between owners), 'and the generosity of the owner who would be satisfied by a lower price, would be advantageous only to the merchants, given the competition among consumers' (Cournot, *Principes de la théorie des richesses*, § 63, p. 112). Mill is, therefore, quite incorrect when he asserts that the price of products may fall when production costs decrease even if the output and supply of these products have not altered (see Mill, Vol. 1).

Mill assumes that the reason for a fall in price in this case would be the *fear* of sellers that the large profits obtained by them would attract new competitors into this industry. The reasoning is downright naive: quite apart from the fact that such behaviour would contradict correct economic calculus (the entrepreneurs themselves would have *entirely* to renounce *excess* profit for fear that . . . this excess *might in the course of time* be reduced under the influence of competition!), the whole of the modern trading system, which is based precisely on the pursuit of market-determined profit, contradicts what is assumed by Mill.

Marginal utility theory was further developed in the writings of Dupuit, who was the first to give it mathematical (graphic) expression.[1]

In Dupuit we already find fully expressed the *contrast* between *total* utility, i.e. the sum of the utility incorporated in a known quantity of a product, and *marginal* utility, i.e. the utility of the last unit to be added,

---

[1] We do not include Cournot among the theoreticians of marginal utility (as is done, for example, by Zalessky, 1893, p. 188, who even regarded Cournot as the *first* to establish this theory), since in his writings the 'demand curve' expressing the relationship between the volume of demand and price level *is assumed to be empirically given*. We cannot therefore find any *explanation* in Cournot of the fact that price falls when sale expands, and this is the very essence of marginal utility theory. In Cournot's most recent essay we also find only isolated references to the shape of the 'demand curve' for different categories of goods (see Cournot, 1863, § 54, pp. 95, 96 and some other places). It is interesting to note a remark by Cournot (which is also important for marginal utility theory) that although 'In general, demand for a commodity should increase when price falls' (Cournot, 1863, p. 95), there are nevertheless things for which demand increases only within certain narrow limits when the price is reduced, and that further reduction of price may completely eliminate the demand. Precious stones are said to be a case in point; 'in this case a large price fall would reduce demand almost to zero' (Cournot, 1863, p. 95).

which also determines the price which the consumer will be prepared to give *for the total* quantity, although Dupuit still does not use any special term to denote the utility of the last unit to be added (we know that the term 'marginal utility': 'final degree of the utility' was first established by Jevons: Wieser rendered it in German by the term '*Grenznutzen*'; Gossen and Menger also did not have a special term to denote marginal utility. Walras used the term *rareté* to denote this concept, defining it as 'the intensity of the last want satisfied by any given quantity consumed of a commodity' (p. 119 of the English edition)).

Dupuit states:

'The various points about utility which have been developed above may be presented geometrically in a very simple manner.

If it is supposed, as in Figure 3.1, that along a line *OP* the lengths

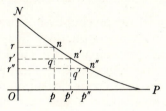

Figure 3.1

Op, *Op'*, *Op''*, ... represent various prices for an article, and that the verticals *pn*, *p'n'*, *p''n''*, ... represent the number of articles consumed corresponding to these prices, then it is possible to construct a curve *Nnn'n''P* which we shall call the curve of consumption. *ON* represents the quantity consumed when the price is zero, and *OP* the price at which consumption falls to zero.

Since *pn* represents the number of articles consumed at price *Op*, the area of the rectangle *Ornp* expresses the cost of production of the *np* articles, and, according to J-B. Say, also their utility. We trust we have demonstrated that the utility of each of these *np* articles is at least *Op* and that for almost all of them the utility is greater than *Op*. Indeed, by raising a perpendicular from *p'* it can. be seen that for each of *n'p'* articles the utility is at least *Op'*, since they are bought at that price. Of the *np* articles there are therefore only *np − n'p' = nq* for which utility is really only *Op* (or rather the average between *Op* and *Op'*); for the others it is at least *Op'*. We are thus led to the conclusion that for *nq* articles the utility is represented by the area *rnn'r'*, and that for the remainder, *qp* or *n'p'*, it is greater than the rectangle *r'n'p'O*; by supposing a further rise in price *p'p''* we could show that for *n'p' − n''p''* =

193

$n'q'$ articles the utility is an average between Op' and Op'', and is measured by the area $r'n'n''r''$ and so on. By continuing this process it can be shown that the absolute utility of the np articles to the consumer is the mixtilinear trapezium OmP. The relative utility is arrived at by subtracting the costs of production, shown as the rectangle mpO, which leaves the triangle npP; this, according to our view, is the utility remaining to the consumers of the np articles after they have paid for them. It is seen that the area of this triangle on one side of the line np has no relation to that of the rectangle on the other side.

The utility of a natural product the acquisition of which requires no expense, is expressed by the large triangle NOP.

It may be noticed that as the price of an article rises, the utility diminishes, but less and less rapidly: and that, on the other hand, as the price falls, the utility increases more and more rapidly; for it is expressed by a triangle which shortens or stretches as the case may be.'[1]

Dupuit does not consider the psychophysiological causes of a reduction in the utility of a product as its quantity increases. Another French economist, who wrote at approximately the same time, and whose views on value undoubtedly make him one of the forerunners of the developed theory of marginal utility, paid greater attention to this question. This is Gustave de Molinari, who gives a complete solution of the question of the relationship between utility and value in two theories of marginal utility in his article on price formation which appeared in *Journal des économistes* (Vol. 29, p. 117) in 1851 (see also his *Cours d'économie politique*, the chapter on exchange and value). Furthermore, Molinari attempts to base his basic formula of price change on statistical data ('when the ratio in the quantities of two commodities offered in exchange alters in arithmetical progression, the ratio of the value of these commodities, or their price, alters in geometrical progression', see *Cours*, p. 80) and in this respect he comes close to the other trend in political economy, the main representatives of which were Gregory King and Tooke, who attempted to arrive at an empirical formula for price change by analysing the history of prices. We know that Gregory King attempted to establish, on the basis of the very limited amount of material at his disposal, a general law between a *deficit in corn and the increase in its price*.[2]

---

[1] J. Dupuit, *De la mésure de l'utilité des travaux publics*, Annales des ponts et chaussées, 2nd series, Vol. 8, 1844; translated in *International Economic Papers*, n. 2, 1952, pp. 83–110; pp. 106–7 of the English translation.

[2] King was writing at the end of the seventeenth century. He compiled the following table, which is also reproduced by Tooke, to express this relationship.

A deficit of corn of	increases the price by
10%	30%
20%	80%
30%	160%

Tooke, more cautiously, avoided establishing any general law, even one for corn alone. He stated that the most that could be asserted was that a deficit in the amount of corn caused a greater increase in price, considerably exceeding the proportion of the deficit, than did a deficit in many other articles. He later attempted to explain this fact (cf. Tooke, *A History of Prices*, Vol. I, Ch. 2 'Effects of Quantity on Prices', pp. 10–17). This explanation was however superfluous because a similar disproportionately large alteration in price is also observed for other commodities which are not such prime necessities as corn.[1]

In general the analysis of the history of prices has hitherto contributed very little to an 'explanation' of the determination and movement of market prices (detailed consideration will be given in the second part of this work to the importance to *theoretical* political economy of the quantitative data provided by reports on *wholesale* prices).

Finally, there appeared in 1854 an essay by Gossen.[2] By comparison with this work the arguments of the most recent members of the marginal utility school (with the exception of the mathematicians) are poor stuff indeed, and are verbose and confused by comparison with the original. For instance, a great deal of confusion has been introduced into the theory of the value of complementary goods (in Menger's terminology) by the most recent members of the school. In this connection it is interesting to note the strange lack of familiarity of the theoreticians of the Austrian school with the previous literature on the question they are attempting to solve. For example, the question of the value of complementary goods, to which they devote so much space in their writings (especially Böhm-Bawerk: *Grundzüge der Theorie . . .*, pp. 56–9 and von Wieser: *Der näturliche Werth*, pp. 81–4) had already been analysed in Cournot's first publication in 1838 (Sections 55–65; pp. 99–116 of the English translation) and an acquaintance with this faultless analysis, which leaves nothing further to be desired, could have helped to clear up

---

40%	280%
50%	450%

(See T. Tooke, *A history of prices and of the state of circulation from 1793–1837*, 2 Vols., London, 1838, Vol. I, p. 12; see also Roscher, *Grundlagen*, Section 103, p. 300.)

[1] Cf. e.g. the example given by Scharling ('Werttheorie und Wertgesetze', *Jahrbuch fur Nationalökonomie und Statistik*, Band 16, 1886, p. 557); cotton production was 30% less than usual in 1864 and the price rose by 384%.

[2] H. H. Gossen, *Entwickelung der Gesetze des Menschlichen Verkehrs*, Braunschweig, 1854. Bruno-Hildebrand and Knies are usually included among the economists who 'prepared the ground' for the theory of marginal utility, but the solution which they propose in their writings to Proudhon's 'contradiction' in fact has *nothing in common* with the ideas of *marginal utility* (see B. Hildebrand: *Die Nationalökonomie der Gegenwart*, Frankfurt, 1848, pp. 318–19; Karl Knies: 'Die Nationalökonomie Lehre vom Werth', *Zeitschrift für Staatswissenschaft*, 1885, pp. 433–8 *et seq.*). Moreover, all this naive reasoning can scarcely lay serious claim to the significance of a 'scientific theory' (even in the most modest sense of this word).

the whole confusion introduced by the imprecise and verbose arguments of the most recent dialectical economists. However, Cournot's writings have remained unknown to German economists (the only exceptions are once again the *mathematical* economists: Auspitz and Lieben, Launhardt and others).[1]

To avoid repetition, we shall not give an account of Gossen's theory, which is moreover quite well known, even if only from its reproduction in the writings of Menger and others,[2] but shall proceed directly to an account of the theory of marginal utility in its most developed form, following mainly Walras, Launhardt, Jevons and Auspitz and Lieben.

We shall make only one preliminary remark: most proponents of the theory of marginal utility who have solved the problem of price determination by considering cases of *isolated exchange* have turned their attention in the main to the aspect of utility. On the effect of the *total purchasing power* of consumers on the establishment of market price they have confined themselves to the most general arguments, and even then have not attempted to give precise quantitative expression to the effect of this factor. Only the mathematical economists have given full consideration to this aspect since, for them, the complexity of the relationship between data and variables has not been an obstacle to a precise solution of the question. However, the effect of a difference in the purchasing power of consumers on the determination of market prices had been the subject of economic analysis far earlier, when it was considered *separately* and not in relation to the theory of marginal utility (the 'statistical law of demand' of French authors).[3] Although the explana-

[1] It should moreover be noted that Jevons himself, who is known as the *head* of the mathematical school, was not ashamed to admit that he was not competent to understand Cournot's writings (owing to his inadequate knowledge of higher mathematics: see W. S. Jevons, *The Theory of Political Economy*, 1871, Preface, p. 58 of the Pelican edition, 1970).

[2] See H. Gossen, *Entwickelung der Gesetze des Menschlichen Verkehrs*, second edition, Berlin, 1889; concerning the law of the distribution see pp. 33, 39, 45. '... man must allot his time and effort to the preparation of various pleasures so that the value of the last atom of utility created by each pleasure is equal to the magnitude of pain which would be caused if this atom were created in the last moment of the exertion of his effort.' See p. 85 concerning the equation of marginal utility in exchange; 'Each of the two objects must be divided between *A* and *B*, after the exchange, in such a way that the last atom each partner obtains from each object creates equal value for both.' See pp. 90–8 on the mechanism of the distribution of producers by individual branches in accordance with the established law of the equalisation of utilities; and pp. 4–5 on the psychological law of decrease in utility.

[3] Here, for example, is how the popular French economist J. Garnier formulated the effect of this factor (following J-B. Say) in one of his early works.
He states: 'Suppose that the pyramid in Figure 3.2 represents the wealth of the citizens and that the prices of the products are written on the side. We can see that, when the products have a zero price, all the citizens whatever their wealth represented on the basis of the pyramid can afford them. At a certain price, say 100 francs, only a few individuals forming the top of the pyramid will be able to buy them; and finally, at 125 francs

tion provided by the 'statistical law of demand' is crude and primitive, this theory has nevertheless given a correct indication of *one* of the reasons for a reduction of demand when the price of a product increases. The effect of the purchasing power of consumers on the market price of products has found its true place in the theory of marginal utility in the *developed form* given to it in the writings of L. Walras and other members of the 'Mathematical school'.

We shall proceed to an exposition of this 'developed' theory of marginal utility in the next section.

2. AN ANALYSIS OF THE RELATIONSHIP BETWEEN PRICE OF A PRODUCT AND DEMAND

The problem posed and solved by the marginal utility school was the determination of the factor or factors affecting the price of a product when 'actual' supply (i.e. supply equal to demand) expanded and contracted. Why did the price fall when supply increased and rise when supply decreased? Finally, was this relationship an economic fact (i.e. dependent on the economic calculus of the parties to the exchange), and therefore amenable to further economic analysis, or should this phenomenon be taken as an empirical fact in political economy, and its analysis be the province of other scientific disciplines? The school of marginal utility *in its developed form* (in the writings of Walras and some other mathematicians) provides a quite definite answer to all these questions.

Let us assume in the interests of simplicity that only two products, A and B, are exchanged in the market. Let us denote the price of product A in terms of B by p_a, and the price of B in terms of A by p_b (so that if m units of product A are exchanged for n units of product B, $P_A = n/m$; $p_B = m/n$). Let us further denote the supply of the product A by O_a and the supply of product B by O_b; the demand for the product A by D_a and

---

nobody will be able to afford them or, which is the same thing, all of them will refuse to buy. . . . Each section of the pyramid can also represent the share of one's wealth that each

Figure 3.2

individual may and wishes to devote to the purchase of a product at a given price. These figures are arbitrary; but they can be easily replaced by actual data' (*Abrégé élémentaire des principes de l'économie politique*, Paris, 1796; pp. 195–6 of the 1846 French edition).

the demand for the product B by D_b. Since the demand for a product invariably equals the supply, we invariably have: $D_a = O_a$; $D_b = O_b$.

D_a, i.e. the volume of demand for the product A, depends on the price of A in terms of B, i.e. on the value of p_a; D_b is also itself dependent on the level of p_b. We therefore have

$$
\left.
\begin{aligned}
D_a &= O_a = F_a(p_a) \\
D_b &= O_b = F_b(p_b).
\end{aligned}
\right\} \tag{1}
$$

We understand by D_a and D_b the total demand for products A and B. If we denote the partial demand for the product A by a purchaser (1) by d_{a1}, that of a purchaser (2) by d_{a2}, and so on, and the partial demands for the product B by d_{b1}, d_{b2}, ..., we shall have

$$
\left.
\begin{aligned}
D_a &= d_{a1} + d_{a2} + \cdots \\
D_b &= d_{b1} + d_{b2} + \cdots
\end{aligned}
\right\} \tag{2}
$$

The quantities d_{a1}, d_{a2}, ...; d_{b1}, d_{b2}, ... will in turn depend on the price of products A and B, so that we have

$$
\left.
\begin{aligned}
d_{a1} &= f_{a1}(p_a); \quad d_{a2} = f_{a2}(p_a); \quad \cdots \\
d_{b1} &= f_{b1}(p_b); \quad d_{b2} = f_{b2}(p_b); \quad \cdots
\end{aligned}
\right\} \tag{3}
$$

If the functions $f_{a1}, f_{a2}, \ldots$ are given, F_a is also given, since

$$
F_a(p_a) = D_a = f_{a1}(p_a) + f_{a2}(p_a) + \cdots \tag{4}
$$

The same also applies to F_b.

Therefore, analysis of the relationship between the quantitites D_a and D_b, on the one hand, and between p_a and p_b, on the other, is reduced to an analysis of the relationship between the quantities d_{a1}, d_{a2}, ...; d_{b1}, d_{b2}, ... and p_a and p_b.

Is it possible to analyse further the expression $d_a = f_a(p_a)$, i.e. the relationship between the price of a product and the volume of the partial demand (*demande partielle*)? Walras's answer is yes. In his *Utility curves or want curves – the theorem of maximum utility of commodities* (Lesson 8,

p. 115 of the English edition) he shows that 'the individual demand equation $d_a = f_{a1}(p_a)$ when solved for d_a becomes $\phi_{a1}(d_a) = p_a\phi_{b1}(q_b - d_ap_a)$' (Walras, p. 132 for the English edition); the equation $\phi_{a1}(d_a) = p_a\phi_{b1}(q_b - d_ap_a)$ is itself derived from the equation: $r_{a1} = p_ar_{b1}$ (where Walras understands by r the 'marginal utility', or in his terminology the 'scarcity' [*rareté*] of the quantities of the product at the disposal of a given individual) by substituting for r_{a1} and r_{b1} their magnitudes yielded by the equations $r_{a1} = \phi_{a1}(q_a)$ and $r_{b1} = \phi_{b1}(q_b)$, which are the equations of the 'curves of utility or want' (*courbes d'utilité ou de besoin*), where it is assumed $q_a = d_a$ and $q_b = (q_b - d_ap_a)$ [sic]. Equations $r_{a1} = \phi_{a1}(q_a)$ and $r_{b1} = \phi_{b1}(q_b)$ *are not themselves amenable to further economic analysis*, since the relationship between marginal utility and the quantity of goods is *psychologically* conditioned, and should be accepted as empirically given in *economic* research.[1] The equation $r_a = p_ar_b$ is the mathematical expression of the 'theorem of maximum utility' (*théorème de la satisfaction maximum*) proved by Walras (in Sections 76–83, pp. 120–31 of the English edition).

Both the explanation of the concept of 'marginal utility' and the proof of the theorem of 'maximum utility' (*théorème de la satisfaction maximum*) given by Walras are to some extent artificial because of his attempt to avoid the use of higher mathematics. We shall therefore turn to other members of the marginal utility school.

Jevons states: 'It is clear then, that utility is not proportional to commodity' (p. 53). 'Utility is a quantity of at least two dimensions, one dimension consisting in the quantity of the commodity and another in the intensity of the effect produced upon the consumer' (p. 56).[2] 'We are now in a position fully to appreciate the difference between the *total utility* of any commodity and *the degree of utility* of the commodity at any point' (p. 58). 'Let u denote the *whole utility* proceeding from the consumption of x. Then u will be, as mathematicians say, *a function of x* . . .'

[1] The view of the theory of value as 'applied psychology' is therefore completely incorrect. See von Wieser, *Ueber den Ursprung . . .*, p. 39.

[2] Jevons uses the following construction to clarify the concept (see Figure 3.3). Line segments corresponding to the 'quantity of the commodity' are plotted on the horizontal

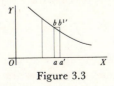

Figure 3.3

OX; the 'intensity of utility' is expressed by perpendiculars to OX. The product 'whole utility' expressed by the area $abb'a'$ corresponds to an infinitely small increment in the quantity of the commodity aa'; 'the intensity' is then expressed by this area divided by the quantity aa', and will equal ab, i.e. the height of the rectangle.

(p. 59). 'The increment Δx corresponds to the increment of the function Δu... the degree of utility, is represented by the fraction $(\Delta u/\Delta x)$'. If we have made the increment $x'a$ infinitely small, we shall have: du/dx, i.e. '*the degree of utility* is in mathematical language *the differential coefficient of u considered as a function of x* and will itself be another function of x'. The 'final degree of utility' is 'the degree of utility of the last addition, or the next possible addition of a very small, or infinitely small, quantity to the existing stock'. 'We may state, as a general law, that it varies with the quantity of commodity, and ultimately decreases as that quantity increases' (Jevons, *The Theory of Political Economy*, 1871; pp. 110–11 of the Pelican edition, 1970).

Having therefore clarified the concept of marginal utility, we shall turn to the basic point considered by the theory, to proof of the hypothesis referred to by Walras as *Théorie de satisfaction maximum* and by Launhardt as *Das Grundgesetz des Tausches* [the fundamental law of exchange]. Let us follow Launhardt, whose exposition is the most concise and clear.

'Suppose there is an owner who has at his disposal good A, whose utility function is $y = f(x)$, in a quantity a; suppose there is a second owner with another good B in quantity b, with a utility function $y = \varphi(z)$. Both owners are then able to exchange certain quantities of their goods with each other and they will do this up to a point, inasmuch as they can gain by it, or at least gain in utility.'

'At first it may be assumed that the utility of each of the two goods is estimated in the same way by both owners. In other words, it is assumed that the utility function $y = f(x)$ for good A and $y = \varphi(z)$ for good B is used by both owners to estimate values.'

'If in an act of exchange p_{II} units of good A are exchanged against p_I units of good B, and if x units of good A are exchanged against z units of good B, we must have $z = (P_I/P_{II})x$. Both these relative numbers p_I and p_{II}, giving the terms of the exchange, are obviously nothing else but the unit prices p_I for good A and p_{II} for good B, expressed in any standard. After the exchange, owner A will have retained a stock $(a-x)$ of his original good, and will have a quantity z of the other good, so that the utility attained by his property is

$$N = f(a-x) + \varphi(z). \tag{5}$$

The value of x for which this utility is maximised is found by differentiating with respect to x, and by equating the derivative with zero. One obtains:

$$-f'(a-x) + \varphi'(z)\frac{dz}{dx} = 0 \tag{6}$$

200

2. The relationship between the price of a product and demand

or, since $z = (p_I/p_{II})x$, and since therefore $dz/dx = p_I/p_{II}$,

$$\frac{f'(a-x)}{\varphi'(z)} = \frac{p_I}{p_{II}}. \tag{7}$$

This equation is the *fundamental law of exchange*, which, spelled out, says: an owner obtains the greatest utility in exchange if the degrees of utility of the goods he owns are in the same proportions as the unit prices of the goods' (Launhardt, 1885, § 4, pp. 16–17).

Consequently, by virtue of the tendency of the exchange parties to pursue the greatest possible advantage we invariably have the following relation between the price of a product and the demand for it on the part of a given buyer:

$$\frac{f'(a-x)}{p_I} = \frac{\varphi'(z)}{p_{II}} \tag{8}$$

or

$$\frac{p_{II}}{p_I} f'\left(a - \frac{p_{II}z}{p_I}\right) = \varphi'(z). \tag{9}$$

If we follow Walras in using the notation p_a for p_{II}/p_I, d_{a1} for z and q_b for a, and if we finally denote f' by ϕ_{b1} (since the differential coefficient of the function is a new function of the variable) and φ' by ϕ_{a1}, we have

$$\phi_{a1}(d_a) = p_a\phi_{b1}(q_b - d_a p_a). \tag{10}$$

Since the magnitude q_b is given, the solution of this equation with respect to d_a gives us the magnitude d_a as a function of a single variable p_a. Therefore, *provided that we are given the relationship between the quantity of a good in the possession of a given individual and the quantity of use* (satisfaction[1]) *which this quantity affords him* (i.e. provided that we are given Launhardt's equation $y = f(x)$ and $y = \varphi(z)$), then $f_{a1}(p_a)$ *is also given; and provided that we are given* $f_{a1}(p_a)$, $f_{a2}(p_a)$ *and so on*, then as we have shown above $F_a(p_a)$, i.e. *the dependence of total demand on price, is also given.*

---

[1] It is interesting in this connection to quote Ingram's remark that 'Units of animal or moral satisfaction, of utility, and the like, are as foreign to positive science as a unit of dormitive faculty would be' (J. K. Ingram, *History of Political Economy*, 1888, p. 234). It is difficult to display greater lack of familiarity with the conclusions and methods of positive science.

Auspitz and Lieben derive the 'total demand curve' somewhat differently. In order to simplify the analysis they take as the measure of the utility of a given quantity of a good to the individual the *sum of money* possessing the same utility for him as the given quantity of the consumer good, on the assumption that the *intrinsic utility of the money to the individual is a constant* (a completely arbitrary assumption having no other backing than the practical considerations of simplification of the analysis. This technique had previously been used by Dupuit and a criticism of it may be found in Walras, § 387, pp. 445–6 of the English edition).

Let us take quantities of some consumer good *A* as the abscissae, and let us take as the ordinates the utility of these quantities to a given individual, expressed accordingly as sums of money having subjective value (utility) equal to that of the corresponding quantities of the good *A*. Auspitz and Lieben formulated the following psychological law: 'an additional small stimulus acts less, the more similar stimuli have preceded it; and beyond the boundaries of total satisfaction, each additional small stimulus will be found increasingly unpleasant (Auspitz and Lieben, *Untersuchungen*, 1889, p. 11). According to this law of the increase in the subjective value of a good as a function of the quantity at the disposal of the individual (which we shall discuss below), in our cases the curve will assume the form *ON* depicted in the Figure 3.4. It will be a significant

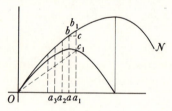

Figure 3.4

property of this curve that each subsequent tangent will have a smaller slope than the preceding one, so that the curve will be concave relative to the horizontal axis.[1] Let us now assume that the abscissa is divided into

[1] The utility curve proposed by Auspitz and Lieben has the form depicted in Figure 3.5, i.e. they assume that the utility of the *whole amount* will decrease when this amount increases beyond a certain quantity, and will finally reach zero. Obviously this hypothesis would agree with facts only if consumers had to consume the quantity *acquired* by them *whatever*

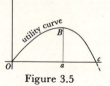

Figure 3.5

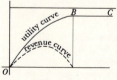

Figure 3.6

2. The relationship between the price of a product and demand

equal parts, which may be made arbitrarily small, and that perpendiculars are dropped from the points of division.

If we now construct from the point b a horizontal line to intersect with a_1b_1, we shall obtain a segment b_1c expressing the addition of utility corresponding to an increase of the quantity Oa by aa_1. Clearly the individual considered will agree to acquire the whole quantity Oa_1 only if the price of the last units aa_1 of the product A which he buys does not exceed b_1c; otherwise he would restrict himself to a quantity less than Oa_1 (since if he paid more than b_1c for aa_1 units, he would be giving up a greater utility for a lesser, which is contrary to economic calculus). If b_1c equals the price of aa_1 units of the product, the price of one unit will equal $\tan b_1bc$ and, consequently, the maximum sum the individual considered will be willing to pay for Oa_1 units will equal the segment a_1c_1 cut off from the ordinate a_1b_1 by a straight line constructed from O parallel to bb_1 (this follows from the hypothesis that several prices for one product cannot exist in the market). If we take the segments a_3a_2, a_2a, aa_1, ... to be infinitely small quantities, the straight line Oc_1 will be parallel to the tangent to the curve ON at the point b_1.

By repeating a similar construction for all quantities of the product (i.e. for all values of the abscissae) from zero to infinity we shall obtain a new curve of the form of ON', which Auspitz and Lieben call the 'demand curve' [gross revenue curve]. Having taken as the abscissae the quantities to be compared, if we now take as the ordinates the tangents of the angles formed with the horizontal axis by straight lines from O through the corresponding points of the curve ON' we shall obtain a new derived curve which will demonstrate the variations of partial demand as a function of market price. This is the curve of the equation $d_a = f_a(p_a)$ already known to us from Walras's exposition. Walras's *courbe de demande totale* is obtained from the partial demand curves by simple summation. The problem is therefore fully solved for our case. The *difference* between the subjective valuations placed on goods by different individuals, which

---

happened, in which case the consumption of the quantity *greater than normal* might in fact be harmful and thus reduce the *total* utility of the whole quantity. But this contradicts the basic assumption of theoretical economics that each individual acts to his greatest advantage: by virtue of this basic assumption the individual (with the exception of pathological cases) will consume from the stock at his disposal the quantity which will afford him the greatest total utility. It is then obvious that the utility curve will assume the form depicted in Figure 3.6: having reached its highest point, the curve will extend parallel to the horizontal axis of coordinates. Auspitz and Lieben were correct in a formal sense in taking the *quantities consumed* as the abscissae in constructing their curve, as depicted in Figure 3.5; the error is in their assumption that these quantities *consumed* equal the quantities *acquired*, which holds only within the amount Oa. According to the actual form of the utility curve, the curve of total demand will also assume a different form, depicted by a dashed line in Figure 3.6.

The theory of marginal utility

was a stumbling block for so many economists,[1] is here no obstacle to the most precise solution of the problem: mathematical analysis enables us to express the effect of all these valuations on the market price.[2]

The most general case, in which not only the number of individuals involved in exchange, but also the number of products entering into exchange in the market, is assumed to be arbitrarily large, presents no difficulty. Walras's Lesson 21 is devoted to an analysis of this case (see Walras, pp. 243–54 of the English edition). The solution proposed by Walras may be considerably simplified: let

$$q_{a1}, q_{b1}, q_{c1}, \ldots; \qquad q_{a2}, q_{b2}, q_{c2}, \ldots; \qquad q_{a3}, q_{b3}, q_{c3}, \ldots \qquad (11)$$

denote the quantities of the products a, b, c, $\ldots$, in the possession of economic individuals (1), (2), (3), $\ldots$ *before the beginning of exchange*.

Let $\phi_{a1}, \phi_{b1}, \phi_{c1}, \ldots; \quad \phi_{a2}, \phi_{b2}, \phi_{c2}, \ldots; \phi_{a3}, \phi_{b3}, \phi_{c3}, \ldots$ express the relationship between the quantities of the goods a, b, c, $\ldots$ at the disposal of the individuals (1), (2), (3), $\ldots$, and their utility for these individuals (so that $y = \phi(x)$ will be the equation of the 'utility curve' of Auspitz and Lieben).

Finally, let $y_{a1}, y_{b1}, y_{c1}, \ldots; y_{a2}, y_{b2}, y_{c2}, \ldots; y_{a3}, y_{b3}, y_{c3}, \ldots$ denote the quantities of the products a, b, c, $\ldots$, which will remain at the disposal of the individuals (1), (2), (3), $\ldots$ *at the end of exchange* (these quantities are the unknowns in our analysis). In that case, if we denote the value of the products a, b, c, $\ldots$ in terms of *some* arbitrarily selected *one of them* by $x_a, x_b, x_c, \ldots$, we shall have three systems of equations

$$\left.\begin{array}{l} q_{a1}x_a + q_{b1}x_b + q_{c1}x_c + \cdots = y_{a1}x_a + y_{b1}x_b + y_{c1}x_c + \cdots \\ q_{a2}x_a + q_{b2}x_b + q_{c2}x_c + \cdots = y_{a2}x_a + y_{b2}x_b + y_{c2}x_c + \cdots \\ \cdots \end{array}\right\} \qquad (12)$$

$$\left.\begin{array}{l} q_{a1} + q_{a2} + q_{a3} + \cdots = y_{a1} + y_{a2} + y_{a3} + \cdots \\ q_{b1} + q_{b2} + q_{b3} + \cdots = y_{b1} + y_{b2} + y_{b3} + \cdots \\ \cdots \end{array}\right\} \qquad (13)$$

---

[1] Most theoreticians of marginal utility (not mathematicians) completely abandon analysis of this question (see, for instance, R. Zuckerkandl, *Zür Theorie des Preises*, Leipzig, 1889, p. 326); others, among them Pantaleoni, attempt to construct an absolute scale of needs, supplementing it by group scales (by sex, race, etc.; see M. Pantaleoni, *Principii di economia pura*, Florence, 1889, pp. 50–2 of the English edition, London, 1898). Pantaleoni himself states: 'The conception of an absolute scale of wants [which is not without a certain amount of truth], has nevertheless, [in its present imperfect condition, probably] given rise to more *economic errors* than sound principles' (*Principii*, p. 54 of the English edition, emphasis added).

[2] When explaining the mechanism of market price determination, the proponents of marginal utility theory themselves proceed from assumptions which completely exclude the possibility of marginal utility affecting price (the cases which they take for analysis are ones in which the 'total demand curve' is *discontinuous* because the number of purchasers is too small). See Böhm-Bawerk, *Grundzüge*, pp. 495–8.

Other representatives of the Austrian school proceed in a similar manner.

2. The relationship between the price of a product and demand

$$\left.\begin{array}{l} \phi'_{a1}(y_{a1}):\phi'_{b1}(y_{b1}) = x_a:x_b \\ \phi'_{a1}(y_{a1}):\phi'_{c1}(y_{c1}) = x_a:x_c \\ \cdots \\ \phi'_{a2}(y_{a2}):\phi'_{b2}(y_{b2}) = x_a:x_b \\ \phi'_{a2}(y_{a2}):\phi'_{c2}(y_{c2}) = x_a:x_c \\ \cdots \end{array}\right\} \tag{14}$$

from which we can determine all the unknowns incorporated in them (and consequently all the prices of the products: x_a, x_b, x_c, ... and so on).*

We shall not go into greater detail, since complete solution of the question of exchange value is outside the scope of the present *critical* study. We shall merely note that, given the vast specialisation of labour existing almost universally at the present time, the producer usually manufactures exclusively one product, and himself consumes only an insignificant proportion of his own product, so that when the volume of production is sufficiently large this quantity may be completely disregarded.

In addition, in order to avoid misunderstanding it is necessary to emphasise that when we refer to prices (exchange value), we always have in mind the *prices* at which products pass into the hands of the *direct consumers*. The prices at which a product passes from the producers to wholesale merchants, and from them to further middle men (merchants of the second, third and subsequent orders) and, finally, to retail traders who deal directly with the consumers, are of no interest from the point of view of *theoretical economics*. In a state of equilibrium, when the volume of the output considered has reached the limit set by the fall of price to the necessary production costs (i.e. to real expenditure + the average ('natural') profit rate on capital existing in a given place and at a given time) all these *intermediate prices* will differ on the one hand from the production price (i.e. the price which the producer of the product should charge for it if the capital expended in production is to bring in at least the normal profit). On the other hand, these prices will differ also from the consumer

* *Ed. note.* If we assume that there are n individuals carrying out acts of exchange, and m commodities, we have n 'budget' equations of type (12), plus m 'conservation' equations of type (13), plus $(m-1)$ first-order conditions of consumption optimisation for each individual, i.e. $(m-1)n$ equations of type (14); second-order conditions for consumption optimisation are implicitly assumed to be satisfied. There are $n \cdot m$ unknowns y's, and m unknowns x's, while the initial endowments q's of individuals are known. There are therefore on the whole $m+n+(m-1)n = m(n+1)$ equations, and $m \cdot n + m = m(n+1)$ unknowns; thus the necessary condition for the existence of a solution that the number of equations should be equal to the number of unknowns, is satisfied. Dmitriev does not deal with the other conditions for the existence of an equilibrium price system, nor with questions of uniqueness and stability of the equilibrium. Since he ends up by rejecting the generality of this approach, an implicit assumption that all these conditions are satisfied does not harm the following reasoning.

price (i.e. the price which consumers agree to pay at the given level of satisfaction of the need, in other words at the given volume of supply) by the amount of profit due to each of the merchant middle men according to the existing average profit rate and with the quantity and turnover of capital (i.e. in conformity with the 'amount of investment of capital', to use the terminology of Jevons) invested by merchants in intermediate trade. In this case intermediate prices will be theoretically fully determined (provided that we are given the volume of intermediate capital of each order and the time for which each of the middle men handles the commodity), but the theoretical interest of these prices is completely the same as that of the *intermediate values of a product at different stages of manufacture within the same enterprise* (should the producer wish for any purpose to determine these intermediate values, he would determine them in conformity with the same principles by which the above-mentioned intermediate prices of a product are determined in a state of equilibrium).

The situation will be different if the industry considered has not yet reached a state of equilibrium. Suppose the difference between gross revenue (which is *exclusively* dependent on demand conditions at a *given* supply of the market) and real production costs (i.e. production costs without profit on capital) expressed in the same units is *greater* than the total profit due on the industrial and trading capitals occupied in the production and sale of the given product, in conformity with the existing average profit rate. The question arises of how this exceptional profit extracted from the consumers of this commodity, above the average rate normally existing under the given conditions of production of the means of subsistence of the workers (see the First Essay), will be distributed.

Will it go exclusively to the retail merchants who deal directly with the consumers of the commodity or, on the contrary, will it take the form of an increased production price when the commodity leaves the owner-producers; or, finally, will it be distributed between all the middle men in proportion to the capital employed (i.e. their expenditure and the time over which it is spent)? The solution of the question of prices of 'production goods of higher orders' will depend on the nature of the solution to this question (since the principles governing both are completely identical). These production goods of higher orders (*Productivgüter, Güter höherer Ordnung*) have been a stumbling block for most theoreticians of 'marginal utility'. However, the difficulty of the question is only apparent, or to be more precise the difficulty does not lie where it is sought by most economists; the question of the distribution of surplus profit above the normal percentage on the capital employed in any industry (before output expands to the limit under the tendency of individual entrepreneurs to pursue 'temporary profit') lies *outside the sphere of economic research.* In fact, under the influence of the pursuit of the greatest advantage, each of the middle men who handles the product, from the start of manufacture until it is transferred to the direct consumer, *will attempt* to obtain *the whole of the excess profit for himself.* But since this attempt will meet with similar attempts by the others, *each will in fact receive* from the surplus *as much as he is capable of winning for himself* in the face of the claims of the middle men above and below him (in the chain by which the commodity passes from producer to consumer). This is a *question of fact for economic theory: in economic analysis the result of the struggle of middle men at the different levels for the excess profit should be a known given quantity,* since economic analysis does not have the means to solve such questions or in general any question passing outside the sphere of (theoretical) economics. If the separate categories of middle men (e.g. producers, wholesalers, small merchants, etc.) are at the same time definite differentiated social classes (groups), the question of the outcome of this struggle may have a general *sociological** solution (but not an *economic* solution, since the subject matter of economics is only *one strictly defined set of social phenomena*). Otherwise we should have to admit that the question cannot have any *general* solution at all, in other words that in the present state of our knowledge the *prices at which a product passes from the hands of some middle men into the hands of others when these middle men are randomly distributed* (i.e. if they do not form definite social groups) *are themselves a random variable.* What has been said about 'intermediate prices' and the prices of 'production goods' ('goods of higher orders') is of course also fully applicable to the price of 'complementary goods' (*Komplementargüter*). In particular, on the assumption that all middle men, or all producers of productive goods or complementary goods *are equally favourably situated* (i.e. on the assumption that *none of them has advantages over the others in the struggle for the excess profit*), the question receives an extremely simple and very precise solution: this is Cournot's solution of the question of the price of 'complementary goods', to which we have already made reference (Cournot, 1838, Ch. 9, Sections 55–65; see above, p. 195); all other related special cases may also be solved by exactly the same methods.

---

* *Ed. note.* In his review of Tugan-Baranovsky's *Osnovy politicheskoi ekonomii*, Dmitriev wrote that, in his deep persuasion, the 'inclusion of the social moment in the system of contemporary abstract-deductive theoretical economy is impossible in principle (by the methodological principles)'. The study of the influence of the social factor on the phenomena of national economic life, in his words, 'can and must represent the object of inductive sociology, having as its own task the establishment of empirical laws of social phenomena' (*Russkaya Mysl'*, n. 11, 1909).

3. THE PSYCHOLOGICAL FOUNDATIONS OF MARGINAL UTILITY THEORY

In conclusion, there are a few things to say about 'utility curves'. We have noted above that the analysis of these curves lies outside the province of political economy, but this does not mean that the form assumed by these curves is a matter of indifference to the economist. All the conclusions we arrive at in the theory of price determination are significantly dependent on the shape of these curves. Therefore, if the data for constructing these curves are taken from the province of other disciplines, extreme caution must be used in borrowing to avoid hasty and false generalisations. In my view all attempts to relate the theory of marginal utility to the so-called 'basic psychophysical law' of Weber and Fechner are false conclusions of this kind (due to a rather superficial acquaintance with psychophysiological data). Fechner's law (see Fechner, *Psychophysik*, Vol. II, p. 33 *et seq.*) concerns only the alteration of *purely objective sensation* (without any emotional overtones) as a function of the strength of the stimulus, and even here the logarithmic relationship between the two holds only within relatively narrow limits (see Fechner, Vol. II, p. 564 *et seq.*; also W. Wundt, *Physiological Psychology* for the more recent literature). We are unable to establish any regular relationship (such as a logarithmic relationship) for an increase in utility as a function of the

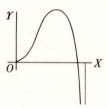

Figure 3.7

strength of a stimulus. If we attempt, by observation, to express schematically the increase in utility as the strength of the stimulus increases, we obtain the curve depicted in Figure 3.7 (see Wundt, *Vorlesungen über die Menshen- und Thierseele*, and *Physiological Psychology*). The ordinates below the horizontal axis correspond to negative utility, i.e. to dissatisfaction. However, even such a schematic picture of the utility curve (as the *average result* of observations of stimuli of *different kinds*) is possible only for products, whose *consumption* arises from their effect on our *external sense organs*. We can only establish in relation to all other products (not consumed but merely used) that as the quantity obtained by the individual increases, the utility of a further unit added to that stock (i.e. the satisfaction derived from the further unit) will, *in general*, be less. We have not got sufficient data for further analysis, and even if we had it would scarcely be possible to establish any *general* relationship for *all kinds* of economic goods (even excluding 'production goods'). As we have seen, the diversity and individuality of utility curves do not prevent us however from giving a quite precise economic solution to the problem of value.

We are unable also to draw any general conclusions (conclusions applying to all kinds of products) concerning the continuity or discontinuity of the functions expressing the relationship between quantities of goods and their marginal utility. This function is discontinuous for most goods (both because the goods are insufficiently divisible and because needs are not sufficiently flexible) and, in accordance with this, *partial* demand curves are discontinuous also. However, because of the individual nature of every partial demand curve (whereby discontinuities in one will not correspond to discontinuities in another), the *total demand curve* obtained by summation of the partial curves will be continuous nevertheless, because of the 'law of large numbers', provided the number of consumers is sufficiently large (see Cournot, 1838, Section 22). It is also incorrect to base the form of utility curves on laws established by mathematicians of the last century (Buffon, Bernoulli, Laplace), who tried to express by abstract (mathematical) analysis the relationship between *fortune physique* and *fortune morale* (to use Laplace's terminology)[1] [or *goods* and *satisfaction*]. Bernoulli postulated that an expected increase in property was divided into equal infinitely small elements. He then assumed that an infinitely small increase in mental satisfaction was directly proportional to the magnitude of the infinitely small increase in wealth to which it corresponded and inversely proportional to the magnitude of the original wealth plus the sum of all the preceding infinitely small additions to this wealth. Denoting the infinitely small increase in wealth by x and the increase in mental satisfaction by dy, we have

$$dy = k\frac{dx}{x} \qquad (15)$$

where k is a constant positive coefficient. Integrating this equation, we obtain

$$y = k\log x + \log h \qquad (16)$$

where h stands for the fixed quantity, determined from the known magnitude of y, corresponding to a given value of x.[2] It is evident that

---

[1] The question is dealt with by Buffon in *Essai d'arithmétique morale* and by Laplace in *Essai philosophique sur les Probabilitës.*

[2] D. Bernoulli, 'Specimen theoriae novae de mensura sortis', *Commentarii Academiae Scientiarum Imperialis Petroplitanae*, 1738, Vol. 5, pp. 175–92.

Bernoulli's formula yields a relationship similar to that reached experimentally by Fechner for the relationship between the magnitude of stimulus and sensation.[1]

It should, however, be remembered that the law established by Bernoulli relates only to an increase in individual *total purchasing power*, rather than the stock of a *specific* consumer good. As the stock of some consumer good increases, new portions of it will be used to satisfy increasingly less important needs (see the excellent clarification of this in Böhm-Bawerk).[2]

Therefore it is possible to observe some regularity in the change of marginal utility of goods when qualities alter only if the same regularity is observed in the degree of urgency of the needs successively satisfied when the quantity of the good considered increases. Consequently, the only assumptions we can justifiably make now, *for all consumer goods in general and all consumption uses* (in other words for all individuals) are as follows:

(1) When the amount of a good at the disposal of a given individual increases, in general its marginal utility is reduced.[3]

[1] This wide applicability of a logarithmic relationship in mental phenomena is the basis on which some psychologists see the Fechner-Weber law as an expression of a general law of judgement. For example, the eminent psychologist Wundt states (W. Wundt, *Vorlesungen über die Menschen-und-Thierseele*, Leipzig, 1892): 'Weber's law allows various interpretations: a *physical* interpretation (it is assumed that it "arises from processes in the nervous system"), a *psychophysical* interpretation ("it is regarded as a specific principle of the interaction between the physical and the mental") and, finally, a *psychological* interpretation ("the law of the logarithmic relationship between sensation and stimuli is the mathematical expression of a *psychological* process of universal import").'

The third (psychological) view of Weber's law is the more correct and better founded. 'In fact, the view of Weber's law as a *psychological* law finds support in a variety of other phenomena of mental life. . . . But the factual generality of the law is not the only evidence of its psychological importance; we can also reduce it to definite physiological conditions that are of general significance.

. . . our measure of sensations always remains *relative*, i.e. it is always a reciprocal relationship of two intensities. This relativity is in no way altered by the fact that we are able to make further new comparisons, and thereby measure all possible intensities.

Therefore, the law of the logarithmic relationship between sensations and stimuli is the *mathematical* expression of a psychological process of universal significance.

The fact that a more powerful stimulus needs a more powerful increment to give rise to a barely perceptible intensification of sensation in itself admits, as we have seen, of a dual interpretation: either a more powerful sensation needs a stronger stimulus to increase by an equal amount; or a more powerful sensation needs a stronger increase in sensation for that increase to be *equally perceptible*.

The reduction of Weber's law to the principle of the relativity of sensations is an argument in favour of the *second* of these two interpretations. For a stronger sensation to increase by the same amount as a weaker sensation, for our relative comparison, the increase in sensation should be correspondingly greater, and two increases in sensations at different points on our scale will be *equally perceptible* when each increase stands in the same relationship to the intensity of the sensation to which it is added.'

[2] Böhm-Bawerk, *Grundzüge*, p. 31 (the colonist example).

[3] This eliminates all objections of the Italian economist Valenti (see C. Valenti, *La teoria del valore*, 1890, pp. 109–15) to the psychophysiological basis of marginal utility theory (these objections essentially are completely correct).

3. The psychological foundations of marginal utility

(2) The quantity of a product may be increased to a point where its marginal utility vanishes.

(3) The quantity corresponding to zero marginal utility is a finite magnitude for all products and all consumers (excluding pathological cases).

(4) However much we increase the quantity at the disposal of a consumer, marginal utility *never becomes less than zero* (once again excluding pathological cases). On this latter point we disagree with Auspitz and Lieben and with Launhardt.

CONCLUSION

SUMMARY AND RESULTS OF THE ANALYSIS IN THE FIRST, SECOND AND THIRD ESSAYS

The essay on the relationship between price and demand ends the *first part* of our attempt at analysing the basic propositions of theoretical economics.

All the essays in this first part constitute a single organic whole: each essay continues the investigation from the point at which it was left in the previous essay. *These first three essays*, which are united by a common plan, *constitute a complete theory of the general elements of value.*

Before proceeding (in the following essays) to a specific analysis of individual elements of price and of the complications introduced into the theory of value by *monetary circulation*, we shall attempt to summarise briefly the results of the analysis so far.

We have shown that Ricardo succeeded completely in the task he set himself, namely to reduce *necessary production costs* to elements independent of the subjective aspect of economic calculus. The reproach usually levelled at 'production cost theories', that they define price in terms of prices, i.e. that they express a sought-after unknown in terms of new unknowns, is therefore completely inapplicable to Ricardo's theory.

Paying particular attention to the main point of Ricardo's theory of necessary production costs, namely, his theory of the profit rate, we have shown that contrary to the common view, Ricardo explained not merely the laws of the *relative* profit rate (i.e. the conditions under which profit rises and falls), but also the laws governing *its absolute level*.

We have further attempted to show that, although Ricardo invariably has in mind *existing* conditions for the production of economic goods, *general principles* valid under *any* conditions emerge from his theory of profit when correctly interpreted.

The essence of Ricardo's views on the profit rate may be briefly summarised: given an industry where production costs may be reduced *ultimately* to the same product A obtained as a result of the production process, the *profit rate* in that industry is determined *independently of the price* of the product.

Now, if the costs of all other industries are also reducible *ultimately* to product A, the profit rate established in that industry will also prevail (because entrepreneurs move from less profitable to more profitable industries) in all other branches of industry, so that the profit embodied in the price of all products will itself be determined independently of market conditions. By algebraic analysis we have shown that no limitations are placed on this theory when the product *A* is not a single but a composite product (as in reality), i.e. a combination of several products (*a*, *b*, *c*, ...) entering into production costs in definite proportions, determined, under present-day conditions, by the consumption budget of wage workers.

By setting out *general* conditions for the occurrence of profit, Ricardo's theory clearly shows that there is no *exclusive* connection between profit on capital and the human labour spent in production. If the profit rate *at the present time* is determined by production conditions *for workers' means of subsistence*, this merely shows either that, in the *existing state* of technology and with man's existing ability to use freely available natural forces, no other production processes exist that could satisfy these requirements, or that if such production processes do exist in general the profit rate they determine is lower than that determined by the production conditions of workers' subsistence.

Hypothetically, however, conditions could exist where the profit rate actually prevailing in all industries (within the limits of validity of Smith's law of profit equalisation) would be determined by production conditions (costs) of the subsistence of some domestic animal. This requires only (1) that all products (or at least the 'greater part', as we have shown in the First Essay) are producible by these animals' work, so that production costs are ultimately reducible in all industries to the cost of subsistence of these animals, (2) that a higher profit rate should exist in the industry producing animal subsistence than in an industry producing workers' subsistence (by human labour).

Finally, conceivably a state of technology could exist where (as shown in the First Essay, p. 63) the profit level is determined in a production process where *no 'living' power is involved at all* and 'reproduction' of goods (including machines) is effected by machines driven by free 'inanimate' natural forces. Therefore, we can imagine a state of society where *wage labour is not used* in production, *but where 'surplus value' will nevertheless arise, and where,* consequently, *there will be profit on capital.*

Continuing our criticism of Ricardo's theory of value, we showed first that Ricardo's views on price determination of products under monopoly were incorrect; we noted that undoubtedly this was the main obstacle to his constructing a correct theory of competition.

Turning to Ricardo's theory of the value of those goods whose necessary production costs depend on the quantity produced,[1] we then showed that Ricardo was completely unable to free the definition of the value of such goods from dependence on market demand conditions (ultimately

---

[1] So that if we indicate necessary costs of a unit of the product by y, and the quantity produced by x, we have: $y = \phi(x)$.

reducible to consumption conditions), since, even for unchanged production conditions (i.e. for a given form of function ϕ), by arbitrarily altering the conditions of demand (consumption conditions) we may arbitrarily alter the price of such a product.

Finally, for the third, most extensive and important category of products, namely those goods infinitely reproducible at constant costs by the use of labour and capital, we showed that Ricardo succeeded in defining their price independently of market conditions only by using an arbitrary hypothesis (which he did not justify anywhere) that unlimited free competition tends to lower the price of products to necessary production costs. Since the validity of Ricardo's whole theory of value and, in general, of the 'production costs theory' depends on this hypothesis, we were obliged to analyse it thoroughly, leading to the writings of Cournot, the only author to give a complete theory of competition.

In the account of the essentials of Cournot's theory, we showed that competition is supposed to lower prices because of the tendency of individual entrepreneurs to pursue *temporary* advantage. As Cournot demonstrated, this compels them to expand total supply beyond the level ensuring the greatest benefit *for each of them*, thus lowering the price below the level a monopolist entrepreneur would seek. Therefore, competition is capable of lowering prices only in the case when individual entrepreneurs can derive a temporary advantage. In the absence of these conditions, competing entrepreneurs lose all incentive to lower the price below the level fixed by a monopolist, since as Thornton excellently put it 'merchants do not undermine one another by lowering prices merely for fun. No merchant is opposed to all other merchants selling as dearly as himself'.[1]

With an analysis of conditions under which 'temporary profit' (*bénéfice momentané*) occurs, owing to expansion of supply by individual entrepreneurs, we showed that this temporary profit occurs only when the reaction from the other entrepreneurs (of a corresponding expansion of supply) reaches the first to disturb the equilibrium, not instantaneously, but after a greater or lesser time lapse. But this condition *invariably* holds only if the quantity of the product offered by entrepreneurs at a given moment *always* equals, precisely, the quantity available to them at that time.

Cournot also makes this assumption when he assumes that the quantity produced in a given time period *invariably* equals the quantity sold in the same period. In criticising this hypothesis, we showed that it contradicts the basic assumption that every economic individual tends to pursue his greatest advantage. Because of this tendency every entrepreneur sells,

[1] Thornton, 1869, p. 58.

at each moment, only that part of the total quantity of the product at his disposal which ensures the greatest possible net profit.

We showed by rigorous analysis that, with a given amount available (potential supply), the sales level (actual supply) is determined by entrepreneurs seeking the greatest benefit in exactly the same way when a monopoly controls the entire quantity available and when it is distributed between any number of competing entrepreneurs.

We showed that, *as a general rule,* the most advantageous sales level (for both the individual entrepreneur and the monopolist) is *less* than the available quantity and, as a corollary of this, that costs to be recouped in the revenue will be *greater than necessary production costs.*

The problem of the level at which potential supply (previously assumed to be a given quantity) is established by economic calculus, as we showed is not difficult to analyse precisely.

We obtained an equation system where quantities dependent on the economic calculus of the economic individual are taken as the unknowns and the quantities not dependent on economic calculus are taken as given (including the technical conditions of production and the psychophysiological conditions of consumption). This system *fully* defines the equilibrium price level. While the technical conditions of production of the product and the psychophysiological conditions of its use remain unaltered, the striving of individual economic individuals after the greatest advantage will not let the market price of the product rise above this level or fall below it. Therefore, despite the complexity of the relationship between the individual factors affecting price, we see that, for *given* technical conditions of production and for given psychophysiological conditions of the consumption of products, *the price of a commodity is a quite definite quantity* provided that our basic assumption that every economic individual tends to pursue the greatest advantage is correct.[1] As Galiani says, 'values differ but they are not capricious'.

The same analysis shows that the price of a product may equal the *necessary production costs* only exceptionally when: (1) the most advantageous volume of sale is equal to the entire quantity in the possession of the seller and (2) the most advantageous level of operation of the enterprise is *full* capacity operation. We have shown by precise analysis that

---

[1] It should be remembered that the proposition that individuals tend to pursue the greatest advantage is not a *conventional* assumption (like other assumptions which we have made use of above to simplify the analysis), but is the expression of a quite real fact. The economic instinct of man (*homo economicus*) is as much a product of the struggle for existence and of natural selection as the sexual instinct or the instinct of self preservation. (See Pantaleoni, *Principii,* Part I, Ch. 2, pp. 17–22 of the English edition.)

On the importance of errors of economic calculus see what we have said with respect to theories of crises seeking the cause of periodic overproduction of commodities in errors of the economic calculation of individual entrepreneurs (Section 7 of the Second Essay).

such exceptional conditions may occur only in a period when industrial technique is imperfect and means of storing products are inadequate[1] and that they inevitably disappear with subsequent progress, so that the equality of price and necessary production costs is a random and temporary phenomenon.

Consequently, whereas Ricardo succeeded in solving completely the first problem, namely that of reducing the *necessary* production costs to elements independent of the subjective factor (economic calculation), the same cannot be said of the second task which he set himself, namely to prove that the market price of products which are infinitely reproducible by the application of labour and capital tends to be established under the influence of free competition at a level equal to the *necessary* production costs. Ricardo was undoubtedly quite correct to assert that, when free competition prevails, equilibrium cannot be established while there exist industries in which the price paid for the product differs by a finite amount from its costs (since as long as this difference exists, the movement of entrepreneurs into these industries cannot cease), but he was undoubtedly incorrect to assert that the level at which equality will be established between the price and the costs, in other words between the price and the value of the product, equals the level of the *necessary* costs of *production*.

We have clearly shown that, *as a general rule*, this level will invariably be higher than the *necessary production costs*. It is precisely because of free competition that the value of products for the entrepreneur inevitably rises above the level of necessary costs, since free competition compels entrepreneurs to expand their enterprises beyond the size naturally required by the volume of sale. As a result of this entrepreneurs are faced with an alternative: *either to operate their enterprises at below their full capacity or*, while operating at full capacity, *to sell less than the entire quantity produced*, and thus *to accumulate non-productive[2] stocks* (increasing the total costs which have to be recouped in the revenue, as does the operation of an enterprise below capacity).

By how much competition between entrepreneurs raises total costs above the level of necessary costs is a question of fact, and will depend in each specific case on the form of the revenue and total costs curves, the

---

[1] We have also shown that even products completely unsuited to storage will be sold at a price exactly equal to the necessary production costs only if these necessary production costs per unit to product are greater than the price corresponding to the greatest gross revenue, which is in general possible only in conditions of extremely low productivity of labour.

[2] Karl Marx refers to such stocks as abnormal, contrasting them to normal stocks, which are an essential condition of regular supply (see *Capital*, 1885, Vol. 2, Ch. 6). We prefer to avoid the term 'abnormal', since it seems to prejudge the question of whether these stocks are in conformity with the *correct* calculus of entrepreneurs.

point of tangency of which determines the equilibrium price in each specific case (i.e. that price of the product at which equilibrium is established both in the sphere of production and of sale of the product considered).

It is sufficient to note that we may arbitrarily raise the level of the equilibrium price above necessary production costs even if production conditions are unchanged, if we arbitrarily modify the form of the demand curve (correspondingly changing the *conditions of consumption* of the product). It would be superfluous to seek a further, more obvious proof of the relationship between the prices of products (even if only those whose necessary costs per unit of product are a constant independent of the total quantity produced) and the conditions of consumption or, in other words, their use value (utility).

We therefore concluded that, to whichever of the three categories established by Ricardo a product belongs, its price cannot be determined independently of the conditions of demand, and therefore of consumption. This led us to an analysis of the 'demand curve' (barely touched upon in Ricardo's writings). We drew the data for this analysis from the theoreticians of marginal utility, who have given a completely scientific solution of the problem of the relationship between the price of a product and the amount of the quantity offered (sold). We also attempted to make some slight corrections to the historical perspective of the development of this theory, by pointing out how little that was new had been contributed to it by the Austrian school, with whose name marginal utility theory is usually linked.

Finally, turning to the clarification of the importance of free competition to the national economy, we made a more detailed analysis of the non-productive expenditure added to necessary production costs because of the struggle of competing entrepreneurs. We showed that these non-productive costs may tend to zero only in an epoch of imperfect industrial technique and that they will rise as labour productivity increases and storage techniques are improved. Under certain conditions these non-productive costs may even exceed the necessary production costs and therefore become a principal element in price.

In our analysis we dealt with only two forms of these non-productive costs, namely those arising (1) from operation of enterprises below capacity and (2) from the accumulation of non-productive stocks. We did this partly to simplify the analysis, but mainly because the third form of non-productive expenditure which plays a prominent role in the present situation of industry could not have attracted the attention of economists at the time when Ricardo wrote the book we were analysing. We have in mind expenditure on advertising, in the broad sense.[1] Moreover, in this

[1] A thorough analysis of this will be made when we study in detail the theory of crises already outlined in the Second Essay.

case, we are not thinking of advertising to expand the market for a given commodity,[1] but only a special category of advertisements to expand sales of an individual entrepreneur *when the total sales level remains the same* (i.e. when the size of the market for a given commodity is the same). A distinguishing feature of such advertisements is that they are effective in expanding sale only if used by one or a few of the sellers of a commodity; they are ineffective once used simultaneously and equally by *all* entrepreneurs. Advertising expenditure of this kind caused by competition among entrepreneurs for a *given* constant (market) raises the level to which competing entrepreneurs may lower the price (selling without loss) in precisely the same way as costs arising from the operation of the enterprise below capacity or from the storage of 'dead' stocks. However, advertising costs have no significant role until supply begins to operate aggressively on demand, as at present (see an excellent description of this phenomenon and the forms it takes in Moffat's book).[2]

When Ricardo was writing, industry was weakly developed in comparison with now, and supply lagged behind demand rather than operated aggressively on it. Therefore Ricardo may not be blamed for this omission.

Following this we noted, in an evaluation of the importance of these phenomena (speculative stocks, incomplete operation of enterprise, advertising costs) to the national economy, that their effect was to completely paralyse all the beneficial results of unlimited free competition in the economy. We clearly showed that *if monopolists use the same method of production as competing entrepreneurs*, monopoly secures a greater 'general advantage' (*Gemeinnutzen*) to the national economy than free competition, since, although consumers pay less to producers under free competition than under monopoly, this price covers a vast *completely non-productive expenditure* representing a loss to the entire national economy. On the contrary, the excess over and above necessary production costs, which consumers pay to a monopolist, will not be lost without trace for the national economy *as a whole*, whether consumed by the monopolist or directed by him to further production; but will increase total satisfaction or benefit. As we have noted (Second Essay, p. 148) we do not deal with the *ethical question* of equity in the distribution of 'total benefit' between separate social classes and individuals.

The cause of all non-productive expenditure, which has to be recovered in the revenue under free competition is either the expansion of enterprises beyond the most advantageous capacity, or the expansion of actual output beyond the most advantageous sales level. Both forms of 'over-production' are not, as we have shown as accurately as possible, *the*

---

[1] This kind of advertisement already existed widely in Ricardo's time.

[2] Moffat, *The Economy of Consumption*, London, 1878, Book II, Ch. 2, 'On the Effects of Over-Competition on the Distribution and Consumption of Wealth', pp. 120–50.

result of errors[1] *by competing entrepreneurs, but are an inevitable outcome of free competition itself* and therefore cannot be eliminated by any palliative measures (e.g. by elimination of speculative manipulation of market values, by the greater comprehension by entrepreneurs of the world market, by their greater enterprise etc.).

Finally, an analysis of the effect of technical progress on the volume of production and sales showed that an increase of labour productivity in any industry gives rise not only to an expansion of output and sales of a given product, but also to an increase in non-productive stocks accumulated as reserves by competing entrepreneurs. This increase in reserve stocks has a twofold influence: first, it increases the additional expenditure (over and above necessary production costs) to be recovered in revenue; second, provided production and trade activities are separate in a society, this over-production will be expressed by *periodic* congestion of the market by commodities for which there is no outlet ('crises'), followed by the elimination of trading middle men and by chronic stagnation, in which case the accumulation of dead stocks will be partly replaced by the *operation of enterprises* below capacity: industrial stagnation will follow trading stagnation.

These *a priori* conclusions are in agreement with reality in the history of countries with a developed manufacturing industry. This makes us believe that our analysis contains a correct explanation both of periodic and of chronic over-production of commodities.*

[1] We noted (p. 177) that there is no foundation for an explanation of present-day over-production of commodities and industrial stagnation *by errors of individual entrepreneurs*. These errors could have a perceptible effect on *total* supply level only if supply is in the hands of *a few* isolated entrepreneurs. When the number of entrepreneurs is sufficiently large, their subjective errors should be mutually compensated as random variables.

* *Ed. note.* The *Essays* end 'The next section of this work will be concerned with the further development of the theory of crises outlined here.' On Dmitriev's plan for a second series of Essays, see the biographical note, p. 30.

BIBLIOGRAPHY

Anon. (L. M. Valeriani), *Apologia della formola* $p = i/o$, *trattandosi del come si determini il prezzo delle cose tutte mercatabili*, Bologna, 1816.

R. Auspitz and R. Lieben, *Untersuchungen über die Theorie des Preises*, Leipzig, 1889.

D. Bernoulli, 'Specimen theoriae novae de mensura sortis', *Commentarii academiae scientiarum imperialis Petropolitanae*, 1738, Vol. 5, pp. 175–92.

E. von Böhm-Bawerk, *Kapital und Kapitalzins*, erste Abteilung *Geschichte und Kritik der Kapitalzins-Theorien*, Innsbruck, 1884; English translation by W. Smart, London 1890.

'Grundzüge der Theorie des Wirtschaftlichen Güterwerts, *Jahrbücher für Nationalökonomie und Statistik*, Neue Folge, Band 13, 1886, pp. 1–88 and 477–541, reprinted in *Reprints of Scarce Tracts in economic and political science series*, n. 11, London, 1932.

Kapital und Kapitalzins, zweite Abteilung *Positive Theorie des Kapitales* (*1889*), Innsbruck, 1909; English translation by W. Smart, London 1891.

P. P. Bois-Guillebert, *Le détail de la France* (1697), in M. E. Daire (Ed.), *Economistes Financiers du XVIIIᵉ siècle*, Paris 1843.

D. Buchanan, *Observations on the subjects treated in Dr Smith's inquiry into the nature and causes of the wealth of nations*, Edinburgh, 1814.

G.-L. L. Buffon, *Essai d'arithmétique morale*, in *Œuvres complètes de Buffon*, edited by J.-L. de Lanessan, Paris, 1884, 14 Vols., Vol. 11.

Bunyakovskii, *Osnovy matematicheski teorii veroyatnostei*, [Principles of the mathematical theory of probability].

J. E. Cairnes, *Some leading principles of political economy newly expounded*, London, 1874.

R. Cantillon, *Essai sur la nature du commerce en général* (London, 1755), edited with an English translation by H. Higgs, London, 1931.

H. C. Carey, *See* McKean.

É. B. de Condillac, *Le commerce et le gouvernement considérés relativement l'un a l'autre*, Amsterdam, 1776.

A. Cournot, *Recherches sur les principes mathématiques de la théorie des richesses*, Paris, 1838; English translation by N. T. Bacon with a bibliography of mathematical economics by I. Fisher, New York, 1897.

Principes de la théorie des richesses, Paris, 1863.

J. Dupuit, 'De la mésure de l'utilité des travaux publics', *Annales des ponts et chaussées*, 2nd Series, Vol. VIII, Paris, 1844; English translation in *International Economic Papers*, n. 2, 1952.

'De l'influence des péages sur l'utilité des voies de communication', *Annales des ponts et chaussées*, 2nd Series, n. 207, Paris, 1849.

221

O. Effertz, *Arbeit und Boden*, Berlin, 1889.

G. T. Fechner, *Elemente der Psychophysik*, Leipzig, 1860; English translation by H. E. Adler, with an Introduction by E. G. Boring, New York, 1966.

B. Franklin, *The works of Benjamin Franklin*, with notes and a life of the author by J. Sparks; Boston and Milwaukee, 1856, 10 Vols., Vol. 2.

F. Galiani, 'Della Moneta', (1750), in P. Custodi (Ed.), *Scrittori classici italiani di economia politica*, Parte Moderna, Vol. III, Milan, 1803.

G. Garnier, *Abrégé élémentaire des principes de l'économie politique*, Paris, 1796.

H. H. Gossen, *Entwickelung der Gesetze des Menschlichen Verkehrs und der daraus fliessenden Regeln für menschliches Handeln*, Braunschweig, (1854); second edition Berlin, 1889.

B. Hildebrand, *Nationalökonomie der Gegenwart und Zukunft*, Bd. 1, Frankfurt, 1884.

J. K. Ingram, *A History of Political Economy*, London, 1888.

W. S. Jevons, *The Theory of political economy* (1871), London, 1971.

K. Knies, 'Die Nationalökonomie Lehre vom Werth,' *Zeitschrift für Staatswissenschaft*, 1885.

P. S. Laplace, *Essai philosophique sur les probabilités*, Paris, 1825 (5th edition). *Théorie analytique des probabilités*, Paris, 1812.

W. Launhardt, *Mathematische Begründung der Volkswirtschaftslehre*, Leipzig, 1885.

G. F. Le Trosne, *De l'intérêt social par rapport à la valeur, à la circulation, à l'industrie et au commerce intérieur et extérieur*, Paris, 177.

J. Locke, *An essay concerning the true original extent and end of civil government* (London, 1690), in *The works of John Locke*, Vol. 5, London, 1823.

A. Loria, *Analisi della proprietà capitalista*, 1889.

K. McKean, *Manual of social science*, being a condensation of the *Principles of Social Science* of H. C. Carey [Philadelphia and London, 1837, 1838, 2 Vols.], Philadelphia, 1864.

T. R. Malthus, *Principles of political economy* (second edition, London, 1836), reprinted in *Series of reprints of scarce works on political economy*, Tokyo, 1936.

K. Marx, *Das Kapital*, Vol. I, (1867); English translation, Moscow, 1962. *Zur Kritik der politischen Oekonomie* (1859); English translation, with an introduction by M. H. Dobb, London 1971.

C. Menger, *Unteruschungen über die Methode der socialwissenschaften und der politischen Oekonomie insbesondere*, Leipzig, 1883; reprinted in *The collected works of Carl Menger*, 4 Vols., Vol. 2, *Reprints of scarce tracts in economic and political science*, n. 18, London, 1933.

A. Miklashevskii, *Den'gi – Opyt' izuchenii osnovnikh polozhenii ekonomischeskoy teorii classicheskoy shkoly* [Money – An examination of the basic propositions of the classical school of economic theory].

J. S. Mill, *Principles of political economy, with some of their applications to social philosophy* (1848); edited and with an introduction by W. J. Ashley, London, 1878.

R. S. Moffat, *The economy of consumption. An omitted chapter in political economy*, London, 1909.

M. G. de Molinari, *Cours d'économie politique*, Brussels and Paris, 1863, 2nd edition, 2 Vols.

Bibliography

Z. Nekrasov, *Teoriya veroyatnostei* [The theory of probability] 1896.

M. Pantaleoni, *Principii di economia pura*, Florence, 1889; English translation by T. Boston Bruce, London, 1898.

W. Petty, *A treatise of taxes and contributions* (London, 1662), in *The economic writings of Sir William Petty*, edited by C. H. Hull, Cambridge, 1899, 2 Vols., Vol. 1.
The political anatomy of Ireland (London, 1691), Cambridge, 1899.

Z. Pichenot, 'The law of supply and demand'.

P. J. Proudhon, *Système des contradictions économiques ou philosophie de la misère*, Paris, 1846, 2 Vols.

D. Ricardo, *The principles of political economy and taxation* (1817), in *The Works and correspondence of David Ricardo*, edited by P. Sraffa and M. H. Dobb, Cambridge, 1951, 10 Vols., Vol. 1.

C. Rodbertus, *Zur Erkenntniss unserer staatswirthschaftlichen Zustände*, 1842.
Zur Beleuchtung der socialen Frage, Berlin, 1890.

W. Roscher, *System der Volkswirthschaft*, Erster Band, *Die Grundlagen der National-ökonomie* (1854), Stuttgart, 1900.

M. P. Rossi, *Cours d'économie politique*, Paris, 1843, 2nd edition, 3 Vols.

J. B. Say, *A treatise on political economy or the production, distribution, and consumption of wealth* (translated from the fourth French edition by C. R. Prinsep), London, 1821, 2 Vols.

W. Scharling, 'Werttheorie und Wertgesetze', *Jarhrbuch für Nat. und Statistik*, Band 16, 1886.

N. W. Senior, *An outline of the science of political economy* (1836), London 1938.

N. Sieber, *D. Ricardo i K. Marx v' ikh ekonomicheskikh issledovaniahk* [D. Ricardo and K. Marx in their economic research] Moscow, 1885.

Z. Slonimskii, Zabytye ekonomisty Kurno i Tiunen' [The forgotten economists Cournot and Thünen], *Vostochnaya Evropa*, October 1878.

A. Smith, *An enquiry into the nature and causes of the wealth of nations* (1776), Edinburgh, 1814.

J. Steuart, *An inquiry into the principles of political economy* (1767), edited and with an introduction by A. S. Skinner, London, 1966, 2 Vols.

H. F. von Storch, *Cours d'économie politique*, St Petersburg, 1815.

W. T. Thornton, *On labour: its wrongful claims and rightful dues, its actual present and possible future*, London, 1869.

J. H. von Thünen, *Le salaire naturel et son rapport au taux de l'intérêt* (translated from German by M. Wolkoff), Paris, 1857.

T. Tooke, *A History of prices and of the state of the circulation from 1793 to 1837*, London, 1838, 2 Vols., Vol. 1.

M. Tugan-Baranovsky, Teoriya predêl'noi poleznosti [Theory of marginal utility], *Yuridicheskii Vestnik*, 1890.

A. R. Turgot, *Réflexions sur la formation et la distribution des richesses* (1770); in *Oeuvres de Turgot*, edited by Dupont de Nemours, E. Daire and H. Dussard, Paris 1844, 2 Vols., Vol. 1.

C. Valenti, *La teoria del valore*, 1890.

P. Verri, *Meditazioni sulla economia politica* (1771), in P. Custodi (Ed.), *Scrittori classici italiani di economia politica*, Parte Moderna, Vol. 15, Milan, 1804.

Bibliography

L. Walras, *Eléments d'économie politique pure* (1874); English translation of the 1926 edition, by and with an introduction by W. Jaffé, London, 1954.

F. von Wieser, *Ueber den Ursprung und die Hauptgesetze des Wirthschaftlichen Werthes*, Vienna, 1884.

Der natürliche Werth, Vienna, 1889.

W. Wundt, *Grundzüge der physiologischen Psychologie*, Leipzig, 1874.

Vorlesungen über die Menschen- und Thierseele, Leipzig, 1892.

V. F. Zalessky, *Uchenie o tsennosti* [The theory of value], Kazan, 1893.

Uchenie o proiskhozhdenii pribyli na kapital [The theory of the origin of profit on capital], Kazan, 1898.

Yu. Zhukovskii, *Istoria politicheskoy uchenü XIX veka* [A history of nineteenth-century political theories].

R. Zuckerkandl, *Zur Theorie de Preises*, Leipzig, 1889.

INDEX

advantage (benefit)
action without, is economically purpose-less, 80
maximum, as *total* income, 76
striving for maximum, as basic premise, 48, 135, 201, 203, 216n; contradicted by assumption that competition minimises prices, 94, 95, 215, by Cournot's assumption that supply equals produc-tion, 21, 118–19, 215, and by Smith's assumption that monopolist will aim at obtaining highest price, 81
advertising (with constant total sales level), as unproductive expenditure, 25–6, 218–19
agriculture in USSR, Chayanov's input–output table for, 11
animals, imaginary system in which work is performed exclusively by, 18–19, 64, 66, 214
Auspitz, R., and R. Lieben, 20, 27, 33, 84, 86, 101n, 113n, 115, 149, 157, 182, 196, 202–3, 204, 211
Austrian school of economists and theory of marginal utility, 20, 26, 43, 181, 195, 204n

Belkin, V. D., 9, 10
Bernoulli, J., 119
Bernoulli, D., 209–10
Böhm-Bawerk, E. von, 26, 50, 78–9, 80, 181, 189, 210
Bois-Guillebert, P., 39n
Bortkiewicz, L. von, 20, 31
Buchanan, D., 84n
Buffon, G.-L. L., 209
Bunyakovsky, 117n

Cairnes, J. E., 182, 183, 185
Cantillon, R., 39, 40, 42n
capital
circulating, 13, 56n
elimination of element of, in calculating production costs, 42–5
expression for price of, 47–8
expression of profit as function of time and, 46–7
fixed, 56n

industrial and trade, 156–7, 161
interest on, *see* interest
profit on, as distinct from other forms of income from ownership, 69n, 77–80
profit defined in terms of demand for and supply of (Smith), 14, 39, 49–50, 58, 92
ratio between demand for and supply of (Ricardo), 51
capitalists, effect on wages of struggle between workers and, 19, 74, 75
Carey, H. C., 37, 83n, 91n
Chayanov, A. V., 11
Chuprov, A. I., 31
Clark, J. B., 19
commodities
amount sold, and price of, 81–3
consumed by workers, *see* wage goods
in hand, postulated to be overvalued in relation to future commodities, 78n, 79–80
infinitely reproducible, in conditions of zero rent, 52; Ricardo's theory of value of, 21, 91–5, 215, 217
labour expended in production of, 8–12, 42–5
perishable, in theory of competition, 22–3, 123–36, 141, 144
relative value (ratio of exchange) of, 41, 46, 49, 71; as ratio of labour expended in production of, 14–15, 52–5; cannot be determined independently of profit rate unless organic composition of capital goods used up in production is identical, 55–6; where composition is not identical, 56–7; when hired labour is withdrawn from market, 71, 72–3; when individual portions have different production costs, 84–9
stocks of, *see* stocks
storable, in theory of competition, 23–4, 136–45
types of: basic, 17; complementary, 195, 207; free (non-economic), 19, 68, 69; 'production', 189, 207, 209; Sraffa's standard, 17
competition
Cournot's theory of, 94, 97–100, 215; assuming production costs are zero,

competition – *contd.*
100–8; assuming production costs are greater than zero, 108–14; equilibrium when prices equal necessary production costs, 94–5, 115–16
critique of Cournot's theory of, 7, 21–4, 116–18; with production costs assumed to be zero, 118–23; with production costs greater than zero, 123–45
effect of number of entrepreneurs involved in, *see under* entrepreneurs
Launhardt on, 149–50
lowering of prices by: (Smith and Ricardo), 48–9, 93–5, 215; (Cournot), 21, 103, 104, 107, 215; (Dmitriev), 21, 23, 90, 111, 136, 147, 219
in national economy, 23, 25, 147–9
non-productive costs unavoidable under, 147, 151, 167, 217, 219–20
perfect, a condition for Ricardo's propositions, 20, 52
tends to the increase of non-productive stocks, 136, 137, 148, of production capacity, 163–7, and of total costs, 23, 90, 95, 136
Walras on, 149
Condillac, E. B. de, 186
constant returns to scale (zero rent), 13, 20
consumers
societies of, 167
total purchasing power of, 196–7
consumption
conditions of, 26
curve of, at different prices (Dupuit), 193–4
costs
average, 20n, 87
total (production+realisation), 23, 90, 95, 136, 217; curves for, 140–2, 152, 159, 165
see also non-productive costs, production costs, realization costs, storage costs
Cournot, A., 20, 21–3, 37, 81, 94, 99–116, 192, 195–6, 215
crises, industrial
technical progress and, 25–6, 173–8, 220
theories about, 173, 216n

demand
for capital, *see under* capital
Cournot's analysis of law of, 99–101
elasticity of, 23, 24
in non-substitution theorem, 13
prices of production cannot be independent of, except under restricting assumptions, 13, 20, 28, 87, 88, 91–2, 214–15, 218

relation between price and, 197–207
'statistical law' of, 196–7
supply and, in marginal utility theory, 182–5
supply 'operating aggressively' on, 219
in theory of monopoly prices, 82
demand curves, 82, 101, 203, 218
elasticity of demand and, 23
form of, depends on economic calculus of consumers, 181
form of, for different categories of commodities, 192n
as gross revenue curves, 33, 101n
intersection of: with production cost curves, 86–91; with supply curves, 160
Denis, H., 19n
Dmitriev, V. K., 7, 29–35
Dobb, M. H., 19n
Dupuit, J., 146, 182, 192–4, 202

Effertz, O., 99n
Eidel'man, M. R., 12
elasticity of demand, 23, 24
entrepreneurs (competitors)
consequences of unequally favourable situations among, 150–61
number of: and potential supply, 130–4; and price, 21, 104, 105–9, 116; and production volume, 21, 23, 129; and supply volume, 21, 22, 103–4; 114; and total net profits, 21, 133
pursuit of temporary profit by, *see* profit, temporary
Ricardo assumes free movement of, into most profitable branch of industry, 88, 93–4
search for most advantageous price by, 145–6
exchange, fundamental law of (Launhardt), 200–1
exchange value, *see under* value

Fechner, G. T., 208, 210
forward markets, lacking for manufactured commodities, 26, 27, 178n
Franklin, Benjamin, 39

Galiani, F., 26, 27, 179, 182, 186n, 187–9, 216
Garnier, J., 196n—7n
Genovesi, A., 183
Georgescu-Roegen, N., 13
Gossen, H. H., 193, 195, 196
Grobman, D. M., 9, 10

Harcourt, G. C., 19n
Hildebrandt, B., 195n

226

income
  Dmitriev's approach to distribution of, 19
  gross, relations of: with price, 98–9; with production volume, 121–3; with quantity sold, 101, 102
  from ownership, profit on capital as special form of, 69n, 77–80
  of rentiers, in crises, 176
  striving for maximum *total*, 76
industrial capital, 156–7, 161
inertia, element of all human activities, 117n, 129
Ingram, J. K., 187n, 201n
input–output analysis
  Dmitriev formulates foundations of, 7, 8, 11
  Leontiev's, 8–10
insurance
  to cover risk in pursuit of market advantage, 163
  in storage costs, 156
interest
  average (Ricardo's 'natural profit'), 123n
  Böhm-Bawerk's theory of, 79
  on capital, as distinct from other forms of income from ownership, 69n, 77–80
  on capital in excess stocks, 156
  as compensation for waiting for an enjoyment, 88n
  striving for highest rate of, 75n

Jaffé, W., 46n
Jevons, W. S., 27, 41, 182, 193, 197, 199–200, 206

Kant, E., 37
Kaser, M., 31
King, Gregory, 194
Knies, K., 195n
Konius, A. A., 15

labour
  in calculation of production costs, *see* wages
  Dmitriev, and Marxian theory of exploitation of, 17–19
  expended in production of commodities 8–12, 42–5
  hired human: imaginary replacement of, by animals or machines, 18–19, 63–6, 214; imaginary withdrawal of, from market, 69–73
  as a production good, 189
  profit as function of quantity of, expended in production of wage goods, 61
  relative value of commodities as ratio of amounts of, expended in production,

14–15, 52–5 (*see further under* commodities)
'socially necessary', 12, 87
specialisation of, 205
value of commodity of which different portions have different production costs is determined by amount of, expended under the most disadvantageous conditions, 87–9
variation of supply of, as function of wage rate, 74n
labour input coefficients
  in Dmitriev's formula for quantity of labour in production of a commodity, 8
  per rouble in different Soviet industries, 12
labour value, term used by Dmitriev in sense of 'exchange value', interchangeably with 'price', 7
  of a commodity, in terms of labour input coefficients and labour values of inputs, 8
  in Marxian theory, 7, 12, 17
  theory of, 39, 71, 87; Dmitriev's synthesis of, with theory of marginal utility, 7, 20; as theory of prices of production, 7n, 20
Lagrange, J. L., 101
land
  need to cultivate less fertile, as population increases (Ricardo), 73–4
  rent of (Ricardo), 83
Lange, O., 11
Laplace, P. S., 119n, 209
Launhardt, W., 27, 74n, 75n, 80, 146, 149–50, 182, 196, 200–1, 211
law, concept of a scientific, 83n
Le Trosne, G. F., 186
Leonardo da Vinci, 37
Leontiev, W. W., 8–10
Levine, H. S., 11n
Lieben, R., *see* Auspitz and Lieben
Locke, J., 39
Loria, A., 71n, 73n
Lunts, A. L., 9, 10

machinery, imaginary system in which work is performed exclusively by, 18–19, 63–5, 214
McKean, K., 83n
Malthus, T. R., 191n
marginal productivity theory, 19
marginal utility, 43, 53; first use of term, 193
  Dmitriev's synthesis of theory of, with theory of labour value, 7, 20
  evolution of theory of, 26–7, 181–97, 218
  as function of quantity bought, 146
  psychological foundations of theory of, 208–11

market, 98n
Marx, K., 12, 17, 39n, 43n, 217n
Marxian economics, 7, 12, 17–18
materials, cost of
    as element in price, 40; can be broken
        down into wages, profit, and rent, 42
mathematics
    Dmitriev, and use of, in Soviet economics
        and planning, 7, 11
    as a logical tool, 37
    in theory of marginal utility, 27, 182,
        192–4
Menger, C., 26, 181, 193, 195
middle men, 157, 178, 192
    and effects of technical progress, 26, 167,
        173–4, 176–8
    prices of products bought and sold by, not
        of theoretical interest, 205–6
Miklashevsky, A., 83n
Mill, J. S., 182, 183, 192
Mirrlees, J., 13n
Moffat, R. S., 219
Molinari, G. de, 194
monetary circulation, theory of, 178
monopoly
    excess production capacity under, 161–3
    and national economy, 25, 147, 148, 219
    most profitable production volume under,
        123, 128–9, 136
    most profitable supply volume under, 103,
        104n, 121, 136, 139; with given pro-
        duction volume, 123–5; with varying
        production volume, 125–8
    prices under, 21, 80–3, 214; effect of
        changes in conditions of production and
        storage on, 155–6; higher than under
        competition, 21, 23, 90, 111, 136, 147,
        219
    total costs under, lower than under
        competition, 23, 90, 95, 136
Montias, J. M., 11n

national economy, significance of unlimited
    free competition for, 25, 147–9, 219
Nekrasov, Z., 119n
Nemchinov, V. S., 9, 31
non-productive costs, 25, 26, 27, 216, 218
    of excess production capacity, 166–7
    unavoidable under competition, 147, 151,
        167, 217, 219–20
    when entrepreneurs are in unequally
        favourable situations, 154–5
    when rent exists, 159–60
non-substitution theorem, Samuelson's, 7, 13
Nove, A., 10

overproduction
    caused by competition, 219–20
    caused by technical progress, 26, 175, 177,
        220
    periodic and chronic, 178, 220

Pantaleoni, M., 204n, 216n
Pashkov, A. I., 19n, 32n
Petty, W., 39, 40
Pichenot, Z., 184
price(s)
    assumed the same for any one product on
        the market, 82, 119, 203
    competition and, *see under* competition
    of corn, effect of short supply on, 194–5
    in Cournot's theory of competition, reach
        equilibrium only when equal to
        necessary production costs, 94–5, 115–
        16; conditions for necessary production
        costs to be equal to, or higher than, 23,
        24, 144–5, 160, 216-17
    demand and, *see under* demand
    fluctuations in, preceding equilibrium,
        145–6
    Marx's theory of, 12
    monopoly, *see under* monopoly
    number of entrepreneurs and, 21, 104,
        105–9, 116; entrepreneurs in unequally
        favourable situations and, 154
    in overproduction, 175
    reciprocal relation between supply volume
        and, 81–2, 181
    Ricardo's theory of, based on production
        costs, *see* production costs, necessary
    tacit collusion of producers on 22, 27
    as wages + outlay on tools and materials +
        profit + rent, 40; reduced in last analysis
        to sum of wages + sum of profit, 13,
        42–3; expression altered to include rate
        of profit, 47–8
price of production, Ricardo's (= necessary
    production costs), 23
probability
    of pursuit of temporary profit by entre-
        preneurs, 109–10
    of sale by different entrepreneurs: taken as
        different, 121, 156; taken as equal,
        119–20
production capacity, excess (under competi-
    tion), 22, 25, 27
    allows immediate expansion of produc-
        tion volume, 163–4
    as alternative to excess stocks, 24, 217, 218
    increased by technical progress, 25
    in industrial crises, 175, and industrial
        stagnation, 177–8, 220

may be advantageous: to competitors, 164–5; to monopolists, 161–3

may be advantageous to competitors to expand, 165–6

and national economy, 166–7

production costs

in Cournot's theory of competition, *see under* competition

curves of (Auspitz and Lieben), 84–6, 152, 157; intersection of demand curves and, 86–8; straight-line, 90–1, and discontinuous, 88–90

elimination of capital in calculation of, 42–5

necessary, *see next entry*

rent vanishes when all units of commodity have the same, 42, 90

theory of, before Ricardo, 39; (Steuart), 40; (Smith), 40–2

of wage goods, *see under* wage goods

production costs, necessary

assumption that competition tends to lower prices to, 94–5, 115–16; conditions for prices to be equal to, or lower than, 23, 24, 144–5, 160, 216–17

average interest on capital related to, 123n

difference between total costs and, 24, 140, 217; *see also* realisation costs

Ricardo's theory of prices based on, 20, 21; disproved by Dmitriev, 24, 26, 86–7, 90–1

storage costs proportional to, 156

storage of 'necessary' stocks included in, 137n, 156

'production goods', 189, 207, 209

production volume (output)

in Cournot's theory of competition, assumed to be equal to supply volume, 21–2, 94, 103, 117, 118, 129; assumption contradicts basic premise on pursuit of maximum advantage, 21, 118–19, 215

effect of competition on, 21, 22, 23, 121–3, 125–7, 129

increased by technical progress, 25, 169, 171

most profitable level of, 81–2, 121, 128–9

most profitable volume of supply: with given, 123–5, with varying, 125–8

number of entrepreneurs and, 21, 23, 129

potential and actual, as independent variables, 161–7

in Ricardo's theory, 82, 86, 90

see also overproduction

productivity of labour, technical progress as increase in, 171, 172, 177, 220

profit

on capital, as distinct from other forms of income from ownership, 69n, 77–80

conditions for positive value of, 15–16, 18, 62–3

in conditions other than those involving hired human labour, 18–19, 61–6, 69–73, 214

as difference between values expended on, and obtained from, production, 69n

effects of higher rate of, in one branch of industry, 48, 66–9

as element in price, 40; price reduced to sum of wages + sum of, 13, 42–5; expression of sum of, as function of capital and time, 46–7; price expressed in terms of wages and rate, of, 47–8

hypothesis of equalisation of, throughout industry, 12, 48, 49, 72, 83, 214

of monopolist, 82, 103, 104n, 139; effect of, on national economy, 25, 147, 148

'natural', 121n

net, 123

reciprocal relation between wages and, 15, 57, 75n

relative values of commodities and, *see under* commodities

Ricardo's theory that level of is determined by production costs of wage goods, 14–17, 57n, 58–61, 73, 214; applied to systems without hired human labour, *see under* labour; failure of critics to understand, 50–2

Smith defines in terms of relation between demand for and supply of capital, 14, 39, 49–50, 58, 92

supply volume maximizing, *see under* supply volume

temporary, *see next entry*

total net, number of entrepreneurs and, 21, 133

profit, temporary (*bénéfice momentané*), in Cournot's theory of competition, 21, 105–9, 116, 215

abolished if supply can be instantaneously increased, 21, 24, 116–18

conclusion on, relate only to production volume (not to supply), 129

equilibrium reached only on disappearance of all incentive to, 142

Proudhon, P. J., 186–7, 188, 195n

psychology, and utility of goods, 199, 208–11

realisation costs (sales costs), 23, 134, 140, 142

increased by technical progress, 169–71

see also non-productive costs

rent
in Cournot's theory of competition, 113n, 116
as element in price, 40; exclusion of, from calculations of price, 42, 46, 52, 61
and equilibrium price, 156–60
exclusion of, from calculation of effects of competition, 137, 147, 151
negative, 87–8
Ricardo's theory of, 50, 61–2, 83–91
Rodbertus's concept of, 77n
vanishes when all units of product have the same production costs, 42, 90
zero (constant returns to scale), 13, 20
revenue, curves of gross, *see* demand curves
Ricardo, D., 14, 15, 17, 18, 20, 21, 27, 28, 47, 50–93, 114, 123n, 141, 145, 156, 186, 213–15, 217, 218–19
risk
associated with disturbance of *status quo* in the market, 117n, 163
associated with transfer of value to other hands, 80
Rodbertus, C., 61, 77n
Roscher, W., 190n, 195n
Rossi, M. P., 182, 184–5, 186, 187, 189, 190–1

sales costs, *see* realisation costs
Samuelson, P. A., 7, 13
Say, J.-B., 193, 196n
scarcity value, 186
Scharling, W., 195n
Senior, N. W., 187, 189–90, 191
Shaposhnikov, N. N., 11n, 29, 31
Sieber, N., 39, 41n
Slonimsky, L., 37, 94n, 99
Smith, Adam, 14, 39, 40–1, 46, 48–9, 58, 72n, 81, 93, 186
social cost, of unrestricted competition, 23, 25, 147–9
sociology, 27, 181n, 207n
Sraffa, P., 13, 16–17, 28
Steuart, J., 40, 184
stocks of commodities, excess (non-productive), 23, 27, 218
compared with peace-time armaments, 25, 148–9
cost of storing, *see* storage costs
effect of liquidation of, by one producer, 148, 419
eliminate possibility of temporary profit, 21, 24, 116–18
equivalent to excess production capacity, 24, 217
middle men and, 173–4
technical progress: decreases value of,

91n; increases amount of, 25, 168–9, 170–3, 175, 220
would be eliminated by forward markets, 26, 178n
storage costs, 22, 23, 137–8, 141, 147, 154
of excess stocks, increase price under competition, 136, 139, 140, 148
insurance and interest on capital as main elements of, 156
of 'necessary' stocks, charged to necessary production costs, 137n, 156
Storch, H. F. von, 183–4
Struve, P., 19n, 20, 30, 31n
subsistence theory of wages, 40, 42, 61, 74–5
supply
of capital, *see under* capital
demand and, in marginal utility theory, 182–5
'operating aggressively' on demand, 219
potential (production volume of a period + stocks), 130–4
supply volume (sales)
in Cournot's theory of competition, assumed equal to production volume, *see under* production volume
curves of (Auspitz and Lieben), 85–6, 157, 159, 160
effects of competition on, 22, 103–4, 114, 121, 122–3
effect on competition of instantaneous expansion of, 116–18
equilibrium conditions for, with entrepreneurs in unequally favourable situations, 154
reciprocal relation of price and, 81–2, 181
yielding maximum profit, 103–4, 119–21, 136; with given production volume, 123–5; with varying production volume, 125–8

technical progress, economic consequences of, 25–6, 91n
where trade and production are combined, 176–8
where trade and production are divorced, 168–76
Thornton, W. T., 21, 94, 97, 215
Thünen, J. H. von, 37, 58n, 75–6, 101
time
needed for expansion of supply, 117
profit as function of, 15, 46–7, 61, 73
utility as function of, 78–9
Tooke, T., 194, 195
tools, cost of
as element in price, 40; can be broken down into wages, profit and rent, 42
trade: divorce of production and, 173–8, 220

trade capital, 156–7, 161
Treml, V. G., 11n, 12n
Tugan-Baranovsky, M., 19n, 20, 45n, 181, 207n
Turgot, A. R. J., 40

utility (use value), 41n, 78
  as basis of exchange value, 190
  'contradiction' between exchange value and, 184, 186–7, 188, 189
  Dmitriev's survey of economic thought on, 26
  as a function of time, 78–9, and of quantity, 190
  prime, depending on importance of need served, and specific, depending also on extent to which need has been satisfied, 187
  see also marginal utility

Vainshtein, A. L., 32n
Valenti, C., 210n
Valeriani, L. M., 183
value: term used by Dmitriev in sense of 'exchange value' interchangeably with 'price', 7; term used both for 'exchange value' and for 'use value', 41
  exchange and use, contradiction between, 184, 186–7, 188, 189
  human needs as basis of, 186
  labour theory of, *see under* labour value
  relative, of commodities, *see under* commodities
  starting points for Ricardo's theory of, 52, 61
  task of theory of, is to determine proportion in which commodities are exchanged, 46

transfer of, to other hands, entails risk, 80
use, *see* utility
Verri, P. de, 183

wage goods (commodities consumed by workers)
  profit rate determined by production cost of, 14–17, 58–61, 73, 214
  upper and lower limits on quantity of, 74–5
wage-profit frontier, 15
wages
  as element in price, 40; price reduced to sum of profits + sum of, 42–5
  level, of, dependent on strength of contending parties, 19, 74, 75
  reciprocal relation between profit rate and, 15, 57, 75n
  relation between supply of labour and level of, 74n
  subsistence theory of, 40, 42, 61, 74–5
  Thünen's calculation of most advantageous rate of, for both capitalists and workers, shown to be erroneous, 75–6
Walras, L., 9, 13–14, 27, 42n, 51–2, 149, 150, 182, 193, 196, 197, 198–9, 200, 201, 202, 203, 204
Weber, 208, 210n
Wieser, F. von, 26, 45n, 181, 189, 193, 195
Wundt, E., 37
Wundt, W., 208

Yurovsky, 31

Zalessky, V. F., 41n, 91n,. 184n, 192n
Zauberman, A., 10
Zhukovsky, Yu., 50, 61, 84
Zuckerkandl, R., 204n